Kierkegaard

Also by Stephen Backhouse

Kierkegaard's Critique of Christian Nationalism
The Compact Guide to Christian History

Stephen Backhouse has given us a wonderfully lively and sympathetic portrait of one of the greatest minds of the nineteenth century, sparing us nothing of Kierkegaard's abrasive, contrarian personality, but also illuminating the extraordinary courage and spiritual depth of the man. We have waited a long time for such an accessible introduction, growing out of deep study of the abundant original sources and bringing them alive with a light and sure touch.

Rowan Williams, Master of Magdalene College and former Archbishop of Canterbury

Stephen Backhouse's *Kierkegaard: A Single Life* is an extremely useful book that makes Kierkegaard accessible to those just beginning to know him. Backhouse's account of Kierkegaard's life is exemplary but particularly useful is his summary of Kierkegaard's works.

Stanley Hauerwas, Gilbert T. Rowe Emeritus Professor of Divinity and Law at Duke University

Drawing on the wealth of new biographical material that has become available in the last twenty years, Backhouse's life of Kierkegaard sets the Danish thinker in his time and place and does so with confidence and verve. Few books about this most subtle and elusive of figures could be described as page-turners, but Backhouse combines a fast-moving style with a strong grasp of the big issues that makes this a compelling read. For those who have not yet read Kierkegaard himself, this will leave them wanting to do so—which must be the best outcome for any work of this kind.

George Pattison, Professor of Divinity, University of Glasgow

This is an extraordinarily likeable book about a not-very-likeable, though fascinating, figure. This is not hagiography; Backhouse gives the full measure of Kierkegaard and loves him in all his weirdness. Backhouse is a great storyteller—witty, imaginative, and with an eye for irony and humor. This book fills a need for an introduction for the educated nonspecialist to Kierkegaard's life and thought, which are inseparable. How lucky we are that this need has been filled with such flair.

Dr. William T. Cavanaugh, Director, Center for World Catholicism and Intercultural Theology, DePaul University

Almost every road in modern Christianity leads back, at some point, to Kierkegaard. Yet few appreciate this fact because we've lacked a knowledgeable and accessible guide. Finally, we have one in Stephen Backhouse. I've waited my whole life for this book. And so has the church.

Dr. Richard Beck, Associate Professor of Psychology, Abilene Christian University

Stephen Backhouse has written a lively, accessible, and expert introduction to an often misunderstood but hugely influential and prophetic thinker. This is an ideal place to start understanding Kierkegaard's life and thought, which has much to say to the contemporary church and world.

Graham Tomlin, Bishop of Kensington, President St Mellitus College

Starting with the astonishing scenes at Kierkegaard's funeral, Stephen Backhouse traces the life and impact of this extraordinary, elusive, passionate critic of passionless Christianity. Backhouse's book is both learned and accessible, so that the issues that Kierkegaard wrestled with walk off the page to challenge us again today, while the man himself haunts us, calling us and hiding from us, as he did his contemporaries.

Dr. Jane Williams, Assistant Dean and Lecturer in Systematic Theology, St Mellitus College

Kierkegaard believed that to understand a historical figure, one must be able, imaginatively, to become the person's contemporary. In this gripping biography, Stephen Backhouse helps us become contemporaries of Kierkegaard himself. In these pages the Danish thinker comes alive. This book gives us an extraordinary portrait of an extraordinary human being.

C. Stephen Evans, University Professor of Philosophy and Humanities, Baylor University

This book is a fascinating read about a fascinating person. Stephen has skillfully created a glimpse into the life and work of a perplexing and brilliant character.

Luke Norsworthy, podcaster and pastor, Organization-Newsworthy with Norsworthy Podcast and Westover Hills Church

STEPHEN BACKHOUSE

ZONDERVAN REFLECTIVE

Kierkegaard
Copyright © 2016 by Stephen Backhouse

Requests for information should be addressed to:
Zondervan, 3900 *Sparks Dr. SE, Grand Rapids, Michigan 49546*

ISBN 978-0-310-52089-4 (ebook)
This edition: 978-0-310-12019-3 (softcover)

Library of Congress Cataloging-in-Publication Data

Names: Backhouse, Stephen, 1976- author.
Title: Kierkegaard : a single life / Stephen Backhouse.
Description: Grand Rapids : Zondervan, 2016. | Includes bibliographical references.
Identifiers: LCCN 2016008389 | ISBN 9780310520887 (hardcover)
Subjects: LCSH: Kierkegaard, Soren, 1813-1855. | Philosophers—Denmark—Biography.
Classification: LCC B4376 .B33 2016 | DDC 198/.9 [B] —dc23 LC record available at
    https://lccn.loc.gov/2016008389

Any internet addresses (websites, blogs, etc.) and telephone numbers in this book are offered as a resource. They are not intended in any way to be or imply an endorsement by Zondervan, nor does Zondervan vouch for the content of these sites and numbers for the life of this book.

All rights reserved. No part of this publication may be reproduced, stored in a retrieval system, or transmitted in any form or by any means—electronic, mechanical, photocopy, recording, or any other—except for brief quotations in printed reviews, without the prior permission of the publisher.

Jacket design: Tammy Johnson
Illustration: © Red Hansen / Shannon Associates
Interior design: Kait Lamphere

Printed in the United States of America

For Norman and Vaila

It is a truth universally acknowledged, that a single man in possession of a good fortune, must be in want of a wife.

Jane Austen, *Pride and Prejudice*

Contents

Preface 11
Acknowledgements 15

1. A Controversial Life 17
2. School Life 35
3. Family Life 43
4. Public Life/Private Life 59
5. Love Life 79
6. Writing Life 103
7. Pirate Life 125
8. An Armed and Neutral Life 145
9. A Life Concluded 169
10. A Life Continued 189

Afterword 209

Overviews of the Works of Søren Kierkegaard 215
Notes 269
Abbreviations 285
Bibliography 287
Index 297
Permissions and Credits 301

Preface

Once upon a time, my colleague Lincoln Harvey asked me for a book on the life and thought of Søren Kierkegaard he could read on holiday. I gave him what I had on the shelf. Upon his return, Harvey, an Anglican priest, teacher, and theologian of considerable insight, confessed he had not been able to get through the first chapter. The Kierkegaard he met seemed dense, distant, and unappealing. I knew then that if a disciple of Karl Barth and minister in the established church of England had thought Kierkegaard was irrelevant to him, then something indeed had gone spectacularly wrong. This was the spur for this book.

Lincoln is not alone. It is not just theologians who find the influence of Kierkegaard hovering behind much of their work, only to find the life and thought of the man himself hard to get to know. Journalists, philosophers, artists, novelists, musicians, psychologists, pastors, politicians, playwrights, therapists, anthropologists, filmmakers, culture critics, historians, and teachers—or anyone affected by these professions—also occasionally stumble across this strange nineteenth-century Danish name (pronounced SOO-ren KEER-ka-gor) and wonder what's up.

To make matters more confusing, Kierkegaard's influence seems to transcend any one of the spheres in which he is encountered. Modernists are suspicious of this apparently postmodern thinker who never said anything directly and wrote mostly under pseudonyms. Postmodernists love the multiple voices but are suspicious of his stubborn adherence to revealed Truth with a capital *T*. Religious people hear Kierkegaard is the "father of existentialism" and suspect he is a secular atheist. Secular atheists steer clear when they hear Kierkegaard lies behind the popular idea of a "leap of faith." Christian apologists love his attack on the idolatry of scientific rationality, but they are less keen on his attack on Christian apologetics. Liberals appreciate his love for the common man and his insights into the vapid nature of market-driven media and politics but don't like his trenchant critique of social solutions to individual problems or the present age's delusional belief in historical progress. Conservatives draw much from Kierkegaard's highly Christian focus on the liberty of the individual but do not like that he finds the main enemies of this liberty to be Christian culture and much that is called traditional family values. Whatever your take on modern life, there are two true things that can be said about Kierkegaard: his influence on our various modes of thought is widespread, and the exact nature of this influence is difficult to articulate.

There are a handful of biographies of Kierkegaard. The books by Walter Lowrie (1938), Josiah Thompson (1973), Alastair Hannay (2001), and Joakim Garff (Danish 2000; English translation 2005) are all excellent in their own right. Lowrie's was the first. It was designed to introduce the Dane to an unknowing public and, as such, reprints large tracts of Kierkegaard's own words, at that time found nowhere else. Besides being perhaps less engaging now than Lowrie intended then, the book also mines Kierkegaard's pseudonymous material for biographical data in a way that is now questionable. Thompson's highly readable biography is the most literary, but he is not a Kierkegaardian scholar, and he largely skates over the content of the authorship. Furthermore, his book, which set out to be a corrective of sorts to Lowrie's hagiography, takes enormous strides into amateur psychology few Kierkegaardians now wish to follow. Hannay and Garff are meticulous in their detail and exhaustive in their dissection of Kierkegaard's life and thought. Theirs are monumental, substantial, and indeed indispensable pieces of work for Kierkegaardian specialists.

The world does not need another academic biography of Søren Kierkegaard. What it can use is something for educated nonspecialists who do not need to know, and do not care, about the depths of

Kierkegaard's intellectual development or the minutiae of his cultural context in Golden Age Denmark. Søren's life had many dramatic, romantic, melancholic, and humorous twists and turns, well-known to experts but perhaps less well-known to normal readers. What is more, Kierkegaard stands as an influence on some of the most important, life-giving, and controversial developments in the modern age. As Charles Williams correctly predicted: "His sayings will be so moderated in our minds that they will soon become not his sayings but ours." Kierkegaard has become part of our culture whether we acknowledge it or not. As it stands, only academics tend to know this. What a shame. What a waste! It is worth trying to redress the balance.

Kierkegaard led an interesting life, but ultimately it was the life of a prolific author.

Inevitably, any account of his life will involve a fair amount of writing about writing. Some of this material is highly technical, and I am well aware it has the potential to clog up the narrative. On the other hand, it is only because of his ideas we know of him at all, and some people care more about his books than his life. To that end I have largely separated biographical discussion from discussion of his works. The present volume contains short overviews of every one of Kierkegaard's published books (both in his lifetime and posthumously). This material is clearly demarcated from the rest of the text and can be easily ignored (or accessed) as the reader prefers.

A word of confession and warning: Kierkegaard himself was disdainful of the practice of overviews. He wrote specifically to avoid summarisation and is all the better for it. If you use these overviews to avoid engaging with the real thing, then it may be small comfort to know the only person Kierkegaard dislikes more than you is me. Kierkegaard can be hard work. My overviews are meant to help orient the biographical reader. They are invariably also my interpretation. You must read the originals and decide for yourself. Another warning: it might change your life. I know he changed mine.

Acknowledgements

Thanks to St. Mellitus College for providing the research leave during which I wrote this book. I love being with all the staff and students at St. Mellitus. It is a remarkable place. Special mention needs to go to Jane Williams, Lincoln Harvey, and Chris Tilling for personal support and practical advice. My busy colleagues Simone Odendaal and Hannah Kennedy read early versions of my opening chapter, and their feedback was much appreciated. I have been fortunate to study and sometimes teach Kierkegaard at McGill University in Montreal and the University of Oxford. I am grateful for the guidance, helpful opposition, and friendly support I received in these places, especially from George Pattison, Joel Rasmussen, Torrance Kirby, Douglas Farrow, Johannes Zachhuber, and Oliver O'Donovan. Elsbeth Wulf was my patient Danish language teacher and first window into Søren's Copenhagen. Conversations with fellow Kierkegaardians Matthew Kirkpatrick and Christopher Barnett helped form my thinking, as did Luke Tarassenko's timely reminder regarding Captain Kierk's changing sense of his role as a poet. Gordon Marino, Eileen Shimota, and the library staff provided help and advice during my time at the excellent Kierkegaard Library at St. Olaf's College in Minnesota. Thanks are also due to Bruce Kirmmse, to Elizabeth Rowbottom and Tom Perridge at Oxford University Press, and to Jon Stewart, editor of C. A. Reitzel's Danish Golden Age series and associate professor at Copenhagen University's Søren Kierkegaard Research Centre. I have very much enjoyed working with my editors Katya Covrett, Bob Hudson, and the team at Zondervan. My wife,

Clare, a historian of clothing and culture, was writing her book at the same time as I was mine. Her selfless sense of fun, patience, and interest during this time was a constant source of joy and a model for me to imitate. Thanks to my father, Norman, and my mother, Vaila. His enthusiasm has given me much encouragement, and her keen reader's eye has provided invaluable editorial suggestions, and it is to them this book is dedicated.

CHAPTER 1

A Controversial Life

The new bishop stands at the window, looking at the crowd milling in the courtyard below. He cranes his neck, trying to get a better view of the church door opposite, but it is difficult. He cannot see, but at the same time he does not want to be seen. That would never do. The bishop has pushed himself to the limits of his reputation to avoid any connection to the distasteful funeral going on across the way. Yet he knows, along with all of Copenhagen, that the events below are all anyone is talking about. They will be in all the papers tomorrow, and the next day, and the next. It is of paramount importance that these papers record that the newly minted Bishop of all Denmark, Hans L. Martensen, shepherd to the nation, was not present at the burial of his former student, now the scourge of all Christendom, Søren Kierkegaard.

Martensen had good reason to expect heightened public interest. All of Denmark's respectable papers, as well as her less respectable (but more popular) magazines had been providing a steady drip of comment on the events leading up to, and following, Søren's passing. The details of his life, after all, were irresistible to any journalist worthy of the name.

An enigmatic, brilliant loner with more than a whiff of scandal about him, Søren Kierkegaard had long enjoyed the reputation as something of a dangerous dandy about town. Every literate citizen, and more than a few who did not read at all, had an opinion. Sophisticated, artistic citizens recognized his talent, even if they did not actually understand his books.

The Church of Our Lady, Copenhagen's "mother church" and the Kierkegaard family's place of worship. Martensen lived just across from the front portico and Søren lived about a five-minutes' walk down the road.

He was the kind of author who it was important either to be seen to be reading or to pointedly ignore. Morally upright citizens admitted he was a good writer, but was he a good man? The constant trips to the theatre and the flagrant gallivanting about town with all sorts suggested an absence of moral fibre. And didn't Søren despise his brother Peter Christian, and didn't he refuse his brother to even attend at his deathbed? In any case, Peter, so earnest and plodding, almost certainly hated his brilliant and infamous younger sibling. Religious citizens remembered him as the promising theologian who spoke and wrote endlessly about Christianity and yet who did not become a pastor and now never even went to church. Romantic citizens vaguely suspected this stillborn church career was somehow connected to the scandal of his broken engagement years before. "Such a sweet young girl," they would whisper to each other, "and taken off by her new husband to the West Indies! It's almost like they were escaping something, or *someone*." Older citizens of Copenhagen could shake their heads and say they always knew Søren would come to a bad end. There was something not quite right about his father, Michael. He was a miserable old miser. And the timing of Michael's second marriage, to Søren's mother, so soon after the death of his first wife was positively scandalous. And she was the maid! Younger citizens knew him from the caricatures and cartoons the satirical magazine the *Corsair* was always churning out. A magazine that they would hastily sneak a peek at when their more respectable elders were not looking. These respectable citizens knew him as the one the King of Denmark had marked out for special favour. Less respectable citizens either knew of Søren as the one who stopped to talk to them on his walks about town or as the one they threw stones at as he passed. Student citizens knew that his first name, when attached to a character in a comedy revue, would automatically get laughs. For the same reason pregnant citizens took this name off their list of potential baby names. The novelists of Denmark's Golden Age, including Hans Christian Andersen, anticipated and yet dreaded Søren's reviews of their latest works. Poets and playwrights admired the man who wrote provocative fiction. Philosophers read him for his statements on the nature of time, existence, and the meaning of life. Conservatives liked Søren for his opposition to democracy and revolution. Liberals liked Søren for his championing of the individual and the common man against the forces of inherited tradition. Atheists loved his attacks on the clergy and official religion of Christendom. Reformers, longing for a renewal of Christianity in the land, also loved his attacks on the clergy and official religion of Christendom. Clearly, this was a man of sharp contradictions and puzzling paradoxes. But all the citizens agreed that he was rich. Wasn't he rich? He must be rich. To whom will he leave all his money?

So it is that when on Friday, November 16, 1855, Denmark's most venerable newspaper announced: "On the evening of Sunday, the eleventh of this month, after an illness of six weeks, Dr Søren Aabye

Kierkegaard was taken from this earthly life, in his forty-third year, by a calm death, which hereby is sorrowfully announced on his own behalf of the rest of the family by his brother / P. Chr. Kierkegaard," it did so with the full knowledge that enclosed in these simple lines raged a storm that threatened to spill out onto the quiet streets of Copenhagen and beyond. Or so they must have hoped. All these citizens had to get and share their opinions somewhere, after all. It was a good time to be a journalist.

Old Copenhagen

If the editors who wrote the bare outlines of the story did hope for someone else to provide the colour commentary, they were not disappointed. Other public figures were not reticent to opine on Søren's passing. Writing in the periodical *North and South*, an editor and journalist (and himself not without literary ambitions), Aron Goldschmidt spoke up for many of Kierkegaard's admirers: "He was without a doubt one of the greatest intellects Denmark has produced, but he died a timely death because his most recent activities had begun to gain him precisely the sort of popularity that he could never have harmonized with his personality. The most dangerous part of his actions against the clergy and the official church is now only just beginning, because his fate undeniably has something of the martyr about it."

The Jewish Goldschmidt was writing outside the walls of the established church. Key figures of Danish Christianity were less distraught about Søren's passing, and more certain about his status as a Christian hero. Namely—he was nothing of the kind. The celebrated Pastor Nicolai Grundtvig, a cultural and ecclesial giant in Danish life then (and now), also spoke for many when he preached a sermon on the day of Kierkegaard's burial, giving thanks that one of the icicles hanging from the church roof had now melted and fallen off. In a letter to a friend, Grundtvig said of Kierkegaard, "I do not wonder that he was surprised by death, for as long as the day of the Antichrist has not yet come, those who tinker with [the national church] will always come to grief, and quickly, just like false Messiahs."

To be labelled a great intellect, martyr, and false messiah all at once was no mean feat, but it was not only the religious and literary establishments that had their points of view. The scientific fraternity also made its voice heard. Kierkegaard was, evidently, a medical marvel according to a group of research students who complained about the decision to bury Søren. He should, they said, have been given an autopsy instead of a traditional burial. A mighty brain like Søren's deserved to be preserved for science. That the engine which powered such a literary output and such a quirky personality should moulder in the ground like any common man was a travesty to research. They complained to the hospital, but the hospital acquiesced to the wishes of the family. This was much to the relief of one of Søren's friends who had been present at the petition and who wrote in his memoirs, "I thought it decent of the hospital, but those who were enthusiasts of science did not think that sort of thing should be taken into consideration." Decency won out, but speculation over the contents of Kierkegaard's skull remained. "He was said to suffer from a softness of the brain," wrote one of Søren's committed enemies. "Was this responsible for his writings, or were the writings responsible for it?"

Here was the rub. It was Søren's writings, especially the writings which made up the final stage of his life and career, which lay at the root of all the fuss. This collection of pamphlets and newspaper articles are now known collectively as Kierkegaard's "attack upon Christendom," and it was while engaged in this attack that Søren died. It was precisely because of these writings that Søren's admirers and enemies alike agreed that he absolutely should not be laid to rest in a traditional manner. And it was precisely because of these writings that many of Søren's family desperately wished that he would.

Henriette Lund, Søren's niece, provided many remarkable eyewitness accounts of her famous uncle. In her later life she jealously protected his reputation.

Søren had said he wanted to upset blind habits and overturn easy assumptions. In this, if nothing else, he had succeeded. His niece, Henriette Lund, was present at the house following her uncle's death. She paints a picture of a family torn between private grief and public responsibility. No one was thinking clearly about the future but were, she says, "living minute by minute in the present." As a result, no one made definite arrangements for the funeral, and each was leaving the decisions up to the others. There had to be a funeral. But when and where should it take place? If it took place quietly, then it would look like the family was ashamed of Søren and his life's work, which was all anyone was talking about at the time anyway. On the other hand, as Søren's nephew (and younger half-brother to Henriette) Troels Frederik notes in his memoirs, a traditional church funeral would have struck a "strongly discordant" note. Troels summarized the quandary well: "Everyone knew that the deceased had characterized pastors as liars, deceivers, perjurers; quite literally, without exception, not one honest pastor."

Søren had publicly stated more than once that the comfortable, civilized world of cultural Danish Christendom had done away with Christianity. He had repeatedly denied he was even a Christian, and upon his deathbed he had sent away his ordained brother, refusing to receive Communion from a clergyman. And now the expectation was that Søren was to be given a full funeral from this self-same established Lutheran Danish Church! The unsavoury rabble who liked Søren's attack and the sophisticated clergy who bore the brunt of it agreed alike that this would be impossible. Yet Søren was the brother of a pastor, the son of a publicly minded churchman, the friend of bishops. What is more, despite his later offensive statements, anyone even slightly familiar with Søren's work could see that his was no simplistic attack on all things holy. He never stopped invoking the name of Jesus Christ in all his works. Surely it was still a Christian heart that stopped beating when the caustic public persona died in its hospital bed.

The way forward was not clear, and the family dithered. According to Henriette, "It was probably in this way that some things were decided by mere chance—for example, the choice of the day of the funeral. This should not have been allowed to fall on a Sunday." Henriette reports that a number of clergy came to Søren's brother, her Uncle Peter, to get him to change the date. But Peter, doubtless with one eye on the inevitable newspaper report, thought that a change would look like cowardice. And so the arrangements went ahead as planned. Peter settled the decision

Hans Christian Andersen, poet, author, and dramatist. Søren and Hans Christian moved in similar circles but were never close friends. One of Kierkegaard's first published pieces was a review of Andersen's novel Only a Fiddler *in which he accused the author of lacking an authentic point of view.*

to bury on a Sunday in Denmark's mother church, the Church of Our Lady. And he would deliver the eulogy himself.

On November 24, 1855, Hans Christian Andersen wrote to a friend about the funeral and its aftermath. His observations help set the stage for the whole scenario as it played itself out.

> Søren Kierkegaard was buried last Sunday [November 18] following a service at the Church of Our Lady. The parties concerned had done very little. The church pews were closed, and the crowd in the aisles was unusually large. Ladies in red and blue hats were coming and going. Item: a dog with a muzzle. At the graveside itself there was a scandal: when the whole ceremony was over out there (that is, when [Dean] Tryde had cast earth upon the casket), a son of a sister of the deceased stepped forward and denounced the fact that he had been buried in this fashion. He declared—this was the point, more or less—that Søren Kierkegaard had resigned from our society, and therefore we ought not bury him in accordance with our customs! I was not there, but it was said to be unpleasant. The newspapers say a little about it. In *Fatherland*'s issue of last Thursday this nephew has published his speech along with some concluding remarks. To me, the entire affair is a distorted picture of Søren K.; I don't understand it!

Andersen was not alone, either in his confusion or in his opinion that with the crowds, colourful hats, muzzled dogs, and graveside protests the whole affair had been grossly mishandled.

Every eyewitness to the scene comments on the packed building, with funereal tourists describing the enormous crowd present at the service where "the church was full to bursting." Many had to be content with their spot of floor space behind a column in the back. Before they were all locked down, Søren's adolescent nephew Troels did manage to find a seat in the pew row immediately behind the family. "A man who I later heard was Prof. Rasmus Nielsen sat in the pew with me and closed the door [to the box pew] so hard that it locked shut." Nielsen, who fancied himself Kierkegaard's disciple and successor, was one of the many people there with mixed motives.

*Troels Frederik Troels-Lund, Søren's nephew.
Troels was one of the last people to see his uncle alive.*

Poor Henriette Lund, there to grieve for her beloved uncle, was overwhelmed by a gang of gawkers who pushed their way into the church. The scene she relates was one of a ceremony on the verge of chaos, much like a restless mob waiting for something, *anything*, to happen. "The tightly packed mass of people surged like an angry sea," she wrote, "while a ring of rather unpleasant-looking characters had placed themselves around the small flower-decked coffin." This group was largely composed of self-declared supporters of Søren, upset that with this funeral the church was attempting to absorb into its own one of its most outspoken opponents. It looked like this group of toughs was going to carry the day when suddenly the church door burst open and a smaller group of "completely different appearance" pushed themselves through the crowd in order to grace "Denmark's great thinker to his grave" with an honour guard around his coffin. These were students from the university, also supporters of Kierkegaard but with a sense of propriety their comrades lacked. "They conquered the space," Henriette tells us, "and their ring replaced the other like a solid wall."

The gang of ruffians, convinced the brightest and best stars of the Danish Church were going to whitewash Søren's legacy with an outpouring of self-serving, Christianised verbiage, need not have worried. In the end all clergy refused to speak. A rumour went about that this was at the behest of Bishop Martensen. The mutual animosity between Martensen and Kierkegaard was well-known, however; his decision here, if indeed it was his decision, was not solely due to petty foibles. The church was in a bind. If pastors spoke harshly of Søren it would be taken as speaking badly of the dead. If they praised him it would seem they agreed with his notorious attack or, worse, were angling for money from the family.

So it was that only two members of the clergy were present in their official vestments. Tryde, the old dean of Our Lady, was there because he had to be. Visibly uncomfortable, Tryde bustled about, pushing his little cap back and forth on his head at a feverish pace, "while his face, usually so benign, wore an expression of profound annoyance." The other clergyman present in his robes was Peter Kierkegaard. He may have been wearing the vestments of his vocation, but when he took his place at the front of the church, he did so not as a priest but as a brother.

Nephew Troels noted, perhaps with some surprise considering Peter's earlier dithering and known antipathy towards Søren, that his uncle's eulogy was powerfully delivered. Other witnesses to the event agree the elder brother was gentle and calm, without directly alluding to the most recent polemics. The eulogy was not published in full until 1881 (which by then was a reconstruction of Peter's own memories in any case). In his reconstruction, Peter tells us he expressed regret that he did not convince Søren to take rest from his labours or to collect himself calmly. Peter talked about their father growing up on the moors of Jutland, how he had loved all his seven children intensely, and how he, Peter, was now the only one left. He did not think this was the time or place to discuss Søren's actions—however, Peter stated plainly that he did not agree with his brother and that Søren did not realize he had gone too far. Finally, Peter said he could not thank the gathered mass on behalf of his brother, pointing out that, after all, Søren had always sought solitude instead of being part of a herd. Showing some of his brother's propensity for honest confrontation, Peter went one further—he could not thank the crowd on behalf of the Kierkegaard family either because he suspected that the crowd was there for mixed motives and wished only to see a spectacle. Peter ended with a prayer that Søren's prodigious efforts would not be misunderstood and that what was true in them would have a positive effect on the church.

Henriette tells us that when her living uncle delivered the eulogy for her dead one, the restless crowd "became still as glass."

Old Dean Tryde in his fussy clerical garb proved less able to preserve the peace when the crowd spilled outside and down the road for the graveside burial service. Tryde was swept along with the throng, whose members were once again jostling for a place with a view. Young Troels was also caught up in the crush. "Everywhere teemed with the tightly packed crowd, which surged over the graves and the latticework fences, forward to its common goal." He arrived, breathless, with the rest of the mob at the gravesite. He saw that the freshly dug earth formed a yellow-grey hill, in striking contrast with the green grass growing under the iron railing surrounding the plot. This fence had been removed to give access to the grave, and the crowd pushed and shoved over the yellowy mud, trampling the grass. Everyone assembled, the dean cleared his throat and began the liturgy of committal.

"*Lovet være Gud og vor Herre Jesus Kristus . . .*" The blessing of "God the Father of our Lord Jesus Christ" faltered on Tryde's lips. One person had broken free and was standing in front of the crowd. From his vantage point, Troels saw a tall, pale young man dressed in black. The man, nervous, looked around and shouted for permission to say a word: "In the name of God—one moment, gentlemen, if you will permit me!" What was this? The dean complained that as the man was not ordained, he was not allowed to speak. Tryde thought it was all highly irregular and deeply offensive. He was right, but the crowd had not come all this way to see a quiet funeral for an ordinary man. They shouted Tryde down and clamoured their approval of the interloper. "Let him speak!"

His name was Henrik Lund. He was unknown to many of the people looking on, but it soon transpired that he was yet another nephew of the dead man, one who also happened to be a doctor at the hospital where Søren had died. "I am bound to him by blood ties," said Henrik, "and I am tied to him, finally, by agreement with his views and opinions, and this is perhaps the strongest tie." Henrik drew a breath. "He, my deceased friend, stands and falls with his writings, . . . but I have not heard them mentioned with a single word; . . . therefore let us investigate here whether his views are true or not!"

The crowd stayed silent, expectant. "It would never happen in a Jewish society, and never among the Turks and Mohammedans: that a member of their society, who had left it so decisively, would, after his death and without any prior recantation of his views, nevertheless be viewed as a member of that society." No! cried Henrik, this crime against honesty is a crime "reserved for 'official Christianity' to commit." Henrik wondered how far the clergy were going to go in their lip service to Kierkegaard—he insinuated that they were only angling for a good fee because they had heard that Søren was rich. If he had been poor, then the clergy would have treated this service differently. All eyes must have turned then to Tryde, unlucky representative of all of Christendom, who stood silently, service book quivering in his hand. "What is this 'official

Christianity' then?" asked the doctor, answering his own question with a quote from the Book of Revelation. "It is the great whore, Babylon, with whom all the kings of the earth have fornicated, the wine of whose whoredom has made drunk all the peoples of the earth. . . . Therefore the deceased was also right when, at the end of his life, he so urgently and incisively said what must be said, namely that everyone, by ceasing to participate in the official worship of God as it currently is will always have one sin fewer—and a great sin!—namely the sin of participating in making a fool of God by calling the Christianity of the New Testament what is not the Christianity of the New Testament." Henrik concluded with a final flourish: "Therefore, both on his behalf and on my own, I protest viewing our presence here as participation in the worship of God sponsored by 'official Christianity'; . . . I have spoken and freed my spirit!"

Some of the crowd yelled "Bravo!" and here and there voices called out, "Down with the clergy!" but mostly there was only scattered applause. Troels tells us that most of the people "stood in tense, silent expectation of what would happen *now*." The young man expected a riot, a great shout, *something*. But nothing happened. "The speaker was gone. I saw the heavy man from the church pew, Rasmus Nielsen—whom I had again discovered near the grave and who had probably wanted to speak out there—depart with an annoyed expression on his face."

If anyone present noticed the irony that the events surrounding the funeral of Denmark's most articulate champion of individuality had largely been dictated by an awkward, shuffling mob, they kept their counsel to themselves. Newspaper comment in the days following was muted, treating the affair briefly and carefully. "As if," said one of Søren's friends, "they were afraid of getting their fingers burnt." The most scathing assessments were reserved for private consumption. They centred less on brother Peter's prayer that Søren's words would not be misunderstood, and more on brother Peter's ham-fisted preparations and on Søren's gauche supporters.

Bishop Martensen had adroitly kept himself from public engagement with the Kierkegaard clan, but that did not stop him commenting archly in a private letter, "Today, after a service at the Church of Our Lady, Kierkegaard was buried; there was a large cortège of mourners. . . . I understand the cortège was composed primarily of young people and a large number of obscure personages. There were no dignitaries, unless one wishes to include R. Nielsen. . . . We have scarcely seen the equal of the *tactlessness* shown by his family in having him buried on a *Sunday*, between two religious services, from the nation's *most important church*." The presumptuous Dr. Lund did not escape notice either. "I still have not been informed about this through official channels, but it has caused a great offence, which as far as I can see must be met with *serious* steps."

The next year, on June 5, 1856, Henrik Lund was fined 100 rixdollars for this illegal speech. He also had to apologise to Dean Eggert Tryde and the congregation of Our Lady for his egregious assault upon the honour of the nation's most important church.

Henrik Lund was concerned about more than just preserving the truth of his uncle's spiritual and literary reputation. The vexed matter of Søren's reputed riches would not go away either. Some of the public may have been reticent to pick sides in Søren's war on Christendom, but they were not shy in speculating about what might have happened to the wealth of this middle-class bachelor. In the weeks following Søren's death there was a rumour going about that all his money was to be given to the poor. Others wondered whether pots of coins were left lying under the mounds of papers and books in his literary abode.

The fact was that no one had yet discovered what Kierkegaard wanted done with his possessions, as Henrik knew full well. As a self-proclaimed guardian of his uncle's legacy, Lund had accompanied the probate secretary on a visit to the house, where he claims to have found a "great quantity of paper, mostly manuscripts, located in various places." They found a lot of books but no will and no money. Indeed, from inspecting his accounts, it seems that Søren had spent all his living on these books, on household expenses, and on people in need. There was nothing left over. In a letter to his brother, Lund wrote with exasperation, "If anyone wants to talk about the great fortune he left behind, just let them talk."

Peter Kierkegaard also made a visit to the house. If he was looking for a plain document that would clear up any confusion, or perhaps a letter that would heal brotherly wounds, he too was sorely disappointed. In a locked drawer of Søren's writing desk, Peter found not one will and testament, but two. Both letters came with firm instructions that they were to be opened only after Søren's death. Both letters were addressed to Peter, yet neither had Peter as their subject. One letter was dated four years previous. It did not contain a single word of rapprochement, but instead read simply: "'The unnamed person, whose name will one day be named' to whom the entirety of my authorial activity is dedicated, is my former fiancée, Mrs Regine Schlegel." The other undated letter, doubtlessly opened with fear and trembling, was similarly terse. It was a will, of sorts, which left all of Søren's possessions to his former fiancée. If Regine refused to accept it for herself, then everything was to go to her so she could distribute it to the poor as she saw fit. "What I wish to express," wrote Søren, "is that for me the engagement was and is just as binding as a marriage."

Søren had left behind another set of instructions, this time regarding his burial site. These papers, dated 1846, listed a set of elaborate details about the placement and decoration of the memorial stone in the family plot. Of particular interest was the poem Søren wished to have engraved on his headstone:

> *In a little while*
> *I shall have won,*
> *Then the entire battle*
> *Will disappear at once.*

Then I may rest
In halls of roses
And unceasingly,
And unceasingly
Speak with my Jesus.

Here was a double curiosity. Of all the chatter in the newspapers, all the talk of the town, the wishes of his family, the statements of his friends and the pronouncements of his enemies, none had settled quite so clearly and simply on the legacy the man himself wished to leave behind. It would seem that this scourge of Christendom died loving Jesus, and the champion of individuality died loving Regine. Let the people say what they wanted about the meaning and purpose of Søren Kierkegaard; no one could deny that his life, indeed, was a singular one.

CHAPTER 2

School Life

"I don't know when S.K. entered the Borgerdyd School . . ." Pastor Frederik Welding sits back and sucks on his pen. Was this a good way to start? How to answer the elegantly phrased—but still rather impertinent—request for information before him? Elegant, because the young man of letters Hans Peter Barfod was always unfailingly polite to his elders and solicitous of their time. Impertinent, because it was clear to Welding, as it was clear to the other men who had received similar letters, that Barfod was staking his claim, seeking to connect his name to that of that old scamp Søren Kierkegaard.

It is 1869. Interest in Kierkegaard has not waned since his notorious burial fourteen years earlier. If anything, thanks to Barfod's recent publication of Kierkegaard's old letters and journals, interest was ramping up. Welding snorts. It seemed to be the way of the world these days that the wrong men got celebrated. Where was the flurry of activity for Welding's own mentor, the late Bishop Mynster? Kierkegaard certainly hadn't done anything to preserve the memory of *that* gentle, civilised man. Why should Søren be treated any differently?

Nevertheless, here it was lying on his desk. Barfod's request for schoolboy memories of Søren from their old days at the Borgerdyd School. How ironic that the most famous graduate of the "School for Civic Virtue" was the one man who seemed to do all he could to offend and reject civilised Christendom! Ah well, Frederik thinks to himself, it wouldn't do to speak *too* ill of the dead hero.

"I don't know when S.K. entered the Borgerdyd School. When

35

I entered the second form—the first form is the highest—in 1826, I met S.K. there. . . . He was always number two or number three in the various classes in which we were students until we were graduated in 1830." There, thinks Welding with grim satisfaction. Let *that* set the record straight about Søren's brilliant mind. "If he was number one in the class, it was only for a few short periods of time." Then, with a pang of grudging honesty: "I was often surprised by his work, but did not really understand why the teachers were pleased with his written compositions."

Welding pauses to consider next how to best describe the character of the blue-eyed, pinched faced, shock-headed boy who was always running about the schoolyard. What word encapsulates the strange mix of reserved inwardness punctuated by unexpected bursts of laughter and taunting that one experienced when around Søren? How to explain to Barfod the way the other boys instinctually kept their distance from the lad and that he too "went his own way, almost self-contained, never spoke of his home"? *Fremmed*. That was it. "Foreigner." Søren was an alien, a refugee. He moved through his world like a stranger exiled to a strange land. "To the rest of us, who knew and lived a more genuinely boyish life, S.K. was a stranger and an object of pity. . . . In most of his contacts with us he showed that he was so foreign to our interests that we quickly broke off contact with him and he often displayed a superior and teasing attitude, which made it clear that he was always a source of the unexpected."

"It seems to me," concludes Welding, "as a boy S.K. usually had a good eye for people's weak points, for the incoherent and offensive features of their behaviour. He therefore pounced upon tall fellows who were intellectual midgets . . . in general upon those who were quick to develop physically but slower intellectually." Frederik sighs as he dips his pen for more ink. "I myself belonged to this latter group."

Barfod would receive a lot of other replies in a similar vein. For instance, "I have now read Welding's letter several times, I doubt that any of S.K.'s schoolmates could do better or write anything more complete about him," wrote Edward Anger, now a pastor, adding, "Despite many battles, it remained an undecided question whether he or I was the weakest and the least capable in sports." The author Hans Holst was keen to point out the regular practice he had with Kierkegaard whereby he would write Søren's Danish composition assignments and Søren would write the Latin ones. "In his boyhood S.K. was not the object of great expectations." Peter Lind (who would one day go on to succeed Søren's brother Peter as bishop of Aalborg) confessed, "We did not have the least suspicion that he would one day come forth as a great opponent of his times. He seemed to be very conservative, to honour the king, love the Church and respect the police."

All the letters were from men who had taken their rightful positions in Danish society for which the School for Civic Virtue had prepared them. Some men recount small moments of friendship. Some, like Welding, remember the teasing wit, designed to exploit weaknesses. Some remember a quiet, aloof boy who never spoke of home or asked for help. Some attest to Kierkegaard's intellect, others cast aspersions on his ability. "*Fremmed*" pops up a lot, which might explain the idiosyncratic memoirs. The pen portraits are inconsistent in minor details, but all agree that Søren struck an odd figure. His character was alien to the other boys, as was his appearance. As a physical specimen Søren seems to have been gangly and fidgety. All of Søren's school contemporaries also allude to Professor Nielsen, usually with a quizzical note acknowledging the preference but failing to account for what the old headmaster saw in the son of Copenhagen's canniest merchant.

> This young man, who has thus been raised and educated in this manner, in keeping with the customs of our forbears and with the discipline that will promote the welfare of the state—and not in the

rash and rebellious spirit of the times—I recommend to you, learned men, in the highest fashion.

With these words on September 29, 1830, Professor Michael Nielsen launched his charge into the bourgeois society for which he had been prepared. Nielsen was the principal of Copenhagen's premier training ground for the sons of the city's merchants, clergy, and civil servants. Søren entered the school in 1821. Nielsen was evidently a better educator than he was a predictor of civic virtue, as Søren's entire life project would eventually amount to an attack on civilised Denmark! Nevertheless, there can be no doubt that the scrawny lad was something of a favourite of Prof. Nielsen, who enlisted Søren to help teach the younger boys Latin and to mark their compositions.

Nielsen's favour is all the more valuable because he was no easy pushover. A dedicated teacher and notoriously imposing figure, Nielsen wanted the boys to tremble when they walked down the street towards the school. He was known to have relaxed his discipline only once in class, and that during a thunderstorm: "When God speaks, I keep silent! But when I speak, you keep silent." Why was Søren so well liked by the old professor?

It couldn't have been because Søren was adept at ingratiating himself with the teaching staff. We are told by former school chums that by and large the teachers "believed [Søren] lacking in diligence, and he sometimes treated them with impudence." Prof. Blindesbøll, the Danish teacher, would complain about Søren to the other students: "Kierkg. is really annoying, because he is ready with an answer before he has got the question." Søren would often finish his Danish compositions earlier than anyone else, having only written a page or two of not very extraordinary prose and claim he was finished.

Poor Mr. Storck, the writing teacher, set himself up for an open goal when, in a test of the students' maturity, he proposed an assignment on any subject. Søren wrote a composition about the area of Charlottenlund—a palace and gardens north of Copenhagen—extolling its fine physical features, amusements, and pleasant places of play. Charlotte Lund just also happened to be the name of Storck's fiancée.

Prof. Mathiessen, a notoriously weak man with no control over his pupils, presided over classes that usually descended into chaos. Fellow students relate how once all the boys set out an entire picnic meal in his classroom—complete with a set table, sandwiches, and small beer—and began to tuck in. Mathiessen threatened to report them to Prof. Nielsen, which set the boys in a whirl of pleading and promises of good behaviour. Søren, however, merely said, "Will you also tell the professor that we are always like this in your class?" Mathiessen did not report to the boss.

Even Søren's obedience could have an air of impudence. Once, when Mr. Muller, the Hebrew teacher, tried to discipline Søren, he was met with laughter. Muller, with great anger and a show of gathering his stuff to quit the room, said, "Either you leave or I will."

Søren thought for a bit, then said, "Well, then, it's best that I leave." And he did.

Søren would frequently satirise teachers who were not there, such as Mr. Warnecke, the history professor who had trouble asserting himself. ("Søren had a good eye for people's weak points.") When supposedly reciting passages and poetry from memory, it was not unknown for the cheeky chap to read from a text hidden on his lap.

In the upper years, Søren had his brother Peter as his teacher in Greek. Here, he "deliberately made things difficult" by teasing his brother and bringing their relationship into the classroom.

Perhaps it was something like these moments of independence of mind and sharpness of wit which impressed Nielsen when he reported of Søren:

> When he was entrusted to our care at the age of nine he did not permit himself to be confused by those who are ignorant of how

they should act and who are like those who swim into a strong current and are swept along with bad companions as if by a powerful river.

The independence of mind certainly did not endear Søren to many of the other boys. As Barfod discovered, by all accounts Søren had few friends at school. As an adult, his diary entries and autobiographical writings also bring to mind a lonely younger self who relied on his wit:

> Slight, slender, and frail and, compared to others, with practically none of the physical qualifications making for a whole man, melancholy, sick at heart, profoundly and inwardly ravaged in various ways, I nevertheless was given one thing: eminent sagacity, presumably to keep me from being completely worthless. Already as a young lad I was aware of my intellectual gifts and that they constituted my power over these far stronger companions.

A pre-emptive attack is often the best defence. Søren was an inveterate teaser. Although the "least and weakest at sports," Søren especially targeted the bigger, taller, and more powerful boys and had a knack for making them look ridiculous. When his classmate Hans (he of the Danish homework help) attempted to read his poetry aloud in his halting schoolboy manner "SK was always one of the first to interrupt his reading by throwing a book at his head." Besides suggesting an early and highly attuned appreciation for poetry, the incident reinforces the idea that Søren was adept at exploiting weak points to get the best of a room. Søren's teasing sometimes caused boys to cry. Once, when a teacher heard about this, he said to the bigger boy, "So what? You could easily put him in your pocket."

Søren may have been a stranger in a strange land, but he did not enjoy diplomatic immunity. His language was "annoying and provocative, and he was aware that this had this effect even though he was often the one who paid for it." He would pull faces and give nicknames to other boys "even though it often earned him a beating." One day, some of the boys decided to teach this strange little upstart a lesson. Throwing him over a desk, two held down his legs while others pinned Søren's thrashing arms. Then they set to his britches "with rulers, book straps, etc."

They were not stylish britches. All Barfod's sources agreed that Søren's wiry frame sported a deeply old-fashioned rough tweed jacket with short tails, shoes, and knee-high woollen stockings. "Never boots" like all the other boys wore. "Søren Sock" he was called, or "Choir Boy," in connection to his anachronistic uniform and his hosier father.

In a roundabout way this leads to the main reason for Professor Nielsen's appreciation. Michael Pedersen Kierkegaard was a notoriously sensible man, tight with money and stern in outlook. Although one of Copenhagen's most successful merchants, and an importer of wool, linen, and silk to boot, he did not permit any of his seven children to dress with panache. His daughters were shabby. His sons utilitarian. Although a leading public figure in commerce and religious circles, Michael only allowed himself to turn his reversible coat inside out when the original side was fully worn out. The strict stance against spending money on frippery spoke of a serious man, heading up a home of true civic virtue. Thus it is that Prof. Nielsen's school leaver's report appears to be less about Kierkegaard and more about the *Kierkegaards*:

> From the very beginning [Søren] was steeped in his parents' seriousness and in the good example of their strong sense of religious reverence, devotion to God, and moral responsibility, and this was subsequently nourished in early childhood with instruction provided by teachers who had been carefully chosen with this goal in mind. . . . One may certainly hope that he will be his brother's equal, since he is his equal in talent.
>
> The root of these virtues is the pure devotion to God that was implanted in his character from the very beginning of his life.

Indeed, his father has conducted his business in accordance with the precepts of philosophy, and he has united his business life with the reading of works of theology, philosophy and literature. . . . Because his father's home is thus such a model . . . and is arranged in conformity with the principles by which children are trained in virtue and in the wisdom which is given by God, he has enjoined his son to view all things in the light of the fear of God and a sense of duty . . . And he has done everything to awaken the boy's love for scholarly culture, which is the foundation of all praiseworthy endeavours.

The good headmaster was certainly right to accredit Søren's family more than his school for the forces which were shaping the man-to-be.

CHAPTER 3

Family Life

Young Søren is asked what he wants to be when he grows up.
"A fork."
"Why?"
"Well then I could spear anything I wanted on the dinner table!"
"What if we come after you?"
"Then I'll spear you."

Søren Aabye Kierkegaard was born May 5, 1813. He joined mother Anne (aged forty-five), father Michael (fifty-six), sisters Maren (sixteen), Nicoline (thirteen), and Petrea (eleven) and brothers Søren Michael (seven), Niels Andreas (five), and Peter Christian (four). They all lived at Number 2, Nytorv ("New Square"), a solid and respectable house for a solid and respectable family. No. 2 was a ten-minute walk from the school, and five minutes down from the Church of Our Lady. The spacious plaza out front hosted Copenhagen's principal meat market and was full of the bustle and pageantry of city life. To the right were the offices of the city hall and high courts. To the left a pharmacy, and further up, the Gammeltorv ("Old Square") with its famous fountain where patriotic townsfolk would float golden apples on the King's birthday.

What might the atmosphere of the Kierkegaard family have felt like? Like any family, the tone of the Kierkegaard home was created by the striking of a few notes in repetition.

Number 2 Nytorv, the Kierkegaard family home. Søren occupied rooms on the second floor. The house was located next to the city hall and a five minutes' walk away from the Church of Our Lady. The building was torn down at the beginning of the twentieth century.

One such note was that of money. The Kierkegaards were comfortably well-off, their security overseen by a frugal and serious man who had acquired his wealth through a mixture of hard work, canny investments, and sheer good fortune. Michael Pedersen Kierkegaard was born into a family of sheepherders in 1756. His family were bonded peasants, traditionally attached to church land in Sædling, a village on the moors of West Jutland (hence the name *Kierkegaard*, or "church yard").

When Michael was twelve years old he was sent to work for his uncle, a wool merchant in Copenhagen. The event saved the hardscrabble family another mouth to feed, just as it saved Michael from a life doomed to poverty. As a mark of his salvation he proudly kept amongst his possessions the document from the village priest releasing Michael from bonded servitude in 1777. In 1780 Michael obtained citizenship and five years later he set up shop with another hosier named Mads Røyen. The mercantile world of Copenhagen was highly regulated, and Mads and Michael had to fight in the courts for the right to sell all kinds of goods normally barred from merchants of their sphere. In 1788 Michael won another concession from the King, gaining Royal permission to deal in East Indian and Chinese textiles, and West Indian sugar, syrup, and coffee beans. Michael was fast becoming more than a humble hosier. In 1794 Michael married Mads' sister, Kirstine Røyen. Kirstine died, childless, in 1796, as did Michael's uncle, who left everything to him. Michael married again and began a family. For ten years Michael's fortune seemed assured, but in 1807, world events caught up with the sleepy market town and its litigious merchants.

Napoleon Bonaparte was striding across Europe. As part of his long war against England, Napoleon was seeking to close all European ports to British trade. For officially neutral Denmark, the pressure was mounting. The British, fearing Denmark's prevarication and mistrustful of King Frederick VI's ultimate allegiance, engaged in a controversial pre-emptive strike. In August 1807 the British Navy placed Copenhagen's ports under embargo and demanded the surrender of the Danish fleet. No answer was forthcoming, and so the British Navy attacked, relishing the opportunity to try out their latest military technology—William Congreve's rocket-propelled bombs. Copenhagen burned, many people died, and King Frederick was forced into a humiliating stand-down.

The cost of rebuilding the city after the bombardment was expensive enough, but combined with punitive measures arising from the King's continued association with Napoleon, Denmark was plunged into economic chaos. Increasing inflation led the National Bank to declare bankruptcy and in 1813 the Danish "rixdollar" (r.d.) was drastically devalued. In adult life, Søren was clearly aware of the pall that money matters cast over his own identity and that of his family:

> I was born in 1813, in that bad fiscal year when so many other bad banknotes were put in circulation, and my life seems most comparable to one of them. There is a suggestion of greatness in me, but because of the bad conditions of the times I am not worth very much. A banknote like that sometimes becomes a family's misfortune.

There is, however, layer upon layer of irony here, as Søren knew full well. For the Kierkegaard family's misfortune was not monetary.

Through clever investments and good luck, Michael actually emerged from this time of financial chaos in fine fettle. It was announced that the Royal Bonds that he had invested in would not become "bad banknotes" like the rest of Danish currency. Spared from the effects of inflation, the Kierkegaard family was not forced into poverty in 1813. Indeed the money would go on to become the foundation for Søren's inheritance, underwriting his literary career and attack upon the Establishment. Michael was wealthier than ever, the Kierkegaards were supported, and, much to his family's future chagrin, Søren was set up to lob a different kind of rocket-propelled bomb at the sleepy citizens of Copenhagen.

The constant awareness of money in the family took the form of frugality, which itself was inextricable from the note of tight paternal control that pervaded the home. Henriette Lund remembered of her grandfather: "Obedience was for him not merely a thing of great importance . . . it was the main prop of his life." A servant recalled how Michael "was not to be trifled with when he became angry. Not that he shouted or used abusive language, but the seriousness with which his reproaches

Michael Pedersen Kierkegaard, Søren's father

were uttered made them sink more deeply than if he had made a scene." Once, when sister Nicoline dropped an expensive soup tureen, Michael did not say a word. He did not need to. His silent disapproval was keenly felt. If he had flown into a rage, it might have been easier to deal with—easily mollified, soon dissipated, quickly forgotten. That this apparently trifling instance survived as a family anecdote long after the principal members had died is testament to the power Michael's stern silence had over the children. More serious is the story of Søren's elder brother Niels Andreas. Niels was a bookish lad who was keen to go to university. Michael decided instead that another Kierkegaard was needed to go into business. The two clashed. Niels lost to his implacable father and spent a few dutiful years trying his hand at Copenhagen trade. Niels was unhappy and unsuccessful, and he soon left to seek his fortune in America. The breach with his father was never healed.

Niels' story is especially sad because, in fact, Michael also loved reading and sported a keen intellect. Thus another dominant family note was that of lively debate, learned discussion, and constant discourse. In other words, the Kierkegaards liked to talk. A lot.

When Søren set about crafting an intellectual autobiography of sorts in 1842 he had his pseudonymous stand-in, "Johannes Climacus," recall the formative times the young lad had with his father. He was "a very strict man, seemingly dry and prosaic, but beneath this rough homespun cloak he concealed a glowing imagination that not even his advanced age managed to dim." Johannes asks to go out to play, but the father offers an imaginative conversation instead. Taking his son by the hand, the old man walks around and around the room. "While they walked up and down the floor, his father would tell about everything they saw. They greeted the passers-by; the carriages rumbled past, drowning out his father's voice; the pastry woman's fruits were more tempting than ever." Is the story true? In later life, Søren's family acquaintances affirmed that it could be, one friend recounting Michael proudly stating: "When I can't sleep I lie down and I talk with my boys, and there is no better conversation here in Copenhagen."

Michael Kierkegaard was not only a canny businessman, he was also a self-made scholar. Michael was justly proud of his literary accomplishments and was often seen book in hand. He favoured German and had taught himself the language, advising his sons not to become too attached to their native tongue lest they become small-minded and provincial. Michael would faithfully work his way through the latest philosophical systems or religious treatise. Unlike much of what passed for intelligent discourse amongst Copenhagen's chattering class, Michael actually understood what he was reading and could defend his informed opinions. In the Kierkegaard household, articulation was a highly prized commodity. The young Kierkegaard brothers would often sit at their father's feet while Michael entertained a guest, engaging him in conversation about some latest theological innovation or other. In his unpublished autobiographical account, Søren relates how his heart thrilled at his father's mastery of argument. Michael, calmly and seriously, would allow the visitor his say, giving him time to build up his case. It was a trap! Just when it seemed that the visitor had created an unassailable fortress, with a few deft questions Michael would bring the whole edifice crashing down. "My father," said Peter Christian, "was the most gifted man I have ever known."

The note struck by the gifted Kierkegaard family conversations was strictly male. Michael did not value educating his three daughters and did not include them in the salon environments he had created at home. Neither did Søren's mother, Anne, enter into the intellectual cut and thrust of family conversations. Indeed, she was probably illiterate, if the guided pen used on the few official documents she had to sign is any indication.

Anne Sørensdatter Lund was born in 1768. A distant cousin of Michael's, she too was of peasant stock. She first properly entered the Kierkegaard sphere when, in 1794, she was hired as housemaid to Michael's first wife, Kirstine. In 1796 Kirstine died of pneumonia, childless. Within the year Anne and Michael were married and the Kierkegaard clan began. Her one surviving portrait reveals a double chin and a satisfied smile. Anne's grandchildren remember a genial woman who loved to fuss over her sons and was especially pleased when they fell ill so she could care for them without competing with their father's witty repartee. Anne lived in her family's shadow, and it is likely she retained something of the servant in their attitude towards her. Perhaps not even that. Michael did the daily shopping and did not entrust the household accounts to her. Anne was not relied upon to educate their sons, and Michael enlisted the assistance of another woman to train up their daughters. Nevertheless, the union was evidentially successful to a certain degree. Anne and Michael's marriage was long, peaceful, and fruitful with children. When Anne died, Michael arranged for an ostentatious funeral cortege to take her to her final resting place. Anne's graveyard memorial (where Michael too would be buried four years later) reads:

> Anne Kierkegaard, born Lund, went home to the Lord July 31, 1834, in the 67th year of her life, loved and missed by her surviving children, relatives and friends, but especially by her old husband, Michael Pedersen Kierkegaard, who on August 9, 1838 followed her into eternal life in his 82nd year.

Anne Sørensdatter Kierkegaard, neé Lund, Søren's mother

We must hope that she was loved and missed. We do not know if this is the case because the most significant thing about her, from the point of view of a biography of Søren Kierkegaard, is that in the thousands of pages of his copious journals, diaries, articles, and books, Søren Kierkegaard does not directly mention her once.

People seeking any morsel of Søren's allusion to his mother must remain satisfied with this thin gruel: in *Sickness Unto Death*, there is passing mention of a "deeply humbled" wife of an "earnest and holy man" who despairs of forgiveness. The woman must be Anne because the man is certainly Michael Pedersen.

If Søren was *Fremmed* to his school friends, then the word most used to describe his father was *Tungsind*. Melancholy. Weighed down with a heaviness (*tung*) of spirit (*Sind*). Throughout his writings Søren often reflects on the note of guilt repeatedly struck in the melancholy Kierkegaard home.

> It is appalling to think even for one single moment about the dark background of my life right from its earliest beginning. The anxiety with which my father filled my soul, his own frightful depression, a lot of which I cannot even write down.

That their father's heavy spirit pervaded the family is not in question. Where it came from will always remain a matter of conjecture. What burden did Michael Pedersen Kierkegaard bear? The question is one upon which many people have wondered, not least Søren himself. In a famous diary entry, set apart from the rest of the entries, Søren wrote the following lines:

> Then it was that the great earthquake occurred, the frightful upheaval which suddenly drove me to a new infallible principle for interpreting all the phenomena. Then I surmised that my father's old-age was not a divine blessing, but rather a curse, that our family's

exceptional intellectual capacities were only for mutually harrowing one another; then I felt the stillness of death deepen around me, when I saw in my father an unhappy man who would survive us all, a memorial cross on the grave of all his personal hopes. A guilt must rest upon the entire family, a punishment of God must be upon it: it was supposed to disappear, obliterated by the mighty hand of God, erased like a mistake, and only at times did I find a little relief in the thought that my father had been given the heavy duty of reassuring us all with the consolation of religion, telling us that a better world stands open for us even if we lost this one, even if the punishment the Jews always called down on their enemies should strike us: that remembrance of us would be completely obliterated, that there would be no trace of us.

Søren's "Earthquake" has joined the ranks of the great literary mysteries of the ages. He deliberately suppressed the details, but two stories especially come to the fore.

"How appalling for the man who, as a lad watching sheep on the Jutland heath, suffering painfully, hungry and exhausted, once stood on a hill and cursed God—and the man was unable to forget it when he was eighty-two years old." So wrote Søren in a diary entry in 1846. It has the artistic flourish of one of Søren's many thought experiments. Yet when Barfod found the entry going through Søren's papers, he showed it to brother Peter. Yes, confirmed the last of the Kierkegaards, weeping. That is father's story, "and ours too." There was enough truth in the story at least that out of respect for the family, Barfod suppressed its publication.

The second story was less obscure, and more socially sensitive. Søren was not illegitimate, but his sister almost was. The upstanding citizen Michael Kierkegaard married Anne Lund a year after the death of his first wife. That Anne was a cousin and an illiterate housekeeper would have been enough to raise Copenhagen's collective eyebrow. To make matters worse, their first child, Maren, was born only five months after the hasty wedding. Michael was aware of the impropriety of the union, formalising his reticence in the marriage contract itself. A strange, idiosyncratic document, the contract needed special dispensation from the royal courts to confirm its legality. It explicitly mentions the possibility that it may be that "the temperaments cannot be united" between man and wife. In this case, a specific sum was set apart for Anne to go her separate way, and the contract went out of its way to deny her the rights and status of a normal wife. The agreement spelled out the exact amount she would receive in case of death or divorce but denied her the usual rights of inheritance. A yearly amount of 200 r.d. was apportioned to her—equivalent to the yearly wage of an apprentice craftsman.

Michael would later amend his will to include his wife, and clearly love and affection grew in the marriage. Yet that inauspicious start of his family, coupled with the youthful rebellion of the deeply pious man must have contributed to Michael's melancholy. Far from dissipating the cloud of doom, Michael's financial success and his growing family seems to have had the opposite effect. He was waiting for the other shoe to drop.

For people already predisposed to melancholy, the sense of a looming day of reckoning was not wildly implausible: another note struck repeatedly in the Kierkegaard family was that of accident and death. As a young boy, Søren Aabye fell from a tree, landing hard on his back. His family were understandably alarmed and attributed Søren's ensuing health problems to this event. Much worse, on September 14, 1819, the twelve-year-old Søren Michael died of bleeding in the head after a schoolyard accident when he crashed into another boy on the playground. The sudden death traumatised the family. Three years later on March 15, 1822, Maren died as a result of convulsions. She was twenty-four, the eldest child and the offspring of Michael and Anne's ill-judged union. Maren had never been well and her death was not a surprise. Middle sister Nicoline died of a fever on September 10, 1832, a few weeks after giving birth to a stillborn son. It was Michael who arranged to tell his beloved daughter straight of her fatal condition. The doctor had wanted to soften the blow but the father insisted. "No, my children have not been brought up like that." She left behind her husband, Johan Christian Lund, Henrik (aged seven), Michael (six), Sophie (five), and Carl (two).

Upon breaking with the family, brother Niels Andreas had immigrated to America. Less than a year later, after moving from Boston to Providence, and then to New York, he eventually tried his fortune in Paterson, New Jersey. It was there Niels succumbed to "galloping consumption" (tuberculosis) on September 21, 1833. News of his death struck the family hard, the news made even worse by the apparent omission of his father in Niels' deathbed utterances. Michael was convinced that the slight was deliberate and was plunged into inconsolable grief.

In the same year that her mother, Anne, passed away, youngest daughter Petrea gave birth to a boy in December 1834. The boy, Peter Severin, was healthy, but Petrea would not live to see the New Year. She left her husband, Henrik Ferdinand Lund, the single father of a two-week-old infant, as well as Henriette (five), Vilhelm (three), and Peter Christian (one). Like her sister Nicoline, Petrea was thirty-three years old. The age would acquire a totemic significance in the Kierkegaard household. Michael became convinced that he was doomed to see none of his children live past thirty-three, an age heavy with meaning.

Now rattling around in a house with only Michael and Peter for company, Søren too absorbed something of this morbid symbolism.

> It is really remarkable that Christ came to be precisely 33 years old, the number of years which according to general reckoning denotes a generation, so that here too there is something normal, in that whatever goes over this number is accidental.

Søren was well aware of the absurdity of the superstition, but it gripped his imagination nonetheless. On their respective thirty-fourth birthdays, Søren and Peter would share letters, congratulating each other for proving their father wrong.

Religion constituted the final note that created the tone of Søren's household. "I acquired an anxiety about Christianity and yet felt powerfully attracted to it." As with any deeply embedded and historical expression of Christianity, the Christian culture of Denmark was far from monolithic. All the various permutations of political and theological liberalism, conservatism, renewal movements, missionary zeal, rationalistic analysis, militaristic patriotism, peace movements, apologetics, philosophical challenges, Bible studies, cultural accommodation, personal devotion, doubt, faith, hope, and love that one can witness in the Christian world today were present in Denmark in the nineteenth century. Throughout his life, Søren would have cause to engage with all of these aspects and their figureheads.

For the young Søren, however, two main stars dominated the night sky of his Christian galaxy: the religion preached by Mynster and the faith of the Moravian Brotherhood. As with everything else in the family, Christianity was taken seriously in the Kierkegaard home. The easy-going religiosity of the cultured citizens of Copenhagen was not for Michael! His piety was no mere lip service. Like most good Danes, Michael faithfully had his children baptised and confirmed in the Lutheran State Church.

A year before Søren's birth, a young Lutheran minister named Jakob Peter Mynster had been appointed to the church down the road. The earnest young preacher had set out his stall *against* the intellectualism and Enlightenment rationalism that was fashionable in the universities, and *for* personal devotion and commitment to biblical revelation. He was also a firm defender of the cultural sophistication of the Danish Church and had a lively sense of the gospel as poetry. These qualities proved attractive to Michael, and Mynster became the Kierkegaards' family friend and pastor. He would remain so even when he became prime bishop of the national church years later.

Mynster's brand of Christianity was especially appealing because it seemed to offer Michael the best of both worlds. On the one hand, he could instil in his children a sense of socially acceptable, civic-minded Christianity. On the other hand, he could be sure that Mynster was not going to deny the personal, serious aspect of the faith, which for Michael was the most compelling version of all.

Michael was a lifelong Moravian, or *Hernuter*. An off-shoot from the Lutheran Reformation, the Moravian Brotherhood had a strong hold on the rural and peasant population of Denmark. It was a version of Christianity diametrically opposed to the high-minded philosophic liberalism of large swathes of the established church. The Moravians practiced the priesthood of all believers, sought inner renewal, and fostered emotional responses to gospel texts. It was a Moravian who was preaching when the Anglican priest and soon-to-be Methodist reformer John Wesley felt his heart "strangely warmed" in England in 1738, and it was Moravians in Denmark who similarly sought to convert the baptised citizens of Copenhagen. Michael was a patron of the Brotherhood, helping them move to a new, larger meeting house in 1816. The Kierkegaard children would attend Moravian prayer meetings with their father on Sunday evenings, after attending to Mynster's sermons on Sunday mornings.

The Moravian emphasis on the tortured and crucified Christ, rather than the Holy Spirit or the Resurrection, did nothing to assuage Michael's sense of impending doom and unforgivable sin. His Christianity was serious and suffering, not joyful or graceful. Søren's later pseudonyms refer more than once to a young boy being shown a picture book of national and mythic heroes. Here was a general who rescued his people. Here was a brave man, feted by his fellows. And then the boy comes across another picture nestled amongst the heroes, deliberately laid across the pages. Here is a man tortured, with wounds in his hands, and blood streaming down his arms. Who did this? Who would harm such a man? The boy is told that it is he who did this, and that this is the way of the world. In later life Søren would recall how he was brought up to believe with a firm conviction that in this base and corrupt world, everything that was Right and True would be spat upon.

Michael and the Moravians may well have been largely correct in their worldly analysis, but the effect on young Søren was deleterious. The unrelenting gravitas proved too much:

> As a child, I was rigorously and earnestly brought up in Christianity, insanely brought up, humanly speaking—already in earliest childhood I had overstrained myself under the impression that the depressed old man, who had laid upon me, was himself sinking under—a child attired, how insane, as a depressed old man. Frightful! No wonder, then, that there were times when Christianity seemed to me the most inhuman cruelty, although I never, even when I was furthest away from it, gave up my veneration for it . . .

It is no wonder that as a young man Søren would prove to be so ambivalent about his theological studies and the expectation that he would take his rightful place in society as a serious man.

CHAPTER 4

Public Life/Private Life

Stefan and David are drinking coffee at the A Porta cafe, watching the world bustle by Kongens Nytorv. The King's New Square is one of Copenhagen's main plazas, a place to see and be seen. Prominently situated on the square, A Porta is an excellent location for both activities. The men are too venerable to promenade now, but as long as young ladies are pretty and young men are cocky, looking at others will never lose its appeal. Stefan has just spotted one such lad now, a fine figure of a tall man with broad shoulders, making his way across the square.

"Ah, you take young Kierkegaard there," he says, jabbing his coffee spoon emphatically to prove the point, "a credit to his father's ideals. I've said it before, my friend, and I'll say it again. No man is fully grown till he leaves Copenhagen. This city's too small to form people properly. Look at that chap now—lived in Paris during the riots, Berlin, Utrecht, who knows where else? Now he's back from Germany, and with a doctorate to boot!"

David has heard this line before. Having never left the market town himself, he can't help bristling. "I don't know, Stefan. I hear he's arrogant. Always arguing—they call him the 'devil debater.' And do you know he turned down a perfectly good church appointment in Jutland, and for what? Ambition, pure and simple, *I* think. A country parish isn't good enough for the likes of *him*."

Stefan is quick to defend his champion. "Arrogant? Maybe. But who can blame him? He's clever. Sped through his finals. There's a line as long as this street of parents hoping to get him to tutor their sons.

59

He's got a good position at the university, and he's got friends in high places—"

With a tap of his hand, David stops his companion mid-flow. A young lady has just honed into view. It's the daughter of old Bishop Boiesen. With a shy smile, the girl waits while the man makes his way purposefully towards her.

"You mark my words," says Stefan, his spoon clattering into the cup with a ring of triumph, "that young Kierkegaard is going places."

"Aye," David concedes, "we certainly have not heard the last of Peter Christian."

Gammeltorv Square and the King's New Square, Copenhagen, from a lithograph by Danish artist Emil Bærentzen. The Kierkegaard family lived in the building just to the right of the archway on the left.

❖

Stefan and David were so intent on watching Peter stride towards his respectable and serious life, they missed the other of Michael Kierkegaard's sons striding, no less purposefully, the other direction into their cafe. So it was they failed to notice the young man who, with his "strange, confused look" and hair in a "tousled crest" almost six inches over his forehead, was sometimes mistaken for a shop clerk in the wrong place at the wrong time. They did not see the "witty, somewhat sarcastic face" with its "fresh colour," perched above shoulders "hunched forward a bit" with eyes "intelligent, lively and superior" with a "mixture of good nature and malice."

They did not see Søren coming, but as this odd man lurched by their table, arm outstretched to order his third coffee of the day to go with his fourth cigar, they would have been jostled. Unlike his older brother, this Kierkegaard was no sportsman with easy grace. Built lopsided, he never could seem to walk in a straight line. Companions were always being pushed one way or the other when walking with Søren, and they were forever having to slip round to his other side to steer him back on course, ducking under his wildly gesticulating arms as they did so. Undoubtedly, the old men would have been annoyed by this awkward adolescent, but they probably would not have recognised him. Unlike Peter, Søren was not making a name for himself amongst their kinds of circles.

When piecing together the story of the young Søren Kierkegaard, it is worth considering in what sorts of circles Søren *was* becoming known and in which ones he was *not*. One public sphere that did not see much of Søren was the Divinity Faculty. Søren entered the University of Copenhagen to read theology in 1830. He was eighteen. When Peter had entered the same department at the same age, he had passed easily, taking the degree in four years to great acclaim. Yet by 1835, when his contemporaries were graduating and finding jobs, Søren had yet to take his final exams, and his name is often absent from attendance registers. Søren's life has many mysteries. The reason for this failure to graduate is not one of them. Søren was bored. In 1835 he wrote to his brother-in-law, "As far as little annoyances are concerned, I will say only that I am starting to study for the theological examination, a pursuit that does not interest me in the least and that therefore does not get done very fast." To the utter consternation of his family it would be almost another five years from this point before Søren would think about taking his exams. Far from pursuing the serious life of a pastor-in-training, in the 1830s Søren was a dandy, working hard on cultivating the aura of a man-about-town. Upon leaving high school, "Søren Sock" had become, in his own words, "a man dressed in modern clothes, wearing spectacles, and smoking a cigar."

One of the public arenas particularly affected by Søren's gentrification was the marketplace. Tobacconists, restaurateurs, grocers, theatre operators, baristas, booksellers, and tailors all benefited from Kierkegaard's lifestyle choice. When they could collect on the bills, that is. By 1837 receipts reveal that Søren owed a tea shop 235 r.d., the tailor 280 r.d., and almost 400 r.d. to bookshops. The Student Union of the university threatened to ban Søren until he paid his dues. The family account books reveal other debts of various magnitudes. One entry from this time shows a repayment of 1262 r.d. These are enormous bills that the feckless Søren could not possibly pay. It was Michael Kierkegaard who was prevailed upon to meet the costs, and again and again that is what he dutifully did. We can only speculate what he would have thought when paying these bills.

Actually, speculation about Michael's attitude is not too hard to fathom. Michael's celebrated financial acumen did not magically desert him when looking over the eye-watering sums. It would not have escaped his notice, for example, that Søren's 1837 bookseller's tab alone amounted to double the yearly amount Michael had apportioned to his wife Anne in their first marriage contract. Michael was an assiduous bookkeeper, moral as well as financial. The ledgers that record his payments are sometimes accompanied by handwritten notes from Søren. These are *aide memoirs* of shame, such as the entry for the 1262 r.d. which reads: "In this way my father has helped me out of financial embarrassment, for which I give my thanks."

The old man managed the paradoxical feat of being indulgent and grudging at the same time. The indulgence led to resentfulness at home. Michael, frugal and self-made, resented paying. Peter, ever the dutiful brother, resented the apparent favour shown to this prodigal son. Søren resented the straightjacket life and constant comparisons with his brother. His journals contain multiple ruminations on the family dynamic: "Peter has always regarded himself as better than I and pettily [regarded me] as the prodigal brother. He is right in so thinking, for he has always been more upright than I. His relation to Father, for example, was that of an upright son—mine, on the other hand, was often blameworthy: ah, but yet Peter has never loved Father as I did." The three were often not on speaking terms with each other. This was true of the brothers especially. Their silent feuds prompted Michael to comment with exasperation more than once that he simply did not know what was the matter with Søren.

One window into the family relationship at this time comes from another public arena, that of the church. Here, attendance records reveal how often—or how little—the three attended Communion together. There is record of father and sons attending separately, and occasionally in pairs. Peter especially is conspicuous by his absence. He often suffered bouts of depression, which he linked in his mind to various religious crises. In March 1834, for example, Peter withdrew from communion, giving as his reason Matthew 5:23–34: "But I tell you that anyone who is angry with a brother or sister will be subject to judgement." The adult Søren would come to admire a man who takes seriously the commands of Jesus in the New Testament. However, as an adolescent, Søren felt he suffered on account of his brother at these times, "when he became morbidly religious."

The dynamics were to change again when Peter introduced Marie into the mix. The daughter of a recently deceased bishop and a keen singer, Marie Boiesen accepted Peter's proposal in June 1836. They were wed in October of that year. Rather than take this event as an opportunity to flee the family homestead, Peter brought Marie to live at 2 Nytorv. He later recalled how she brought a note of happiness to the home. It would be a fleeting note however. By July 1837, weakened by a bout of influenza and afflicted with gastric fever, Marie was dead.

Søren's journals at this time make no direct reference to the death. This is in fact typical for his entries, which are often less like daily diaries and more like "thought experiments." However, around this time there are numerous allusions to sadness, tragedy, and the pointlessness of petit-bourgeois life. True to form, Peter's diary is more prosaic and informative: "Søren these days is perhaps more than ever before weighed down with brooding, almost more than his health can stand . . . A recreational trip he began the very day of the funeral had to be cut short towards the end once it went wrong, it didn't help at all." Marie's passing evidently did nothing to bring the Kierkegaards closer together. In the same month as her funeral, another of Søren's notes appears in Michael's account book. Next to yet one more of Michael's repayments on his son's behalf, Søren is forced to write: "Since from the coming first of September 1837 I will leave my father's house and cease to be a participant in his household, he has promised me 500 r.d. / year for my subsistence." Five hundred a year was not much, especially in light of Søren's profligate lifestyle. To supplement his income, Søren took work teaching Latin for Professor Nielsen at the old School for Civic Virtue.

Søren's leaving home in 1837 obviously marks a turning point of sorts. Yet for the roving gadabout, the wrench could not have been too great. In any case Søren was rarely at his father's home. The enormous restaurant bills are testament to that. Instead of conducting morally improving discussions about politics and theology with Peter and Michael over a sensible supper, Søren at this time was seeking out less salubrious company.

One such person was Jørgen Jørgensen, ten years Søren's senior. Jørgen had a reputation for living off the wealth of others, getting them to stand for his drinks and cigars. In return, Jørgen would ply them with stories from his days on the police force. He was a well-known raconteur, and Søren retained an acquaintance with him for some years, evidently enjoying the worldly atmosphere that Jørgen supplied. It all seems to have been fodder for Søren's written thought experiments. Although there was some ambiguity over the matter (thanks to a handful of typically cryptic comments in the journals), it is doubtful that Søren actually accompanied Jørgen on any of his drunken escapades to the bars and brothels of Copenhagen's seedier districts. There is no record of this, which there would have been for a public figure like Søren in the goldfish bowl that was Copenhagen. Even if Søren kept quiet in his diaries, his contemporaries certainly would not have. They were not shy of gossiping about each other's comings and goings.

One such source of public chatter was the theatre, where Søren could be found almost nightly. Søren loved the melodrama of opera, and he was a keen observer of the actor's craft. And if the eyes of a beautiful woman just happened to be caught from across the stalls, what harm was there in that? Copenhagen's Royal Theatre, however, provided more than merely drama or an occasion for innocent flirting. The place was a meeting of likeminded souls. Søren was part of a group (which included Hans Christian Andersen) of civilised contemporaries, up-and-comers in Copenhagen's chattering class. Every night, literary figures, ambitious politicians, newspaper men, and students would congregate. In between acts, the theatre would be alive with the buzz of witty men discussing the latest ideas when they weren't discussing each other.

Søren was gaining a reputation as one of the wittiest and cleverest of the bunch, due in large part to his student activities. Søren may not have been a keen theologian, but he was active in other university circles and he was making a name for himself in this sphere. Søren attended lectures in psychology, poetry, history, and philosophy. He does not seem to have loved any of these subjects, but two philosophy lecturers in particular were to catch his attention, and he theirs. Søren became friendly with Frederik Christian Sibbern, who taught aesthetics. Sibbern was a serious man, averse to affectation. He wrote complicated, dense texts, but he was also a poet. His daughter remembered Søren's visits to the family home, where the two men talked into the long evening "when the fire gleamed in the stove."

The other key person in Søren's education was Poul Martin Møller. Of the two favourite professors, Møller's life was the more colourful. Before taking up his post at the university, Møller had served as a ship's chaplain. He too was a poet and a celebrated public figure. There is little indication of how much Søren actually learned from Møller's philosophy lectures: it was Møller's style and personality that won him over. Møller also lived in a house on Nytorv and was known to frequent the same cafes as Søren. An early champion of the idea that one should authentically inhabit one's ideas, Møller was a sharp critic and a keen satirist, who, to Søren's delight, could easily puncture the pomposity of Copenhagen's intellectual elite.

The prime source of puffed-up cultural superiority in nineteenth-century Europe was the German thinker Georg Wilhelm Friedrich Hegel. One of Hegel's Big Ideas was that the historical development of art, religion, and philosophy told us something true about the development of the Divine Mind in the universe. The revelation of God was not to be found in a person or a holy text but in the development of a culture's history. The unfolding Spirit is first encountered in a society's art. This artistic expression is then given meaning and explanation in that society's religion. Finally, it is philosophy that explains the religion. The Spirit is ever developing and thus the Divine is revealed in mankind's highest achievements. To see the latest and best manifestation of the Divine Mind in the world, all one has to do is look at the latest and best manifestation of the world's civilisation. The reader will be given no prizes for guessing whose art, religion, and philosophy the Western European Hegel thought was currently sitting on the top of the civilizational pile.

Hegel was (and is) a towering figure in Western philosophy. His influence was (and is) immense, even where his name goes unacknowledged. Hegel and his followers have a hand in such apparently opposite movements as the Manifest Destiny of American exceptionalism, the class-war struggle of Marx's dialectical materialism, and the triumphalism of the Third Reich. Both the liberal myth of progress and the conservative myth of the Golden Age owe Hegel a debt of gratitude. Wherever one finds a commitment to one's culture and history as itself being a vehicle for truth, one finds Hegel's fingerprints.

If you were an academic or literary figure in Denmark in the 1830s, Hegel was inescapable. Either you were setting yourself against him and his systematic view of culture or you were seeking to align your favoured theories with his. Either way, you were grappling with the knotty Swabian. As with the rest of Europe, much of the Danish scene at this time saw authors, philosophers, theologians, and churchmen finding ways to articulate their innate sense of cultural superiority along Hegelian lines.

Sibbern and Møller were no different. Sibbern had to account for Hegelian dialectic in his own aesthetic philosophy. He questioned the Hegelian presumption that one could approach a subject without presuppositions and attain some sort of neutral, objective point of view. By 1837 Møller was offering a sympathetic critique of Hegelianism, based in part on Hegel's inability to account for individual experiences. What marks Sibbern and Møller apart from many of their contemporaries at the university is a healthy scepticism about the pretensions of many of Hegel's Danish followers. It is from them that Søren must have begun to form his own approach to Hegel: a respectful yet critical reading of the master coupled with fierce and unrelenting attacks on the affections of his self-styled disciples. Hegel yes, but especially the Danish Hegelians would be a primary target for the rest of Søren's life.

The main disciple was Hans Lassen Martensen. Long before he became the bishop overlooking Søren's funeral from afar, Martensen was a promising young theologian. In the 1830s he was gaining a reputation in church and university circles as an exciting communicator of complex ideas, especially Hegelianism, of which Martensen was an early champion. In his lectures and publications throughout this time Martensen developed his take on the typical Hegelian view that the established church, culture, and state are crucial to religion and part of Christianity's inevitable progress. Martensen was also adept at teaching on subjects such as Cartesian philosophy and modern theology, and Søren engaged him as a personal tutor in the summer of 1834. True to Søren's form, studies with Martensen were not focussed, and Martensen seems to have been given free rein to choose the subject. Martensen led Søren through readings of Schleiermacher, the eighteenth-century "father of liberal theology." Open warfare between the two men was still years away, but it is safe to say the two did not hit it off. At twenty-six, Martensen was five years older than Søren, not old enough to command respect yet still young enough to pose something of a professional rival. It is clear that Martensen's popular style rankled Kierkegaard as much as his subject matter. That a complex set of thoughts could be packaged and presented in an easy manner bothered Søren. In later years, he would cast a critical eye on the young Martensen who "fascinated the youth and gave them the idea they could swallow everything in half a year."

For his part, Martensen claims not to have been impressed with the callow Søren either. In his memoirs, also written long after Kierkegaard had become an avowed enemy, Martensen paints a picture of a mentally sharp but emotionally unbalanced man with "a crack in his sounding board." It is from Martensen's memoirs that we get a unique anecdote, which Martensen intends to demonstrate Søren's temperament. Søren engaged Martensen in the same summer of 1834 that his mother, Anne Kierkegaard, died. At this time Søren paid a visit to the Martensen family home and met with Martensen's mother. "My mother has repeatedly confirmed," Martensen writes, "that never in her life . . . had she seen a human being so deeply distressed as S. Kierkegaard by the death of his mother." From this Mrs. Martensen concluded that Søren had "an unusually profound sensibility." Why did Martensen include this curious story? It was certainly not to redress the utter lack of mention of Anne Kierkegaard in Søren's own writing. Instead, Martensen offers this incident as demonstration of how Søren's development became stunted. As the years passed "the sickly nature of his profound sensibility" increasingly got "the upper hand." Of their tutorials together, Martensen comments, "I recognized immediately that his was not an ordinary intellect but that he also had an irresistible urge to sophistry, to hair-splitting games, which showed itself at every opportunity and was often tiresome."

Hans Lassen Martensen, a promising and popular academic and a private tutor to Kierkegaard. Søren dismissed Martensen as one who "fascinated the youth and gave them the idea they could swallow everything in half a year." For his part, Martensen claimed that Kierkegaard had "a crack in his sounding board."

It was not only Søren's enemies who noticed his tendency to latch, terrier-like, onto an argument and not let go. His friends too were concerned that his contentious nature would get the best of him. After one social engagement, Møller berated Søren for being so polemical all the time, a caution that Søren took to heart and mentioned in his journals more than once. Nevertheless, it was his arch, argumentative manner that catapulted Søren into the public consciousness.

Søren's first published works were examples of rhetoric and juvenile satire. An 1834 essay entitled "A Defence of Woman's Superior Capacity" was printed in *The Flying Post*, a showcase for new writers and their ideas. The piece strains to be clever and funny about serious issues, a form typical to student journalism then as now. More significant for his reputation was the public debate that Søren undertook in the autumn of 1835. In November, J. A. Ostermann, an up-and-coming political leader, gave a paper to the Student Union in favour of increased liberalised press freedom. Two weeks later, Søren volunteered to offer a rebuttal. It would be his first foray into public debate. In the talk, titled "Our Journalistic Literature," Kierkegaard took the position against freedom of the press and, crucially, its sense of self-importance. He argued that the recent political reforms the press had been claiming responsibility for had, in fact, originated from the government. The presentation was hailed as a success from many quarters. Ostermann was impressed by the "brilliant dialectic and wit" Søren showed at puncturing his arguments, but he did not bother to engage further with the dilettante. Ostermann recognised that Søren was not a serious political sparring partner. "I knew [he] had only a slight interest in the reality of the matter." Søren seems to have chosen the position for largely polemical, rhetorical reasons, but in any case he continued the attack in the newspapers for the next few months under the pseudonym "B." These pieces were also feted and after a bit of speculation in the student press, Søren was "outed" as the true source.

As a result, Søren garnered a reputation amongst Copenhagen's literati. The circle was led by Johan Ludvig Heiberg and his wife, Joanna,

A view of old Copenhagen

an actress and celebrated beauty. A leading light of what would come to be known as Denmark's "Golden Age," it was J. L. Heiberg who was one of the first to introduce Hegel to the Copenhagen scene. He was also an accomplished playwright and dramatic theorist who aligned his aesthetics with Hegelian systematics. Heiberg was the editor of *The Flying Post* and other literary journals. His attention could make or break careers, and he knew it. It is not hard to imagine young Søren's beating heart and trembling fingers as he cracked the seal on the invitation to his first Heiberg soiree.

Søren was a hit. He soon gained a reputation for his quick mind and witty repartee. Kierkegaard would go on to become a regular fixture at the salon parties, which included luminaries of the age such as the scientist H. C. Ørsted, Hans Christian Andersen, Møller, and Martensen. Søren seemed to be taking to this world like a duck to water. Yet the journals of this time reveal the furious paddling going on just under the surface. In one entry Søren likens himself to a two-faced Janus: "with one face I laugh, with the other I cry." "People understand me so little that they do not even understand my laments over their not understanding me," he wrote after one such soiree. And after another:

> I have just now come from a gathering where I was the life and soul of the party; witticisms flowed out of my mouth; everybody laughed, admired me—but I left, yes, the dash ought to be as long as the radii of the earth's orbit———and wanted to shoot myself.

❖

The public could see the comparison between Søren and his brother Peter, his relationship with his father, his spending habits, odd ways, desultory studies, sharp wit, polemical manner, impressive friends. They saw a cocky young gentleman with little practical sense, too much spare time, too much money, and a lot of unfocused talent. And they saw rightly. What no one could know, however, was that Søren saw it too.

Søren began keeping a journal in 1833 and would continue to fill pages of volumes until his death in 1855. It is not a conventional diary by any means and rarely mentions the sort of daily events that other people tend to include in their log books. Most of the journal entries are undated. Some read like rough drafts of essays or written psychological experiments tracing the implications of this or that supposition. Some entries are rough-and-ready fragments; others are carefully edited with the full realisation that they would one day be read by others. The tone of the entries from the early stage of Søren's life are introspective, demonstrating a high level of self-awareness and insight into what is going on around him. His role of the arch-observer who participates in sophisticated society at the same time as he winkles out that society's weaknesses was one Søren recognised but did not relish. His journals reveal a growing distaste at events and of the part he was playing in them.

"Blast it all, I can abstract from everything but not from myself; I cannot even forget myself when I sleep."

In the 1830s Søren was using the journals to test out different parts for himself, some of which he was to play for the rest of his life. One such role is that of "the master thief." These early entries see Søren working on the theme of a rebel outsider who takes on the system and suffers punishment as a result. The journals are not all doom and gloom, even when they are morbid. Like the soldier in the trench or the nurse on the ward, Søren, the "master thief" awaiting his punishment, was adept at gallows humour. "One who walked along contemplating suicide," he wrote in 1836, "at that very moment a stone fell down and killed him, and he ended with the words: Praise the Lord!" Or in 1837: "Situation: A person wants to write a novel in which one of the characters goes insane; during the process of composition he himself gradually goes insane and ends it in the first person." Søren is alert to the ridiculousness of his own ennui: "I don't feel like doing anything. I don't feel like walking—it is tiring; I don't feel like lying down, for either I would lie a long time, and I don't feel like doing that, or I would get up right away, and I don't feel like that either . . . I do not feel like writing what I have written here, and I do not feel like erasing it."

The restless spirit accompanying the apparently carefree gadabout had in fact been awakened in 1835. Father Michael was concerned and flummoxed about his wayward son. That year, in order to get Søren away from the deathly atmosphere at home and the witty time-wasters of his Copenhagen circle, Michael paid for Søren to spend the summer well out of town. In June, Søren travelled to Gilleleje in North Zealand, the area from which the Kierkegaard family hailed. For the twenty-two-year-old urbanite, the time of country living in the fresh air was a revelation. If Michael had been hoping to occasion in Søren a sense of perspective, it is likely he never knew how successful his scheme had been. Outwardly and in public Søren would appear to continue with his dilettante life for years to come. Inwardly, however, the journals from Gilleleje suggest serious work had begun. The entry for August 1, 1835, has become particularly famous. Its theme is about knowing oneself and one's way in the world and it deserves quoting at length:

> What I really need is to get clear about what I am to do. . . . What matters is to find my purpose, to see what it really is that God wills that I shall do; the crucial thing is to find a truth that is truth for me, to find the idea for which I am willing to live and die. Of what use would it be to me to discover a so-called objective truth, to work through the philosophical systems so that I could, if asked, make critical judgments about them, could point out the fallacies in each system; of what use would it be to me to be able to develop a theory of the state, getting details from various sources and combining them into a whole, and constructing a world I did not live in but merely held up for others to see; of what use would it be to me to be able to formulate the meaning of Christianity, to be able to explain many specific points—if it had no deeper meaning for me and for my life? . . . [Truth] must come alive in me, and this is what I now recognize as the most important of all. This is what my soul thirsts for as the African deserts thirst for water. This is what is lacking, and this is why I am like a man who has collected furniture, rented an apartment, but as yet has not found the beloved to share life's ups and downs with him. But in order to find that idea—or, to put it more correctly—to find myself, it does no good to plunge still farther into the world. That was just what I did before. . . . I have vainly sought an anchor in the boundless sea of pleasure as well as in the depths of knowledge. I have felt the almost irresistible power with which one pleasure reaches a hand to the next; I have felt the counterfeit enthusiasm it is capable of producing. I have also felt the boredom, the shattering, which follows on its heels. I have tasted the fruits of the tree of knowledge and time and again have delighted in their savouriness. . . . Thus I am again standing at the point where I

must begin again in another way. I shall now calmly attempt to look at myself and begin to initiate inner action; for only thus will I be able, like a child calling itself "I" in its first consciously undertaken act, be able to call myself "I" in a profounder sense. But that takes stamina, and it is not possible to harvest immediately what one has sown. . . . I will hurry along the path I have found and shout to everyone I meet: Do not look back as Lot's wife did, but remember that we are struggling up a hill.

Søren's quest for truth that was personally engaging—for which he could "live and die"—led to an early rejection of much of the Christianity he had so far encountered. In an 1835 letter to his brother-in-law, Søren admits, "I grew up in orthodoxy, so to speak," however, "as soon as I began to think for myself the enormous colossus gradually began to totter." This was, undoubtedly, an awkward position to be in for someone training to be a minister in the established state church. Søren's prevarication did not spring from hostility to Christianity as much as aversion to the way Christianity took the form of coteries in Christendom. Brother Peter seemed to be able to align his religious seriousness with a willingness to associate with specific factions in church politics. For some years Peter had been a supporter of N. S. F. Grundtvig, a Danish nationalist, poet, populist politician, and church reformer whose group set Creedal Christianity against the liberal Christianity of Mynster *and* Bible-minded enthusiasts like the Moravians, who in turn were set against the cultured elitism represented by Martensen and Heiberg. The endless, noisy tribalism of Christendom was wearing on Søren. He did not mean to find his life's purpose by joining a *group*. Søren often writes of the enthusiasm to band together and defend a certain expression of Christianity as a type of betrayal of the original ideal.

Christianity was an impressive figure when it stepped forcefully into the world expressing itself, but from the moment it sought to stake out boundaries through a pope or to hit the people over the head with the Bible or lately the Apostle's Creed, it resembled an old man who believes that he has lived long enough in the world and wants to wind things up.

The coteries of Christendom did not seem to be good news for Christianity, or for individual Christians either.

When I look at a goodly number of particular instances of the Christian life, it seems to me that Christianity, instead of pouring out strength upon them—yes, in fact, in contrast to paganism—such individuals are robbed of their manhood by Christianity and are now like the gelding compared to the stallion.

Unbeknownst to others, at the same time that Søren was accruing debt, waging snarky student politics, and climbing social ladders, he was also busy working out his relation to Christianity. It was increasingly becoming something that Søren knew he had to make a personal choice about. As a result, Søren became fascinated with the forms of life on offer for people who reject Christianity. His private writing from this time is filled with reflections on three legendary figures. Don Juan, Faust, and Ahasuerus the Wandering Jew represented, for Søren, different modes of life outside of religion. Søren primarily met the figure of Don Juan through repeated attendance of Mozart's *Don Giovani* at the Royal Theatre. Don Juan was a serial seducer and hedonist. He lives the immediate life of sensuality. Faust was singleminded and monogamous in his pursuit of knowledge and power. He is a doubter who delves into deep secrets for selfish ends. Ahasuerus is supposed to have mocked Jesus on the way to the cross and as a result was cursed to wander the earth undying until Jesus should return. In Søren's mind, the three exhibited ascending stages of rejection of Jesus Christ, culminating in Ahasuerus whose rejection was conscious and mocking. He represents the pinnacle of despair because only he recognises how deeply personal the relation to Christianity is.

Søren clearly intended that his reflections on these three figures would form the basis for his first proper publication, the book that would put him on the map as a serious writer. He had been working over the material for years. Sadly, Søren's musings would remain largely confined to his private papers. He had been pipped to the post. In 1837, in one of Heiberg's edited journals there appeared a significant new essay by his despised tutor: "Oh how unhappy I am—Martensen has written an essay on . . . *Faust*"!

Never mind. There would soon be more subjects to occupy the young man's attention. For, over coffee at a friend's house one chilly morning in May 1837, Søren Kierkegaard met Regine Olsen.

CHAPTER 5

Love Life

It is 1837. May 8. Mid-morning. Early spring and the chill is still in the air. As he often does, Søren drops by unannounced for a visit to his friend Peter Rørdam. Peter is a family friend and a fellow teacher at the School for Civic Virtue, but in fact it is Peter's sister Bolette who is the main reason for this visit. At twenty-one years of age and from a comparable family, Bolette seems a natural prospect for the twenty-four-year-old Søren to marry. However, it is not romance that is on his mind this morning. The polemical spirit and witty atmosphere in which Søren operates has been getting to him lately. Søren has been worried that sharp retorts and arguments are becoming a habit. He lives too much in his head and he knows it. Can he even converse normally anymore? Today, Søren is simply looking for real conversations with real people. In Bolette, Søren hopes to find someone to help get "the devil of my wit to stay home."

When Søren arrives at the Rørdam house he finds a party of young ladies already there. His plan for simple interaction seems to be fading fast, and in any case it's too cold to be out walking with Bolette. Søren agrees to join the girls over coffee in the sitting room, and it is here that he meets Regine Olsen. She is fifteen years old, intelligent, composed, strikingly pretty. Søren does not mention her by name in his journal that night, but he does note the occasion and will later describe her effect over him as akin to a magic spell. Søren is smitten. Out of nervousness, a desire to impress, or perhaps simply muscle memory derived from habitual use, he reverts back to his witty ways. His words pour forth unceasingly, he overtakes the conversation and impresses everyone.

Regine does not show it at the time, but she will one day describe her young self as extremely captivated.

❖

Later that night and in the days to follow, Søren reflects on the event. Even though he had originally gone to the Rørdams' as a way to escape rhetoric, he does not now berate himself for dazzling the party with his words. As with much in life, Søren begins to see that his curse can also be a blessing of sorts. As much as he recognises his predilection for witticism to be troublesome, in this instance it has protected him from something more dangerous. Writing about the day, Søren thanks God for not letting him lose his mind. The devil wit now becomes an "angel with the flaming sword," and he is thankful that it interposed itself between him "and every innocent girlish heart." Søren quotes Jesus in Mark 8:36: "For what shall it profit a man if he gains the whole world but loses his soul?" The fact is, before he even met Regine, Søren had begun questioning whether the path marked out for him was one that should—or could—include another. These themes will grow to prominence in Søren's later writing career, but for now in these journals we see a young man beginning to wonder whether he might be being called to something besides the comfortable married life of the bourgeois citizen. Glittering wit, like the angel's flaming sword in the Garden of Eden, helps to bar Søren's heart from going to places where it should not go.

This might be God's will, but it is still a lonely life and Søren is ambiguous about his prospects. Like a brick thrown into a pond, Regine has messed up Søren's sense of himself and his plans, causing waves and ripples he never expected:

> ... good God, why should the inclination begin to stir just now—how alone I feel—confound that proud satisfaction in standing alone—everyone will now hold me in contempt—but you, my God, do not let go of me—let me live and reform—

Søren Kierkegaard. This idealized portrait from around 1840 is by Niels Christian Kierkegaard, one of Søren's cousins.

Søren is conflicted. He does not know whether it is better to be a witty loner or an honest lover and is unsure how either fits with the idea to which he wants to devote his life. The journals from this period are confused, repetitive, and self-reflective. They can be annoying in the way that only self-indulgent adolescent diaries the world over can be. But it is good not to judge too hastily. Let the one who has never been young, serious, religious, and in love cast the first stone!

Regine is lodged in Søren's heart, but he does not pursue her further.

The fact is, Søren has a lot of other things going on: spiritually, mentally, and physically. Søren is not well. His back, while not quite hunched, is certainly lopsided, and he suffers from a number of muscular and nervous complaints in connection with what appears to be a twisted spine. His letters and papers contain many references to headaches, insomnia, aversion to bright light, sensitivity to temperature changes, cramps, constipation, and pain. There is some suggestion that he suffered fits and seizures, although Søren's journals offer scant evidence on this front. In Søren's lifetime and beyond, a litany of diagnoses have been suggested to account for his condition: compression of the spinal cord; temporal lobe epilepsy; complex partial seizure disorder; Landry-Guillain-Barré's acute ascending paralysis; acute intermittent porphyria; camphor-induced porphyria; syphilis (contracted); syphilis (inherited); syphilophobia; Potts paraplegia; myelitis. Each item is contested and no one knows for sure. For his part, Søren attributed his fragility to the childhood fall from the tree, but whatever the case, it remains true that he is not what anyone would describe as a strapping young lad.

The physical frailty had a mental and emotional component. One armchair diagnosis that occurs from time to time is that of depression. It is easy to look at the steady stream of gloomy writing (in journal and published form) and conclude that Søren was depressed. Søren describes his melancholy as "depression" time and again too. Yet the diagnosis is too pat. For one thing, depression is a debilitating illness. Truly depressed people do not tend to produce reams and reams of material, working and reworking their ideas long into the evening. For another thing, Kierkegaard's writing is not all miserable. His journals, and later his books, reveal a man fascinated with *all* the twists and turns the inner life takes. The events of Søren's life sparked feelings, thoughts, and reactions in him that everyone experiences but most of us allow to dissipate. Søren captured these sensations, turning them around and around, sometimes spinning dross into gold. Sadness, yes, but also joy, humour, worship, and puppy love can be found in the pages.

Rather than depressed, it would be fairer to say that Søren was mercurial. Not only his writing, but also his actions need to be seen in light of a steady stream of highs and lows keenly felt and never forgotten. "When at times there is such a commotion in my head that the skull seems to have been heaved up, it is as if goblins had hoisted up a mountain a bit and are now having a hilarious ball in there. [In margin: 'God forbid!']" This temperament affected all his most important relationships. Søren's father and brother, his tutors and mentors, his girlfriend, and his God: no one escaped Mercury's sphere, especially not himself.

The period between 1837 and 1841 would prove to be highly significant, not only due to the writing Søren undertook during this time, but also because of the things that happened, both to him and within him. From the crucible of these five years emerges Kierkegaard the author, Kierkegaard the plotter, Kierkegaard the wealthy, Kierkegaard the unhealthy, Kierkegaard the independent, Kierkegaard the Christian, Kierkegaard the lover, and Kierkegaard the scoundrel. Almost uniquely for Søren's idiosyncratically documented life, we can trace the key events of this time, by the month, often by the day, and occasionally by the hour.

July 1837. Marie, Peter Christian's sweet, young wife has died. Everyone is melancholic and Søren feels unwell. In an attempt to clear his head, he arranges to go away to the countryside the day of Marie's funeral. But the trip doesn't come off and it's no use. Relations with brother Peter and father Michael are as bad as ever. The debts are piling up. On July 28 things come to a head. In return for his father's paying off the bills, Søren agrees to leave the family home by the end of the summer.

September 1, 1837. Søren moves into a set of apartments with enough room for his ever-growing library. Michael Kierkegaard values reading, but this enormous collection is a constant reminder of his son's unfocused and profligate ways. Surely he won't be sad to see these books leave his home. Let Søren pay for everything with his own money and see how he likes his library then!

In the autumn following Marie's death Peter's morose religiosity once again rears its head. For his part, Michael can't help but see her passing as yet another flash of lightning from the divine doom cloud looming over his life. Regarding his own faith, Søren remains a conscious outsider. He continues to work out his attitude to Christianity apart from his brother, his father, and other forms on offer. Living on his own, with no family to answer to and a breach between father and sibling, Søren ceases to attend Holy Communion.

Also at this time Søren begins to make tentative steps towards a doctoral thesis project. He has not yet started, let alone finished, his undergraduate exams, but already the wheels are spinning. In November he muses, "It would be interesting to follow the development of human nature . . . by showing what one laughs at on the different age levels." Søren continues attending lectures on various topics. As an alternative to either rote orthodoxy or vacuous faddish theology, Søren explores philosophy as a way of supplying the idea for which he can live. He attends Martensen's celebrated lecture series on the history of philosophy but finds Descartes' *cogito ergo sum* ("I think therefore I am") a "hackneyed proposition" and Martensen's own appropriation of Descartes' maxim "doubt everything" ridiculous. "Philosophy," writes Søren, "sheds its skin every step it takes, and the more foolish followers creep into it." Around this time Søren worked out his frustrations with the university scene by sketching out a satirical play called *The Battle Between the Old and New Soap Sellers*. The play (never finished) likens the intelligentsia and their philosophical schemes to the real-life competition currently being waged between Copenhagen's soap merchants who were using increasingly complicated advertisements to sell the same basic product. The play is sophomoric and would be largely unremarkable if not for the fact that it reveals how much of Søren's attitude towards the various philosophic and religious schools of thought had been set, even at this early age.

1838. Early spring. There is a gap in the journals. In April, Søren breaks his silence, revealing why. "Such a long period has again elapsed in which I have been unable to concentrate on the least little thing—now I must make another attempt. Poul Møller is dead." Møller was forty-four years old. He was Søren's teacher and confidante and the model for the way Søren would carry himself as an assessor of the foibles of public life. One day Søren would go on to dedicate a book to Møller, the drafts of the *Concept of Anxiety* dedication reading: "To the late Professor Poul Martin Møller . . . the mighty trumpet of my awakening . . . my lost friend; my sadly missed reader."

The dedication lies in the future. At the present moment, matters are made even more galling because Martensen has attracted the patronage of Heiberg. As a result, he is appointed to replace Møller's position at the university. It is a temporary position but one he will hold for the next two years before being made a full professor. Lest it be forgot, at the same time as Martensen is taking on the mantle of Copenhagen's golden boy, Søren, only five years younger, has yet to complete his undergraduate degree.

The events seem to have catalysed the young would-be writer. Later that same April, Søren's journals go silent again. This time the lack of journal writing is not because of grief but because of a renewed spurt of applied productive energy. Søren is writing in earnest, getting his first proper piece ready for publication. Martensen may have pipped him to the post when it came to Faust, but now Søren has another project in mind that will get him on the literary map. Over the next few months he applies himself to his extended essay and review of Hans Christian Andersen's new novel *Only a Fiddler*.

May 5, 1838. Søren celebrates his birthday. Against the odds, he has survived yet another year. The occasion leads to a renewed spiritual reflection on work, life, family, and God.

On May 19, precisely timed at 10:30 in the morning, Søren records an experience he has just undergone:

> There is an indescribable joy that glows all through us just as inexplicably as the apostle's exclamation breaks forth for no apparent reason: "Rejoice, and again I say, Rejoice."—Not a joy over this or that, but the soul's full outcry "with tongue and mouth and from the bottom of the heart" . . . a heavenly refrain which, as it were, suddenly interrupts our other singing, a joy which cools and refreshes like a breath of air . . .

July 6, 1838, Sunday. The spiritual experience is not repeated, but the effects seem to have taken root. Pastor Kolthoff—one of the few clergymen for whom Søren retained respect—records in his notes that Søren attended confession and Communion at the Church of Our Lady just down the road from the old family home. There is no question of familial pressure, however, for Søren attended alone. Indeed, the summer marks a time of reconciliation between the three Kierkegaard men, which Søren and Peter especially had been working on for some weeks.

On July 9, Søren rejoices in his journal that his "Father in Heaven" has kept his earthly father alive long enough for Michael to take pride in his reformed child. The son prays that the father will experience "greater joy in being my father the second time than he had the first time." The reconciliation is evidently bound up with Søren's renewed confidence in his faith and his ability to articulate a personally engaging relation to Jesus Christ, for the same entry concludes,

> I am going to work toward a far more inward relation to Christianity, for up until now I have in a way been standing completely outside of it while fighting for its truth; like Simon of Cyrene (Luke 23:26), I have carried Christ's cross in a purely external way.

August 8, 1838. Michael Pedersen Kierkegaard is proved mistaken in his conviction that he was cursed to outlive all his children, for by 2:00 a.m. Michael Pedersen Kierkegaard is dead. He was eighty-two. In a journal entry marked with a cross, Søren writes:

> My father died on Wednesday . . . I so deeply desired that he might have lived a few years more, and I regard his death as the last sacrifice of his love for me, because in dying he did not depart from me but he died for me, in order that something, if possible, might still come of me.

The entry concludes, "He was a 'faithful friend.'"

Michael died reconciled to his son. But he also died without seeing his son marry, finish university, take up a position, or publish anything of significance. To the end of his life he was convinced that Søren had not, and perhaps would not ever, live up to his potential. In later years Peter admitted that Michael was disappointed in Søren for frittering away his talent. Søren too was well aware of the debt he owed to his father that would now never be paid. Many of his most important and spiritually serious books would be dedicated to the memory of the merchant hosier. At the same time, Søren was not blind to the ambiguous nature of the debt. His father loved him and he loved his father, but their life together was still "insane."

Not at all insignificantly, the passing of the older Kierkegaard means the Kierkegaard boys are rich. The brothers inherit Michael's wealth and Michael's house. Peter moves into his father's set of rooms, and Søren moves back to his old rooms, where he will stay for the coming year. He also inherits over 33,000 r.d., a tidy sum that means Søren will not have to earn a living from whatever it is he decides to put his hand to. In other words, he's set for life.

It is a good thing that Søren did not need to rely on his writing to pay the bills, for this would never become a reliable source of income. Some books made a slight profit while others did not, but throughout it all it was Søren's inherited wealth that subsidised his writing career, beginning with his first book, until he ran out of money at the end of his life. Søren had completed the manuscript of his critique of H. C. Andersen in July, before his father's death, so its cryptic title *From the Papers of One Still Living* does not refer to Søren's relationship to Michael. Instead, the title alludes to the content of the book, which substantially criticises Andersen for writing his novels without a committed "life view." Andersen has not invested his characters with a clear point of view, thus they (and the author) cannot be said to be fully living. Søren presented the manuscript to Heiberg for publication, but it was rebuffed. Heiberg—the great arbiter of Danish literary taste—did not like Søren's style.

So it is that on September 7, 1838, just shy of a month after Michael Pedersen was put into the ground, Søren's first book is self-published, the dead man's money paying to launch the career of the still-living son. The book sells fairly well, but it cannot be called a runaway success. It displeases Andersen and confuses most readers. By December, the piece is perhaps more discussed than actually read, but even so the mission is accomplished. Søren has made his literary mark and is beginning to be noticed as more than merely a sharp-tongued wag who is good at parties. As a nod of respect he is asked to be the president of the Student Union.

The short book is impressive, but a sophisticated take-down of a popular teller of fairy tales is hardly the sign of a serious man. In the months following Michael's death, those familiar with the family fully expect that Søren, flush with cash and free from the heavy eye of his father, will now live the sort of indolent life that only a wealthy, foppish rake with a four-cigar-a-day habit can live. "Now you will never get your theological degree," says Sibbern, resigned to losing his young friend and student.

Another of Søren's tutors, Hans Brøchner, questions Søren's dedication to completing his finals. The doubters will be confounded, for they've got Søren all wrong. Here is a lad, Søren "the Fork," raised from childhood to debate, argue, and talk his way through everything. The relationship between father and son was constituted upon verbal sparring—combative conversation was both the punishment and the reward. With Michael gone, Søren has no one left to define himself against. To his journal he will later confide, "If Father had lived, I would never have gotten it." To Brøchner he replies, "As long as Father was alive, I could defend my proposition that I ought not to take the degree. But after he died, and I also had to assume his side in the debate, I could no longer resist and had to make the decision to prepare for my degree."

With the book published and the father buried, at long last it is time to buckle down. A year's worth of university study has to be crammed into a handful of months. Søren employs Brøchner to prepare him for the finals. He dedicates himself to memorising lists of popes, Hebrew lexicons, Greek verbs, church history, and all the other paraphernalia of a nineteenth-century Danish theology exam. He dutifully attends the required lectures. It is dry and uninspiring and everything else has to be put on hold until it is over. Søren calls this time from autumn of 1838 through to the summer of 1840 "the longest parenthesis I have experienced." By and large the journals and thought experiments are included in the parenthesis, and he writes to his diary,

> I must bid farewell, and you, my thoughts, imprisoned in my head, I can no longer let you go strolling in the cool of the evening, but do not be discouraged, learn to know one another better, associate with one another, and I will no doubt be able to slip off occasionally and peek in on you—Au revoir!

By and large, the journals are thinned out but they do not cease altogether. One common theme running through the remaining entries is Søren's continued winnowing of authentic Christianity from its debased forms and his frustration at poseur philosophers (like Martensen) who align Christianity with Hegelianism. Another theme is love.

Søren never forgets Regine, and he keeps up a sociable relation with her family during this time. "Even before my father died my mind was made up about her." The father's death and the son's inheritance made the union even more feasible, and during his subsequent parenthetical phase, thoughts of Regine continue to grow. "During all that time I let her life become entwined in mine." Yet accompanying all this is a continued reticence about marriage itself and what it implies for Søren's future life. A study in theology is naturally a precursor to ordination, which for the established church in Denmark is akin to a comfortable life as a sort of clerical civil servant. Is the role of the husband, father, citizen, and clergyman the role Søren the witty, caustic writer is supposed to play?

On February 2, 1839, for the time being, the romantic poet wins out over the prophetic loner or the dutiful academic. Søren, using the Latin form of his beloved's name, bursts into celebration:

> You, sovereign queen of my heart, *Regina,* hidden in the deepest secrecy of my breast, in the fullness of my life-idea. . . . Everywhere, in the face of every girl, I see features of your beauty, but I think I would have to possess the beauty of all the girls in the world to extract your beauty, that I would have to sail around the world to find the portion of the world I want and toward which the deepest secret of my self polarically points—and in the next moment you are so close to me, so present, so overwhelmingly filling my spirit that I am transfigured to myself and feel that here it is good to be.

Still Søren does not directly approach the lady in question. She is young. He is conflicted. And that list of popes is not going to memorise itself.

July 3, 1840. At last the work is done. Søren passes his exams with a "commendable" grade, firmly in the middle of his cohort. His examiners praise Søren's maturity of thought but note the paucity of acceptable theological material in his written answers. To mark the end of his studies, two weeks later, Søren takes himself north to Jutland. The trip is a holiday after the great parenthesis, but it is also a pilgrimage to Michael's childhood home and to the infamous hill. ("Here on the heath, one must truly say, 'Whither shall I flee from thy presence?'") Søren is touched by the beauty of nature, bored by the company he meets along the way, and dogged by sadness over his father. "I am so listless and dismal that I not only have nothing which fills my soul, but I cannot conceive of anything that could possibly satisfy it—alas, not even the bliss of heaven," he writes.

Through it all, Søren is also itching to get back to Copenhagen. Before his Jutland trip he had paid a friendly visit to the Olsen home, exchanging pleasantries and lending them a book or two and some sheet music. It is all part of the plan to break the ice with Regine, and now Søren is keen to follow up the next stage. Finally, late in the evening on August 6, Søren returns home. Two days later, Søren calls on the Olsens to enquire after his books and to see if they enjoyed the passages he had marked out for them. The scheme works. From August 9 until September he visits the family often and draws close to Regine. She is eighteen. He is twenty-seven.

September 8. Søren sets off from home, "determined to resolve the whole thing" once and for all. Sure enough, he comes across Regine on the street outside her house. He politely requests after her family, but she says there is no one at home. Now is the chance! Søren is rash enough to see this as the opportunity he needs. With heart hammering, he invites himself in.

Regine is a well-brought-up girl, and added to that, she is no fool. She knows something is up, and that it is highly irregular to be in the house alone with a man. He can see she is flustered, so to calm her nerves, Søren asks her to play something on the piano. Regine gets through a piece, while her ungainly visitor, normally so talkative, manages not to say anything at all. The music ends, and still Søren sits and goggles, swallowing nervously. There is nothing for it but for Regine to begin a new piece. Suddenly Søren lurches forward, grabs the music book and dashes it onto the piano. "O, what do I care about music; it is you I seek, for two years I have been seeking you!" The floodgates are open and the rest pours out. Søren does not follow up his confession of love with praise for the beloved or even an eloquent defence of his merits as a suitor. Such actions are for normal citizens. Instead, true to form for one whose life was largely lived inwardly, Søren woos his Heart's Sovereign by confessing his melancholia and warning her away from him. A strange proposal, but, in any case, the deed is done. Now it is Regine who must respond.

She would later describe her young self as "struck completely speechless." Fortunately, her upbringing and good sense kicks in. Without a single word or explanation she bundles her untimely visitor out of the house as quickly as possible.

Regine Olsen. This portrait, by Emil Bærentzen, was done in 1840 when Regine was eighteen years old.

On the street, Søren is left holding his hat and gaping at the slammed door. In a flash he sees the situation from Regine's point of view. All the plotting, prayers, and rhapsodic journaling from the past two years have happened in his head. Neither Regine nor anyone else knew anything concretely of his intentions. If someone had come upon them in the house alone together it would be she, and not he, whose reputation would suffer. There had been no warning, no prior hints, no understanding with her family that would set the context for his visit. They would not see the culmination of a long-gestating romance with theological overtones, only an eighteen-year-old girl playing love songs to a twenty-seven-year-old rapscallion! No wonder Regine was so flustered. Søren immediately resolves to make matters right. He marches to Counsellor Terkild Olsen's offices that very afternoon and tells him all that has transpired.

Regine's father likes Søren and enjoys his company. Søren can tell that he is well disposed to the idea of acquiring a Kierkegaard for a son-in-law. Still, Terkild says neither yes nor no to the young man's proposal. That is for Regine to do. But he does permit Søren to call on the house at an appointed time. On the afternoon of September 10, Søren calls again. This time the Olsen family is present and correct, and here, too, is Regine. "I did not say one single word to fascinate her—she said yes."

Before the happy couple could embark on courtship, there was the little matter of a previous admirer. Fritz Schlegel was Regine's former teacher. They were not engaged, but he was known to the Olsen family as a patiently waiting, hopeful suitor. With some awkwardness, that same day Regine tells Søren about the attachment. Søren bats the rival aside with a wave of his hand. Let the teacher be consigned to the brackets—he has first priority. "You could have talked about Fritz Schlegel until Doomsday," Søren boasts. "It would not have helped you at all because I wanted you!"

What kind of woman is this who Søren thinks he wants? A mutual friend described her at this time as "a profound, powerful soul, as well as lovely and charming." Regine is composed and self-aware. She would rather listen than speak if speaking meant sending more idle chatter into the air. She is an accomplished and intelligent young lady who takes her Christianity seriously. Of all the things with which to take issue in regard to Kierkegaard, in later years it would be the intimation that she was not a spiritually suitable match for Søren that would consistently attract her ire. Since childhood Regine has attended the Moravian prayer meetings (at the meeting house partly financed by Michael Pedersen). Currently she is guided by her reading of Thomas à Kempis's *The Imitation of Christ*. Regine's heroine is Joan of Arc. Like that prophetic warrior of old, Regine too fosters in her heart a desire to be called to a divinely appointed task. Like Søren, she too is the youngest of seven. Like Søren, she too knows what it is to live with a melancholic father. Even accounting for differences in their ages and stages in life, Regine's and Søren's temperaments, personalities, and experiences are well matched. It is no wonder they fall in love.

Their courtship develops over the ensuing months. Søren writes to Regine almost daily with notes of love, arch observations, and funny hand-drawn sketches. The letters are delivered in person, for Søren visits the Olsen home regularly, sometimes twice or even three times a day. They throw parties to introduce Søren's army of nieces and nephews to the Olsen clan. Søren gets on famously with his future in-laws, and he especially strikes up a rapport with Counsellor Olsen, whose gruff businesslike exterior belies a kindred spirit. When the whole city turns out one day to witness the crown prince's new consort, Søren and old father Olsen are content to slip away into the woods for a walk and a quiet smoke.

Søren and Regine also take walks and rides together into the countryside. In these excursions they are often accompanied by Søren's friend and tutor, Frederik Sibbern, who chaperones the young couple and becomes a confidant to them both. He approves of Søren's choice and likes Regine immensely. Indeed, Sibbern comes to suspect that Regine might be too good for Søren, or, at the very least, that Søren might be bad for her. It is Sibbern who first sees that all is not happy with the couple, and he will later reflect that even in these early trips "discord had already arisen in their relationship."

The fact is Søren does not want to dupe Regine with a false bill of goods. He does not hide his conflicted nature from her, and in their walks and rides together, he often pours out his sadness over his father, his broken relations with Peter, and his self-doubt. If the confessions were meant to be a sort of test whereby Regine would freely choose to repel Søren, then the plan did not work. She is no stranger to living with mercurial men. Her father had the highs and lows of melancholy too. Regine is well placed to recognise the symptoms in her newly beloved. It seems the Danish Joan of Arc has found her mission. A passion for the fight is awoken in Regine's heart. For his sake she decides not to give up on her man. Against Sibbern's best instincts and Søren's expectations, the confessions and discord only serve to bind her closer.

Meanwhile, Søren continues to follow the various rabbit trails of his vocation. As winter follows autumn and night follows day, so too do recently graduated theology students with fiancées seek positions in the established church. It is the natural course of things. Søren enrolls in the Royal Pastoral Seminary and, as part of his ordination training, preaches his first sermon on January 12, 1841. The assessors note that the sermon was delivered with a clear voice and a dignified tone. But they also express concern that the wealth of ideas is too rich and that Søren's depiction of the soul's struggle will not appeal to the average churchgoer. It is not hard to imagine Søren's wry smile at receiving this feedback. It is not the average churchgoer's soul whose struggle he is concerned with, but his own.

The journals and sample writing from this period of early engagement and ordination training reveal a man who remains highly alert to the problems inherent in the idea that he of all people is pursuing the married life of a clergyman. Many of these writings will make their appearance in polished form in future publications, such as the passages in *Either/Or* where the young pseudonymous author dithers over the value of marriage: Wed or not—you will regret it either way. Things do not bode well for Regine.

Work on the dissertation also continues apace at this time. Søren had been trying out ideas for some time in his journals. Now, for his master's thesis (equivalent to a doctorate today) Søren decides to title his study *On the Concept of Irony*, a phrase and subject matter favoured by his deceased friend Poul Møller. Thus it is that in-between sermon preparation and daily visits to the Olsens, Søren puts his mind to "irony," a study, in fact, that amounted to a critique of the popular German Romantic movement and comment on Hegel, with, as its subtitle suggests, *Constant Reference to Socrates.*

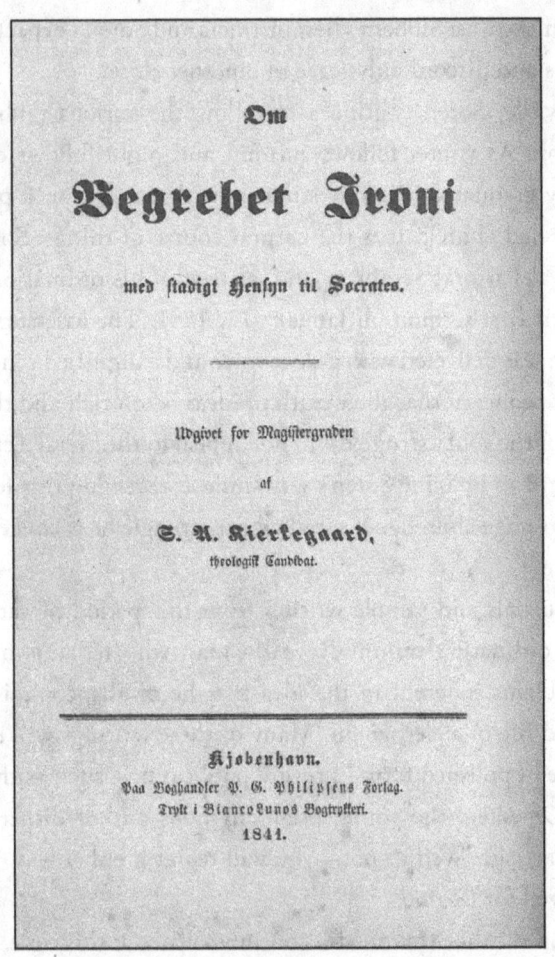

Original 1841 title page for the first edition of
The Concept of Irony, *the published version of Søren's
master's thesis (equivalent to a doctoral dissertation today).*

On June 3, 1841, the work is done. Søren presents the manuscript to the university after receiving official dispensation to submit in Danish rather than the usual Latin. The assessing faculty members included Sibbern (who generally liked the thesis) and Martensen (who did not). In July the committee grudgingly recommends the dissertation's undeniably erudite content while lodging serious issues with Søren's style and mannerisms. "The exposition suffers from a self-satisfied pursuit of the piquant and the witty, which not infrequently lapses into the purely vulgar and tasteless," writes one examiner, concluding that with any other student such elements could be forcibly edited out. Not so with Søren "the Fork" Kierkegaard. "Negations about this would be difficult and awkward. Given the particular nature of the author and his preference for these elements, it would be fruitless to express a wish about this." The university rector (and celebrated natural scientist), Hans Christian Ørsted, concurs: "Despite the fact that I certainly see in it the expression of significant intellectual strengths, I nevertheless cannot deny that it makes a generally unpleasant impression on me, particularly because of two things, both of which I detest: verbosity and affectation." Nevertheless, the work is passed and a date in September is set for Søren's live defence of the thesis.

It is evident from the examiners' comments that they either did not recognise, or at least did not appreciate, that with his tortured prose about irony, Søren was himself making an ironic comment on bloviating academics. The verbosity of the book was part of the point. In light of their inability to take a joke it is a good thing, then, that Søren did not include this idea, found in his jottings from 1838:

> For a dedication copy of my treatise: *Since I know that you probably will not read it, and if you did would not understand it, and if you understood it would take exception to it, may I direct your attention only to the externals: gilt-edges and Morocco binding.*

Perhaps the rest of the committee would have had a better chance of understanding the joke if they had known that Søren was currently living out another ironic campaign of his own. As it is, while the committee decides Søren's academic fate, only Sibbern has an inkling as to what is going on in Søren's private life.

On August 11, 1841, Regine receives a small parcel wrapped in paper. It is the ring she had given Søren on their engagement. For Regine the world goes silent as she reads the accompanying note (a note that would one day be reproduced word-for-word in *Stages on Life's Way*):

> Above all, forget the one who writes this; forgive a man who, even if he was capable of something, was nevertheless incapable of making a girl happy. In the Orient to send a silken cord is a death penalty to the recipient; in this case to send a ring is very likely a death penalty to the person who sends it.

They had been engaged for thirteen months. Søren would later claim that he knew the engagement was a mistake from the first day, but in any case, he had not hidden his ambivalence about his suitability for marriage from Regine. This parcel is unwelcome, but it is not a surprise.

The irony of Søren's breach with Regine is that he never stops loving her, even while he pushes to break the engagement. Søren's reasoning is typically convoluted, hinging as it does on his ideas that marriage is good, but not for him, and that his serious, melancholic life is unsuited to Regine's well-being. To make her happy, he needs to break her heart. Regine has heard something of this tortured logic before on their long drives into the country, while Søren wept and Sibbern pretended not to listen. She is no stranger to the odd combination of self-doubt, principled conviction, and true love in her beloved's breast, so, when she receives the note, she does not take the hit as Søren intends. Instead Regine fights back.

Regine immediately goes round to Søren's apartments and bangs on the door, only to be informed by Anders that the master is out. Regine asks for paper and a pen and produces what Søren will later describe as a note filled with "feminine despair." With tears and prayers Regine stakes her claim. Søren's moods, his convictions, his isolating campaigns are irrelevant. He can do anything, absolutely anything, and she would still love him, being thankful all her life for the greatest of blessings. *"In the name of Jesus Christ and in the memory of your dead father, I implore you not to abandon me!"*

Søren is cut to the heart when he receives this piteous letter. Nevertheless, there is nothing else for it. She has not succumbed to the first sally, so the attack must press on. Søren had at last convinced himself that the break-up was for her own good, as well as his. Thus, he tells himself, "I have to be cruel in order to help her." What follows is a liar's campaign, which Søren refers to as a "time of terrors." To dump Regine now is to publicly humiliate an innocent girl, so Søren needs to convince everyone else that the breach is for her own good and for Regine to think it is her own idea. She believes (rightly) that he still loves her and so will not release him. So he must convince her of that which is not true. Over the next two months he adopts an attitude of cruel and calculated indifference. He refuses to meet. He acts cool towards her in public. He ceases to reciprocate her love letters and sends cold notes instead. He reverts to his old gadabout ways. He acts, in his own words, like a "scoundrel . . . an arch-scoundrel."

As with many of Søren's schemes, it does not work quite as planned. True, most people in town think he is a villain, and even friends like Sibbern become concerned at Søren's high-handedness. Regine's family are confused. Regine's sister Cornelia is puzzled and does not know what to think. Her brother Jonas is more forthcoming, writing an angry letter to Søren claiming that he has never learned what it was to hate until now.

The one person the plan is not working on is Regine. "She fought," Søren would later write, "like a lioness." It is only the belief that he has divine approval of his cause that allows him to persist with his ironic campaign.

"Give up, let me go; you cannot endure it," Søren tells her one day.

"I would rather endure everything than let you go," Regine replies.

"You will never be happy anyway," she says another day with impeccable logic. "So it cannot make any difference to you if I am permitted to stay with you."

Finally Søren cracks. "You should break the engagement," he says directly, "and let me share all your humiliation."

Regine will have none of it. She tells Søren that if she can bear his actions now she can bear the public humiliation. Let them talk, she says, besides, "very likely no one would let me detect anything in my presence and what they said about me in my absence would make no difference."

She is impervious. Søren admires her more than ever. For him too the ordeal was "a frightfully painful time—to have to be so cruel and to love as I did."

They are at an impasse entirely of Søren's making. It is during this stressful time that Søren is called to defend his doctoral dissertation. The work is published on September 16, giving enough time for people to prepare their questions for the disputation panel on September 29. The thesis may have been written in Danish, but the public defence is carried out in Latin. It lasts for seven-and-a-half hours and includes questions from interested members of the public such as a hostile Heiberg and Søren's brother, Peter. History does not record whether Peter was hostile or not. In any case, Søren acquits himself admirably, and, at the end of the ordeal, he is granted the right to use a new title: *Master*.

Less than two weeks later, matters with Regine come to a head. On October 11, the newly minted Master Kierkegaard goes to the Olsens to finish the process begun months before. Even now—*especially now*—at the end of it all, Søren maintains his caddish facade. After breaking the news to Regine, he callously looks at his watch and announces that he is late for the theatre and a meeting with his friend Emil Boesen. "The act," he reports in his journal, "was over."

But Søren has yet again underestimated his opponents. After the play, Counsellor Olsen approaches Søren in the stalls.

"May I speak with you?" he asks. "She is in despair. It will be the death of her. She is in utter despair."

"I will try to calm her," Søren says loftily, "but the matter is settled."

Terkild, normally so staid, has to collect himself. "I am a proud man," he says. "This is hard, but I beg you not to break with her."

Terkild's magnanimity jolts Søren, and at the father's invitation he meekly returns to the scene of the crime. He eats with the family and speaks briefly to Regine. The next day Søren receives yet another note. The girl has not slept, and she begs Søren to come and see her.

"Will you never marry?" Regine asks. What she said about not sleeping is true, and it is clear she has been crying all night.

It is hard, but Søren keeps up the act. "Yes," he replies breezily, "in ten years' time, when I have had my fling, I will need a lusty girl to rejuvenate me."

From her person, Regine takes out a piece of paper containing some lines that Søren had written to her. The paper has been lovingly folded and unfolded many times. Now Regine tears the paper into little pieces. "So you have been playing a dreadful game with me. Do you not like me at all?"

Søren sets his face. "Well, if you keep on this way I will not like you."

"If only it will not be too late when you regret it," she cries. "Forgive me for what I have done to you."

It is altogether too much to bear. Here, at the end, the mask slips. "I'm the one, after all, who should be asking that," replies Søren, broken at last.

"Kiss me," she says. He does.

"Promise to think of me," she says. He does. And takes his leave of the last full conversation the two will ever have.

Outwardly, Søren has attained his aim. The engagement is ended beyond all repair, and the Olsens, finally, are scandalised. Copenhagen's social circle is convinced of Søren's guilt, and the town is filled with gossip about the various ways he has publicly humiliated the longsuffering

Regine. Privately, Søren is distraught. At a family gathering he breaks down weeping in front of his nephews and nieces. He spends his nights "crying in my bed." Peter Kierkegaard, ever vigilant about the family reputation, seeks to limit the damage by putting it about that Søren is not, after all, quite the hard-hearted scoundrel he seems. "If you do that," Søren warns, "I'll blow your brains out."

On October 25, Emil and Peter accompany Søren to the docks. He needs to get away and has decided to live in Berlin for a few months. The trip marks the end of Søren's aborted career as a respectable family man and the beginning of a new phase of Søren the writer. It is in Berlin that Søren will break the back of the first book of his "authorship," and it is in Berlin that Regine the flesh-and-blood girl completes the transmutation into Regine the symbol of faith, marriage, and love unrequited.

No request has been expressed as completely and utterly in vain as was Regine's request that Søren think of her "from time to time." For the rest of his life not a moment will pass when she does not cross his mind. "I was reminded of her every day. Up to this day I have unconditionally kept my resolve to pray for her at least once every day, often twice, besides thinking about her as usual." Søren had given her a diamond ring, set in gold, for their engagement. Upon its return, he had the ring reset, arranging the four diamonds into the pattern of a cross. It was a constant reminder of his renunciation in service of God, and he wore it until his death. Søren never stopped writing about Regine. She and her analogues would haunt his books for years to come, his pseudonyms constantly leaving clues to the relationship for those with eyes to see. The private journals were less mysterious. After Søren's death, they will find amongst his papers reams of writing about Regine, including this entry from 1848: "The few scattered days I have been, humanly speaking, really happy, I always have longed indescribably for her, her whom I have loved so dearly and who also with her pleading moved me so deeply."

CHAPTER 6

Writing Life

It is the winter of 1842, and Søren is walking the streets of Berlin. In fact he is sauntering down the same road that he has walked many, many times. For on this street is located a fine shop with a fine shop window, and in this fine shop window is a fine walking stick. Søren has tempted himself with this stick before, but today, as a little New Year's present to himself, he decides to take the plunge. Søren straightens his coat collar and assumes a nonchalant air before entering the shop. It would not do for the seller to know just how much the buyer wants his wares! Søren is so intent on striking just the right pose of friendly enthusiasm mixed with studied indifference that he becomes tangled on the doormat, breaking the window on the door. "After which I decided to pay for the pane and not purchase the stick."

Søren left for Berlin on October 25, 1841, shortly after breaking with Regine. He would return to Copenhagen on March 6, 1842. There would be two more short trips to Germany in the ensuing years, but these five months mark the longest time Søren ever spent away from home.

He was hapless abroad. Initially, Søren felt real pleasure in speaking another language. At first he wrote with interest about what it does to one's identity to have to express oneself in a foreign tongue. It wasn't long before the bloom wore off that particular rose, however. Søren's ability to speak, write, and think in Danish, Latin, Hebrew, and Greek did not extend to German, and he did not get along well in that language. He was confused by the orders barked at him by train conductors and had difficulty ordering the simplest things, like more candlesticks for his room. One such tortured interaction led to Søren being ripped-off by his landlord.

Søren's uneasiness extended to his manner when out and about in Berlin. For one thing, he felt a stranger in this city that seemed so inhospitable to nature's call. He was discomfited by Berlin's lack of public toilets. In one letter he complained that he had to carefully time his walks so he could arrive at "a particular nook in order to p.m.w. [pass my water] . . . In this moral city one is practically forced to carry a bottle in one's pocket." Another occasion saw Søren enter a fancy restaurant with some friends. On seeing a phalanx of important-looking men wearing starched collars and tails, he made his way over and formally introduced himself. After a few minutes of stilted conversation, Søren rejoined his party at the table, only to discover that the grandees of Berlin society he had been speaking to were, in fact, his waiters for the night.

To avoid the constant *faux pas*, Søren naturally gravitated towards other Danes abroad, such as at Spargnapani's, a cafe that was a favourite haunt of Danish expats. Yet even here Søren was out of place and awkward. Reporting home to his mother about the Danish cafe culture in Berlin, another tourist, Caspar Smith, wrote, "Søren Kierkegaard is the queerest bird we know: a brilliant head, but extremely vain and self-satisfied. He always wants to be different from other people, and he himself always points out his own bizarre behaviour."

What Caspar was never to know was that Søren was carefully managing his appearances amongst the Danish set. Søren did not leave behind his tendency to micromanage his reputation when he left home. If anything, the tendency became more pronounced, and for the same reasons. In Berlin, as in Copenhagen, the (attempted) reputation management was all for Regine's benefit. In letters to his friend Emil Boesen, Søren admits to frequent ill health but downplays it in public and dares not be seen to consult with a doctor, for fear of the expatriate Danes. The danger was that if they wrote home and mentioned the news in passing,

Emil Boesen, Søren's best friend and confidant. Søren occasionally tried to enlist Emil in his campaigns of literary intrigue.

Regine might hear that Søren was not, in fact, living the high life in Berlin. "Here, a groan which might, after all, possibly mean something entirely different, might reach the ear of a Dane, he might write home about it, she might possibly hear it." Søren needed Regine to think he was happy, healthy, and productive, which would supposedly increase her ability to despise him and move on with her life. Søren's frequent letters to Emil are filled with detailed instruction as to how his friend should spy on the girl to track whether his scheme of holy deception was working. He tells Emil where, and at what times, he will be best placed to observe Regine but gives strict orders not to approach or speak with her. In other letters, Søren seems to be feeding information to Emil that he hopes will make its way into general circulation amongst Copenhagen's chattering class. He wants the Olsen family to hate him, and so, for example, he includes in a letter—on a separate sheet of paper—a curious note about having romantic designs on a Berlin opera singer who "bears a striking resemblance to a certain young girl." Søren knows the gossips are out to get him. Is this a roundabout way of tempting Emil to fuel the flames by offering titbits that are easily disseminated? In any case, the Berlin opera singer is never mentioned again. We also do not know to what extent Emil proved pliable as a secret agent. Certainly, we know he disobeyed at least one of Kierkegaard's instructions, for the letters were not burnt as Søren directed.

Ostensibly, Søren had gone to Berlin to attend lectures. The university there was a hive of academic activity, attracting philosophers from across Europe. Søren dutifully attended many different series of lectures, but they all disappointed him in one way or another. An especial low point was the series by Friedrich Schelling. Schelling was a famous opponent of Hegelianism, occasionally singled out by name in Hegel's writing. Kierkegaard was keen to witness Schelling in action, as were many, many others. Attendance was packed, and Søren had to jostle for seating amongst a crowd that also included Friedrich Engels and the Russian revolutionary anarchist Mikhail Bakunin.

The series was celebrated, but Søren was disappointed almost from the start. Early on, Schelling's use of "actuality" as opposed to the vague generalities of Hegelian systematising made Kierkegaard perk up. Soon, however, Schelling's promising start gave way to convoluted systems of his own, delivered in an officious, nasal drone that Søren found extremely off-putting. The great man did not acknowledge Hegel's direct criticisms, and he grew querulous when audience members complained about the length of his sessions, which often exceeded two hours. Surprisingly, Søren persisted for forty-one lectures before finally throwing in the towel. "I am too old to attend lectures," he wrote to his brother Peter, "just as Schelling is too old to give them."

Even so, Søren did not consider his trip to be wasted, for what was really occupying him during this time was his authorship. He wrote to Emil that he was writing like crazy, but he refused to divulge any more detail and asked his friend not to discuss the project with anyone. "Anonymity is of the greatest importance to me." Søren had gone to Berlin to be free from Regine and to focus on learning and writing away from prying eyes. The months away were invaluable for this purpose. It was necessary to separate himself from his old life in order to break the back on this, the first salvo of the authorship. Yet Søren missed home, and he came to realise that its routines and familiarities also provided a release for him. "I am coming to Copenhagen to complete *Either/Or*. It is my favourite idea, and in it I exist."

From October 1841 through to February 1846, Søren would write and publish thousands of pages of text. In less than five years, the Danish reading public were presented with *Either/Or* (two volumes), *Repetition, Fear and Trembling, Philosophical Fragments, Prefaces, Concept of Anxiety, Stages on Life's Way*, and *Concluding Unscientific Postscript*. Many of these volumes were published on the same, or subsequent, days. Running alongside this welter of pseudonymous works, Søren also produced, under his own name, twenty-one "Upbuilding Discourses," which, by and large, he arranged to come out at the same time as the pseudonymous books. Even the shortest of these works are substantial in their own right and have been subject to sustained scrutiny and academic study. The longest are compendious—*Either/Or* runs to 838 pages, *Stages on Life's Way* 383, and *Concluding Unscientific Postscript* 480. Søren carefully edited every one of his pieces, in some cases rewriting them two or even three times. Some books were partially written before being abandoned. Besides this series of publications, which Søren referred to as his "authorship," he continued to fill journals and compose newspaper articles, personal letters, and occasional pieces. He would later sum up this time with pithy accuracy: "To produce was my life." In light of this stupendous output, the question that comes to mind is not "Wherever did he find the time to write?" It is instead "Wherever did he find the time to do anything else?"

Søren returned home on March 6, 1842. Apart from two brief trips to Berlin in 1845 and 1846 (each visit lasting less than two weeks) Søren would remain in Copenhagen for the rest of his life. The city itself became crucial to his writing process. Lengthy walks around Copenhagen were part of the authorial process, because it was on the city streets that Søren "put everything into its final form." Søren "wrote" while walking. The hiking stage was only the first part of his process. The second stage occurred when he got home, where he would be observed by his servant, Anders Westergaard, standing at his desk, hat still on head and umbrella tucked under arm, furiously scribbling down with his hands the words he had already written by foot.

Yet Copenhagen was no mere inert backdrop. The living, breathing people of the city were key.

> I regard the whole city of Copenhagen as a great social function. But on one day I view myself as the host who walks around conversing with all the many cherished guests I have invited; then the next day I assume that a great man has given the party and I am a guest. . . . If an elegant carriage goes by with four horses engaged for the day, I assume that I am the host, give a friendly greeting, and pretend it is I who has lent them this lovely carriage.

Søren called these excursions his "people bath," and he became known for plunging into conversation with everyone and anyone, whatever their age and stage. In 1844 Søren remarked that "although I can be totally engrossed in my own production, and although together with all this I am doing seventeen other things and talk every day with about fifty people of all ages, I swear, nevertheless, that I am able to relate what each person with whom I have spoken said the last time, next-to-the-last time . . . his remarks, his emotions are immediately vivid to me as soon as I see him, even though it is a long time since I saw him." Such a claim might seem an exaggeration except for the multiple eyewitness accounts that appear to affirm the assertion. "He preferred to involve himself with people whose interests in life were completely different from his own or which were diametrically opposed to his own." The sight of Master Kierkegaard gently but firmly taking someone by the arm while walking with them down the street, talking all the while and swinging his walking stick for emphasis, is one well attested by many contemporary Copenhageners.

Some people loved it and found Søren sincere, humorous, and good natured. Others disliked the feeling they were being pumped for information, suspecting they were fodder for a character study in a future book. Both reactions were valid. "His smile and his look were indescribably expressive," remembered his old friend and tutor Hans Brøchner. "There could be something infinitely gentle and loving in his eye, but also something stimulating and exasperating. With just a glance at a passer-by he could irresistibly 'establish a rapport' with him as he expressed it. The person who received the look became either attracted or repelled." Brøchner recalled how Søren would "carry out psychological studies" with everyone he met. The practice sounds more sinister than it really was, however. For Søren, a "psychological study" was synonymous with meaningful conversation focussed on the individual before him. Søren, Brøchner tells us, would "strike up conversations with so many people. In a few remarks he took up the thread from an earlier conversation and carried it a step further, to a point where it could be continued again at another opportunity." Undoubtedly some people felt ill-used by the Kierkegaard treatment, such as his secretary Israel Levin. Levin was employed in 1844 as a proofreader and scribe (he would stay on until 1850). Levin was a notoriously cantankerous individual and seems to have been retained by Søren partly for his ornery (and therefore psychologically interesting) nature. A daily fixture in the home, Levin was often drafted into helping prepare the morning coffee. He hated this duty, as invariably Søren would ask him to choose a coffee cup from the jumble in the cupboard and then demand that Levin give a personal accounting for why he chose that particular cup on that particular day.

Overall, the intense, honest attention was welcomed by others. In personal relations, Søren would often employ a psychological directness that eschewed the normal platitudes of everyday chatter. His letters to mourning or infirm acquaintances, for example, show a man who faces difficulties directly and thereby validates the person experiencing the problem. Hans Brøchner recalled with fondness the way Søren once helped a grieving widow of a friend. "He comforted not by covering up sorrow but first by making one genuinely aware of it, by bringing it to complete clarity." A case in point is Søren's cousin, Hans Peter, who was granted rare permission to visit Søren at home rather than on the street. Peter (as he was known) was paralysed on one side, and the infirmity seems to have awakened in Søren a kinship of feeling for a fellow awkward figure. The two would spend hours talking together, with Søren unapologetically transmuting Peter's condition into a spiritual treatment of a man with physical weakness in a section of *Upbuilding Discourses in Various Spirits*. Peter was deeply touched by the attention. "He is so unspeakably loving and understands me so well, but I am really afraid to make use of his arm when he offers it to me to help me into my carriage."

Back out on the streets, there was another reason for the city walks. At the same time Copenhagen was illuminating the human condition to Søren, it was also helping the secretive author hide in plain sight. In *The Point of View*, written near the end of his life, Søren claims he used these public appearances as a way to keep up his authorial project of indirect communication. The city walks served as a way of disguising just how much time and effort was going into the authorship, which was supposed to be by many different people. Often, while writing and editing these works, Søren had no time to walk as he would like. So instead he arranged to be at the theatre for ten minutes at a time, presumably during the intervals. This way the "gossipmongers" would still see him and the word would be put about that as Søren was always out and about, he couldn't possibly also be the author of all these serious works.

The secretive and pseudonymous element of his project was not incidental to the authorship. It was essential to it. This way deeply autobiographical elements could be obfuscated behind a cloud of misdirection and absurd characters, pious reflections could appear alongside scandalous anecdotes, and letters of protest to newspapers could shift attention from Kierkegaard onto his pseudonyms and *vice versa*. Pseudonymity provided the means by which Søren could explore and present different points of view without having to claim each account as his own. It enabled him to draw from his own personal life without making him and his loved ones the object of direct examination. It was also just a lot of fun.

He may have perfected the art, but by no means were pseudonyms a Kierkegaardian invention. The literary world of Golden Age Denmark was positively lousy with them. In a culture in which newspapers were the medium by which intellectual conversations were carried out in public, pseudonymity (or anonymity) was a literary convention followed by almost everyone. Copenhagen was a small city; pseudonyms allowed people to express their views forthrightly without also having to meet their opponents the next day on the street. The practice could be spiteful, but more often than not it was playful, with authors deliberately constructing pen names that hinted cheekily at the man behind the curtain. (Bishop Jakob Peter Mynster, for example, often wrote under the initials "Kts," the middle letters of each of his names.) Some pseudonyms remained mysterious, while others appeared with enough regularity in journals and newspapers that the true identity of their owners became an open secret. Pseudonymity was a game, and like any game it had rules, the first being that you did not talk about pseudonymity. To publicly identify an author with his pen name was considered bad taste. People who refused to respect the deliberate disguise of others had to be prepared to face the consequences.

It was for this reason that Søren chose an editor of the *Fatherland* newspaper as his prime helper when proofreading the disparate elements of *Either/Or*. During the winter of 1842–43 Søren was a frequent visitor to the offices of J. F. Giøwad. He liked Giøwad because of his reputation for protecting the identity of his anonymous contributors and because of the editor's discretion in other matters too. Often when at Giøwad's, Søren had "strong attacks of his suffering so that he would fall to the floor, but he fought the pain with clenched fists and tensed muscles, then took up the broken thread of the conversation again, and often said: 'Don't tell anyone; what use is it for people to know what I must bear?'" It is clear that Giøwad liked Søren, and the two would talk for hours on end. Their mutual respect did not spill out to the rest of the office. Another assistant editor, Carl Plough, would later bemoan the "impractical and very self-absorbed man sitting in the office, ceaselessly lecturing and talking without the least awareness of the inconvenience he is causing." Søren had enlisted Giøwad for his cause, but to ensure the success of his impending authorial onslaught he used the *Fatherland* to publish a "Public Confession" in the June 12, 1842, edition. The article (written by Søren) urges the good people of Copenhagen never to regard Søren as the author of anything that does not bear his name. (Incidentally Søren was luckier with Giøwad than with his other choices of assistants. Around this time he also enlisted the help of a poor theology student, P. V. Christensen, as a scribe and proofreader. Søren soon regretted letting "my little secretary" in on his secrets, however, and later that year had to fire him on suspicion of plagiarism. "I wager that he is the one who in various ways is scribbling pamphlets and things in the newspapers, for I often hear the echo of my own ideas.")

The ground thus prepared, *Either/Or* was published February 20, 1843. If the literary wags of Copenhagen liked their pseudonyms, they were possibly about to get too much of a good thing. This is the book that began the dialectical movement through the stages of Christendom, but it is also the one that put the complex "Russian doll" pattern of the authorship into play. Victor Eremita is responsible for *Either/Or*, but he claims he is not the author. With Kierkegaard, even the pseudonyms have pseudonyms, and Victor (whose Latin name means "victorious hermit")

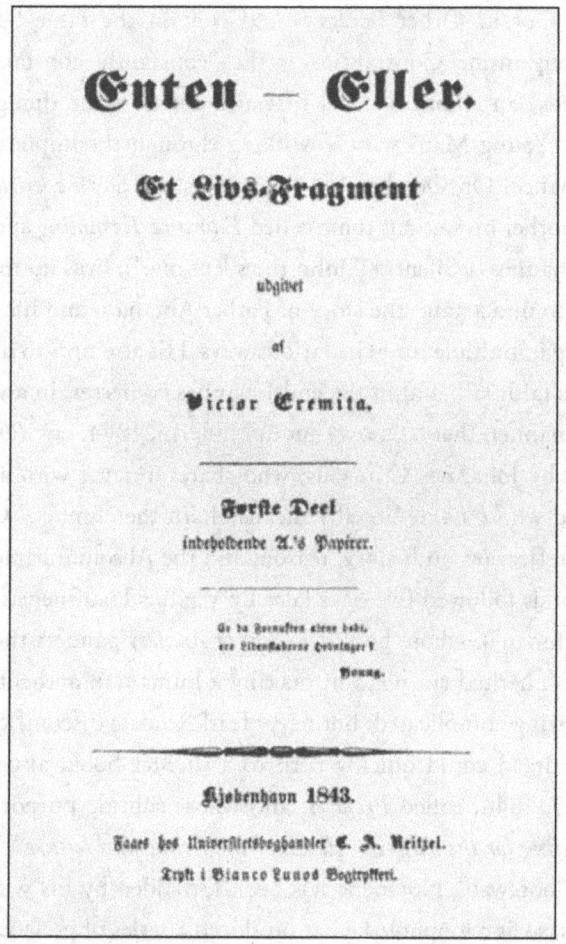

Original 1843 title page for the first edition of Either/Or, *the book Søren considered the true beginning of his "authorship" proper.*

is supposedly merely editing a collection of papers that he found hidden in an old desk, one set written by "A," a young, hedonistic man, and another by "B," who may or not be "A" as an old man but who in any case is actually revealed to be a moral character named Judge William, who supports marriage by objecting strenuously to "A" and to another essay in the book called the "Diary of a Seducer" by someone named

Johannes. Got it? Other books would contain the same bewildering teases. Constantine Constantius is the "constantly constant" author of *Repetition,* an elliptical novel that also contains the thoughts of an unnamed "Young Man" who is working through the implications of a failed romance. On October 16, 1843, the same day *Repetition* hit the shelves, another mysterious tome called *Fear and Trembling* appeared. Its author, Johannes deSilentio ("John the silent one"), lives up to his name by trying to understand the story of Father Abraham and his son Isaac, by retelling it multiple times in various ways. His attempts to understand Abraham's faith fail, and in the end Johannes confesses, in a wordy and eloquent manner, that he must shut up. June 13, 1844, saw *Philosophical Fragments* by Johannes Climacus, who shares a name with a medieval monk, and whose name literally means "John the climber." Climacus's extended reflection on history, reason, and the Absolute Paradox of the incarnation is followed five days later by Vigilius Haufniensis (the "vigilant watchman"), whose book *Concept of Anxiety* ponders the role that *angst* over inherited sin plays in making a human an authentic person. It is all getting complicated, but never fear! Readers discomfited by paradox and dread could quickly turn to a slighter book, also published on June 17, 1844, called *Prefaces,* and whose subtitle purports to offer *"Light reading for the different classes at their time and leisure."* Its author, Nicholas "notewell" Notabene has been forbidden by his wife to write any books, so as a loophole he has produced a series of prefaces to books that have never been written, taking the wind out of public luminaries like Heiberg and Martensen along the way. The next year, on April 30, 1845, Hilarius Bookbinder does one better. His monstrous book, *Stages on Life's Way,* is a compilation of a veritable army of pseudonyms. Here we meet again Johannes the Seducer, Victor, Constantine, a tailor, and Judge William, who is still busy defending marriage. *Stages* also finds room for Frater Taciturnus ("Brother Silence"), who fishes a diary out of a lake. The journal, entitled "Guilty?/Not Guilty?" is by someone named Quidam. It details his descent into madness after breaking troth with the cheerful and beautiful Quaedam. Yet it soon becomes apparent that the waterlogged diary is about more than love, for in it we are also introduced to a "bookkeeper" who bears a striking resemblance to a former merchant hosier of the city and who is labouring under a guilty burden he cannot shake off.

Despite the clear autobiographical elements for those with eyes to see, Søren took pains to distance himself from this portion of his authorship. He would never be able to hide his involvement completely, however, as he was fully aware. All his books, he wrote to Emil, are "healthy, happy, merry, gay, blessed children born with ease and yet all of them with the birthmark of my personality." It is worth stressing that not all pseudonyms were created equal. Søren occasionally prevaricated over to whom he would ascribe an already-written manuscript. For example, *Concept of Anxiety* was going to be published under Kierkegaard's own name until a few days before the manuscript went to the printer. In the end, the book contains a highly personal dedication to Søren's teacher, P. L. Møller, passing without comment over the curious coincidence that Vigilius Haufniensis also considered the deceased philosopher to be a personal friend and inspiration. The case of *Anxiety* highlights the caution one must take over reading *too* much into the pseudonyms, but it also highlights the fundamentally playful nature of the pseudonymous project itself. The pseudonyms are not watertight, neither are they meant to deceive utterly and completely. Instead, pseudonymity is a mechanism by which the reader is forced to pause and consider their own relation to the text rather than to the author. Søren clearly enjoyed playing the pseudonymous game with his public. At various times he arranged for Victor Eremita, "A.F." and an "Anonymous" letter writer to reply to critics in the newspapers, and to offer their theories as to the true author of the books. Anyone familiar with the practice of "sock-puppetry" on internet message boards (where one user creates many aliases and uses them to converse with each other) will recognise what Søren was doing with the newspaper technology of his day. In May 1845, he wrote a letter to the *Fatherland* under his own name, objecting to the free-and-easy association that an enthusiastic reviewer had made between Kierkegaard the author of the *Upbuilding Discourses* and the author(s) of such works as *Either/Or* and *Stages on Life's Way*. Even here, however, the objections are tongue-in-cheek. Everyone knew, or strongly suspected, that Kierkegaard was the real author, and he knew that everyone knew. Still, the playful charade needed to be kept up for the sake of the authorship as a whole.

The pseudonyms were only part of the authorship. Søren considered the self-penned *Upbuilding Discourses* to be as essential to his output as the books ascribed to the others. There are twenty-one *Discourses* in all, brought out in batches that roughly correspond to the pseudonymous publications. The first two arrived on May 16, 1843, a couple of months after *Either/Or*. Three more entered the shops the same day (October 16) as *Fear and Trembling* and *Repetition*. December 6 saw four *Discourses*, March 5, 1844, saw two and June 8 three more, five days before *Philosophical Fragments* hit the shelves and less than ten days before *Concept of Anxiety* and *Prefaces* burst onto the scene. Readers had a couple of months to get their bearings before tackling four more *Discourses* on August 31, but they would have to wait until April 29, 1845, before they could be edified by the final *Three Discourses on Imagined Occasions*, which handily arrived a day before *Stages on Life's Way*.

If the pseudonyms represented the array of non-Christian, anti-Christian, or deluded-Christian characters one finds on Christendom's stage, then the *Discourses* were Søren's attempt at straightforward spiritual nourishment. Or were they? *Straightforward* is not a word easily ascribed to Kierkegaard. The *Discourses* are openly Christian in their language and are usually built around reflection on a biblical passage. Yet they are as challenging to platitudinous religiosity as anything else he penned, and they are by no means easy reads. One cannot shake off the suspicion that "S. Kierkegaard" of the *Discourses* might also be a character playing a role invented by Søren Kierkegaard. The *Discourses* counterbalance material found elsewhere, offering different takes on similar themes. Whatever it is Kierkegaard is trying to say to his readers is not found in any one book or in any one author, named or unnamed. Instead, the truth is found as the reader engages in reflective and dialectical conversation with all the books in the authorship.

The "reader" is a very important aspect of Kierkegaard's output, and he had an active participant in mind when constructing his books. All the *Discourses* bear the inscription: *"To the late Michael Pedersen Kierkegaard formerly a clothing merchant here in the city, my father, these discourses are dedicated."* Yet Michael, as a dead man, was not the ideal reader Søren had in mind. It is in the May 16, 1843, *Discourses* that we first encounter "the single individual." In an 1849 journal entry Søren admits how at first this phrase was "a little hint to her." The *Discourses* are replete with messages and imagery that only Regine would understand. They were intended, first and foremost, for her. In the same journal, Søren records how the scandalous "Seducer's Diary" in *Either/Or* was written for Regine's sake, "in order to clear her out of the relationship." That piece describes the callous seduction and abandonment of an innocent girl. Regine was supposed to be disgusted at *Either/Or* and then reassured that the breakup had a spiritual value from reading the *Discourses*. Only later, as the relationship with Regine receded into the distance, would Kierkegaard's "single individual" come to take on the wider meaning of any reader who takes on Søren's challenge for her or himself.

Søren tells us that the pseudonyms and self-named works contained many nods to Regine. But she was capable of making nods of her own.

Søren and Regine often met on the street. They would acknowledge each other with an incline of the head but otherwise they did not speak. On Easter Sunday, 1843, during Mynster's sermon at the Church of Our Lady, these slight actions took on a significance greater than the sum of their parts. "At vespers on Easter Sunday . . . she nodded to me. I do not know if it was pleadingly or forgivingly, but in any case very affectionately." Søren thrashed out the implications of this momentous event in his journals. Her frank actions made Søren suspect that she saw through all he had done. "I had sat down in a place apart, but she discovered it. Would to God she had not done so. Now a year and a half of suffering and all the enormous pains I took are wasted; she does not believe that I was a deceiver, she has faith in me." Years later Søren would elaborate on the meaning he had ascribed to this, the most indirect of communications. "Her eyes met mine in church. I did not avoid her gaze. She nodded twice. I shook my head, signifying: You must give me up. Then she nodded again, and I nodded as friendly as possible, meaning: I still love you."

Too many assumptions were riding on too little information. The "conversation" was doomed to fail. The crucial piece missing in this puzzle was something that Regine assumed Søren already knew but of which, in fact, he was completely unaware. For Regine was about to become engaged to her original flame, Fritz Schlegel.

When Søren finally found out the news, he saw the nods in a whole new light. "After her engagement to Schlegel, she met me on the street, greeted me as friendly and charmingly as possible. I did not understand her, for at the time I did not know of her engagement. I looked questioningly at her and shook my head. No doubt she thought that I knew about it and sought my approval." He had meant the nods in church and the street to mean that he still loved her but must pursue his project, encouraging her to stay the course with bravery and perseverance. Instead, Regine had taken the nods to mean he was giving his blessing and release for her engagement. "No doubt the decisive turn in her life was made under my auspices." It bears noting that all the "mistaking," "loving," "releasing," "decisive turning," and the rest are *Søren's* interpretations of the nods. Of Regine's opinion there is no record.

The incident sent Søren packing, yet again, to Berlin for his second trip on May 8, 1843. The writing break would prove short-lived, but it was there he continued *Fear and Trembling* and altered *Repetition*. Both books bear the marks of Regine's decisive alteration to the *status quo*. It was in Berlin Søren wrote, "If I had had faith, I would have stayed with Regine. Thanks to God, I now see that. I have been on the point of losing my mind these days." The line illuminates much of the ethos running through *Fear and Trembling* and its heart-wrenching account of a man who gives up what he loves and yet waits, in faith, for it to be returned to him. *Repetition* tells the story of a lovelorn Young Man who returns to a foreign city in an effort to recapture his experiences, only to discover that in life true repetition is impossible. The ending to *Repetition*, especially, reflects a strong editorial hand in the aftermath of Fritz and Regine. A comparison of draft manuscripts and the published version reveals that Søren radically changed the fate of the Young Man. Originally, he commits suicide as a symbol marking the impossibility of ever marrying. In the new version, the Young Man lives on to become a better man, ennobled by the ultimate rejection of his lover.

Like the ending of *Repetition*, some journal entries from this time contain fantasies of benign revenge against Regine. Søren had often claimed that he wanted Regine to move on with her life, but now that it was actually happening, it stung. Søren was hurt and angered by what he saw was her inconstancy. "But so my girl was—first coy and beside herself with pride and arrogance, then cowardly." Here was the woman who once wildly pleaded with Søren, now engaged to the sensible Fritz. In his diaries, Søren tries out various scenarios in which he meets Regine on the street and is able to coolly reprimand her for claiming she would die without him and then getting engaged to another within a year. "I have loved her far more than she has loved me," he tells himself. The entry continues with assurances that his breach with her was a mercy. "I dare congratulate myself for doing what few in my place would do, for if I had not thought so much of her welfare, I could have taken her, since she herself pleaded that I do it . . . since her father asked me to do it." The exact reason for his chivalrous action is lost to history—Søren tore this page from his journal. But he saw fit to leave in more assertions that he was "prouder of her honour than of my own" and defends his loving, deceptive break by claiming that marriage to Regine would have been tantamount to drawing her into his "cursed" life. "But if I were to have explained myself, I would have had to initiate her into terrible things, my relationship to my father, his depression, the eternal night brooding within me, my going astray, my lusts and debauchery, which, however, in the eyes of God are perhaps not so glaring . . ." In Søren's eyes, he may have been guilty of breaking her heart in order to save her, but Regine too was guilty of breaking her promise to love him forever. He took steps to remember her declarations, even if she had supposedly forgotten them. To that end, Søren commissioned to be constructed a tall chest made out of rosewood, in which he kept various tokens of their engagement. "It is my own design, prompted by something my beloved said in her agony. She said that she would thank me her whole life if she might live in a little cupboard and stay with me. Because of that, it is made without shelves.—In it everything is carefully kept, everything reminiscent of her and that will remind her of me. There is also a copy of the pseudonymous works for her. Regularly only two copies of these were on vellum—one for her and one for me."

Statistically at least, brother Peter was luckier in love than Søren. He had married not once, but twice, having wed Sophie Henriette (or Jette as she was called) in 1841, following the death of his first wife, Marie. Since that time Peter and Jette and their son, Paul, had lived in a country parish where Peter served as a pastor of a village church. As a representative of the established state church, it was one of Peter's duties to practice compulsory baptisms of the children of Baptist and other dissenting parents. This practice went against Peter's conscience and his theological association with the Grundtvigian school. Grundtvig was a vocal opponent of the practice, which he saw as religious persecution. Although he too was a senior figure in the official Lutheran church, Grundtvig supported a more *laissez faire* style of populist "People's Church" as opposed to the hierarchical "State Church" model. The position put Grundtvig and his disciple, Peter, in direct opposition to the supreme primate, Bishop Mynster. Their stand-off came to a head in 1845, causing a minor public scandal. Although he was still something of a "Mynster man" out of loyalty to their deceased father, Søren privately agreed with Peter and urged him to stand his ground. The issue was doubly annoying for Søren, because siding with Peter meant tacitly siding with Grundtvig, of whom Søren had almost nothing good to say whatsoever.

Nikolai Frederik Severin Grundtvig, a towering figure in Danish politics, church life, poetry, education, and nationalism. "The Grundtvigian nonsense about nationality is also a retrogression to paganism," Søren complained. "It is unbelievable what foolishness delirious Grundtvigian candidates are able to serve up."

N. F. S. Grundtvig loomed large on the Danish stage. He was a poet, a politician, and a pastor, and the author of endless volumes of history, theology, and hymnody. One of Grundtvig's Big Ideas was his so-called "Matchless Discovery." For Grundtvig the "discovery" was that authentic Christianity does not reside in holy texts written in foreign languages but instead in the public recitation of the Apostles' Creed and the Lord's Prayer in the native tongue of the people. Another pillar of Grundtvigianism was that different nations in history had been appointed divine tasks. Past ages belonged to the Jews, the Greeks, the Romans, and so on. *Now* was Denmark's time. In Grundtvig's voluminous writing, ancient Norse culture is "baptised" and given revelatory status. Søren is scathing about all this. "The Grundtvigian nonsense about nationality is also a retrogression to paganism. It is unbelievable what foolishness delirious Grundtvigian candidates are able to serve up. [. . .] Christianity specifically wanted to do away with paganism's deification of nationalities!"

Søren had little time for Grundtvig's bluster and considered his populist rhetoric, which explicitly combined patriotism with Christianity, to be worse than even the intellectualised religion of the cultured elites. His private writing is full of humorous caricatures of Grundtvig and his followers. He was not, however, simply dismissive of Grundtvig on a personal level. The *Concluding Unscientific Postscript*, Søren's *magnum opus*, published February 27, 1846, is, in large part, his provision of a rigorous intellectual, philosophical, and theological answer to Grundtvig's view of Christianity, history, and nation. To be sure, Hegel, Martensen, and others come in for a kicking, but Grundtvig is one of Søren's major targets in the *Postscript*.

But, of course, it is not *Søren* who wrote the book. It is "Johannes Climacus" who arranged for this finale to his *Philosophical Fragments* to be published. The massive tome, with its comically complicated chapter headings and bewildering arrangement, signals to the discerning reader that part of the book, at least, is a satire on the style favoured by Grundtvig and the Hegelians. Not just the content but the physical dimensions are part of the joke—the "postscript" is four times larger than the book it is supposed to "conclude." Readers who are not turned off by the jocular style are led into a *tour-de-force* of intellectual content. The *Postscript* contains some of the best Kierkegaard (or whoever) has to offer and brings to a conclusion many of the themes in development since *Either/Or*. To the stages of existence—"aesthetic," "ethical," and "religious"—is brought a new form of faithful life. Søren intended this book to be a conclusion, not only to Climacus's works, but to the authorship as a whole. To this end it contains a lengthy section entitled "A Glance at Contemporary Danish Literature," which is, in fact, a review and a discussion of all the works since *Either/Or* up to and including *Stages on Life's Way*. The "Glance" is attributed to Climacus, but inserted at the end are a few pages deliberately kept separate from the rest of the text. "The First and Last Explanation" echoes the letter that Søren had published in the *Fatherland* before launching his authorship with *Either/Or* years before. In it, he finally acknowledges that he, S. Kierkegaard, is the one responsible for the texts "in a legal and literary sense." He asks, however, that the pseudonyms be treated as essential parts of the work and not as optional extras. "Therefore, if it should occur to anyone to want to quote a particular passage from the books, it is my wish, my prayer, that he will do me the kindness of citing the respective pseudonymous author's name, not mine."

The wish, the prayer, brought to conclusion Søren's carefully constructed scheme of presenting Christianity to Christendom. The five or so years of ceaseless writing, endless perambulating, lonely living, and prodigious expenditure were brought to an end, and with it Søren intended to renew his long-postponed idea of taking up a quiet pastorate in a country parish. As with every other of Søren's elaborate schemes, however, this one was not to be.

For one thing, he was a writer, through and through, and the parson's life was not for him. For another, the great revelation of the genius behind the authorship had actually already been made a month before, in a scurrilous rag of a newspaper. In hindsight "The First and Last Explanation" would come to look less like a triumphant *coup-de-grace* and more like desperate damage control for a writing career only halfway finished. In 1846, a tabloid campaign against him was brewing, threatening to crack the edifice of the authorship and bring Søren's world crashing down. And worst of all, he had brought it on himself.

CHAPTER 7

Pirate Life

Catrine Rørdam has a lot to answer for. How much pain, joy, anger, humour, boredom, insight, frustration, spiritual reformation, and existential revolution would have been denied if Catrine Rørdam had cried off her hostess duties? How many sleepless nights and ruined careers, how much spilled ink, and how many trees have given their lives as a result of Catrine Rørdam's coffee klatches? It is because of her hospitality that Søren was put into the path of the two people with the most impact on his writing career. Søren first met Regine in 1837 at a gathering hosted by the mother of his friend Peter Rørdam. And it was that same year at another of her soirees Søren first made the acquaintance of a young Aron Goldschmidt.

It is not easy being Jewish and Danish in the nineteenth century. True, there is no outright oppression, and Russian or German Jews have it worse, but that does not take away from the steady unease one feels in Danish society. No matter how well you fight in the army, teach in the university, or write in the press—any Jewish person in the public eye is always waiting for the other shoe to drop. In Danish Christendom, Danish Jews are considered slightly off. A "cursed race" in popular lore, like Ahasuerus they are doomed to wander as foreigners even in their home lands. A respectable Jew, going about his daily business, is always ready to hear the taunt "Jerusalem is lost!" or to deal with the insinuation that unlike other "civilised" people, he cares only about making money. And woe betide the Jewish man whose concern actually *is* about making money.

*Meïr Aron Goldschmidt. Amongst his many
literary projects, Goldschmidt was the principal
author and editor of the satirical* Corsair.

Meïr Aron Goldschmidt is an intelligent, artistic, empathic, and funny man. He is politically informed and a committed defender of free speech. Aron is a novelist, essay writer, and a journalist, and is making a name for himself in radical, reform-minded government circles. He is also adept at wringing a profitable livelihood from his writing talents. Unbeknownst to the wider public, Aron is the founder and secret chief editor of the *Corsair*, a satirical magazine with literary promise and an enormous influence on public opinion. Like many Danish Jews of his generation, however, Aron is constantly on the back foot, unsure about his place in the world and sensitive to receive the good will that his fellow Gentile Danes take for granted. Even his financial success is a source of potential shame, and he aspires to be taken seriously as an artist, author, and thinker.

Aron is particularly susceptible to the opinions and advice of P. L. Møller. Peter Ludvig (no relation to Søren's old teacher Poul Martin Møller) is an award-winning poet with academic ambitions. He is a friend and early defender of Hans Christian Andersen and a political supporter of Grundtvig's radical Danish nationalism. He is also a notorious womaniser in a city that likes to be titillated by talk of seduction more than it likes actually doing it. In short, Møller is a bad boy with insider privileges. He represents many of the things that Aron both fears and aspires to. No wonder Aron will later devote the main part of his autobiography to Møller, describing him as "looming up" in Aron's young life like a sort of "nemesis."

P. L. Møller first sought out Aron Goldschmidt on the strength of the latter's involvement with the *Corsair*. As the editor of the country's most feared satirical magazine, Aron is a powerful man. He founded the weekly periodical in 1840 as an outlet for radical ideas in opposition to both the conservatism and liberalism of the day. In the first issue, under a pseudonym, Aron wrote that people might object to a newspaper named after a type of pirate ship. Instead, the paper loftily claimed for itself that it was a vessel "manned by courageous young men [who] are determined to fight under their own banner for right, loyalty and honour." The paper never did quite reach these heady heights, however, and soon gained a reputation for censor-baiting character assassination, gossip mongering, and attacks on the great and the good of Danish society, all the while hiding behind a wall of anonymity and secret identities. There was a serious edge to the paper, which had to constantly dodge official censorship by instituting a rotation of straw-man editors who would take the fall if things got really bad. In one instance in 1842 Aron ran out of fake editors and had to face the law himself. He was sentenced to "six times four days" in jail as a result. The events only served to strengthen Goldschmidt's resolve, and the *Corsair* continued its reign of terror unabated. When Møller came on board he joined a small team of writers contributing to a paper read by everyone, high and low, but admitted by none. Hans Christian Andersen noted about the magazine that the elite wouldn't stoop to buying such a rag, but they would "read to pieces" their servants' copies.

On its best days the *Corsair* shows flashes of brilliance, but even Aron knows it is not the ideal vehicle for his skills. Aron has not forgotten his more serious literary and political ambitions. One day in 1844, following an unsatisfying showing at a political event where he and his people were sidelined yet again, Aron shares with Møller his frustrations at being Jewish in Denmark. Møller's advice is direct and to the point. "With feelings like that," he says, "one writes a novel."

A Jew came out in 1845. It was ascribed to the pseudonym Adolf Meyer, but following Copenhagen literary culture, the people who mattered knew Aron Goldschmidt was the source. The novel, recounting the trials and tribulations of a Jewish man in Denmark, is widely praised. Amongst its admirers is Søren Kierkegaard.

Søren had long taken an interest in Aron, who was a few years junior to him. The two had met at one of Mrs. Rørdam's parties, and their relationship developed on the streets where Søren would offer unsolicited advice on everything from Aron's literary output through to his choices in clothing. On one occasion Aron had stepped out in a particularly garish coat, only to be discreetly taken aside by Søren and given some frank advice. "You are not a riding instructor. One ought to dress like other people." At the time Aron was mortified, but also grateful for the paternal attention. On another memorable occasion in 1841 Aron had arranged for the *Corsair* to print a stilted but favourable review of Søren's *On the Concept of Irony*. It was the first time Søren was mentioned by the paper, and he was not overly thrilled. The *Corsair* was generally more suited to caricature and satire, and Søren gently took Aron to task for the clumsy article, encouraging him instead to focus on perfecting his skills at "comic composition." The advice was kindly delivered, and Aron was initially flattered by the attention. Yet as with the frock coat, the feedback was also a source of humiliation.

Now, four years later, Aron enjoys an influential position as an editor of his own paper. He is well remunerated. His novel *A Jew* is well received and widely praised. It has been translated into foreign languages, including English. Søren can boast none of these accolades. Yet here is the Master, once again taking Aron's arm, indicating another serious—and probably condescending—conversation is about to commence. It's all very confusing—helpful and infuriating at the same time.

"Which of your book's characters do you think was the best delineated?" asks Kierkegaard.

"The hero," replies Aron immediately.

"No," says Søren, swinging his cane, "it is the mother."

Aron is surprised. "I hadn't even thought about her at all in writing the book."

"Ah, I thought so!" says Søren, delighted.

Søren then asks Aron whether he has read all the positive reviews his book is getting in the Danish press. "What do you think the point of it is?"

Aron has read them, and he is gratified, but he assumes the kind words are "quite simply intended to praise the book."

"No," Kierkegaard interrupts, "the point is that there are people who want to see you as the author of *A Jew*, but not as the editor of the *Corsair*. The *Corsair* is P. L. Møller."

When Aron hears this, he knows the game is about to change. For a while now, P. L. Møller has been angling for a serious position in the university and aspires to a professorship in aesthetics. If his name is openly associated with the scurrilous and populist newspaper it will ruin his reputation. Møller is a large (even "looming") figure at the *Corsair*, but it is still Aron who is the proprietary editor, a fact of which he earnestly reminds Søren, but to no avail. Upon hearing about the conversation back in Aron's office, Møller panics. Is his cover blown according to general opinion, or is this just another one of Søren's private schemes?

The answer is a bit of both. Unbeknownst to Aron, Søren has taken him on as a sort of paternalistic project. He describes Aron in his journal as "a bright fellow, without an idea, without scholarship, without a point of view, without self-control, but not without a certain talent and a desperate aesthetic power." He thinks that Aron's talents are wasted on the *Corsair*. Søren has no regard whatsoever for Møller, who was likely the model for the perfidious "Johannes the Seducer" character in *Either/Or*. Søren clearly thinks Møller is a bad influence on the pliable Goldschmidt. He writes in his journal that it is his goal to separate Goldschmidt from Møller and to take him from the *Corsair*. "It was my desire to snatch, if possible, a talented man from being an instrument of rabble-barbarism."

The conversation with Aron was Søren's first shot across the *Corsair*'s bow. Søren saw the paper as a blight on society, its form of irresponsible and unethical satire a source of "irreparable harm." Yet Søren's designs to sink the pirate ship while rescuing its captain are not wholly disinterested. As always, he has his own authorship and its reception in mind too.

Søren had an odd relationship to his critics and reading public. In private conversation and in his journals he fretted and obsessed over every review his books received, and he clearly valued the good opinion even of his adversaries. In the public forum, however, Søren actively repelled attention and tended to avoid being drawn into wider conversations about his books. Not that all his books received the same attention. As a general rule the earliest tomes such as *Either/Or* got more discussion than the later ones, probably due to (understandable) reader-fatigue at the ever-increasing complexity of the authorship. The salacious material in "The Seducer's Diary" in *Either/Or* did not hurt either. Heiberg was muted and patronising in his praise of *Either/Or*, describing the "Seducer's Diary" in particular as "disgusting, nauseating and revolting," a designation he meant as a reproach but which tended to attract more readers than it repelled. Søren was affronted by Heiberg's review, prompting Victor Eremita to write an equally sarcastic and patronising "thank you" to the literary doyen in the *Fatherland* four days later. Other negative reviews could expect to receive similar dismissive (pseudonymous) responses. Not all the reception was negative, of course. In fact, the reviewers were often fulsome in their praise. Bishop Mynster (under the pseudonym "Kts") wrote a good review of *Edifying Discourses*. *Fear and Trembling* and *Philosophical Fragments* got some good notices. To Kierkegaard's frustration, however, even the positive reviewers were plodding and didactic in their understanding of the works. "No, thank you, may I ask to be abused instead," he complained in his journal of one enthusiast, "being abused does not essentially harm the book, but to be praised in this way is to be annihilated." Other positive reviews got even shorter shrift, with Kierkegaard (or a pseudonym) going out of his way to alienate potential fans. A glowing write-up in the newspaper *Berlingske Tidende* ("Berling's Times"), which too closely identified Kierkegaard with the pseudonyms, prompted Søren to write indignantly in the rival paper *Fatherland*. The *Times*, he sniffs, is fit only for wrapping one's sandwiches! This was all perfectly in keeping with the campaign of indirect communication. After all, if Søren had been trying to gather followers he would not have created such an elaborate cloud of pseudonyms.

The *Corsair* was one of the founding members of the Kierkegaard fan club. It had praised Søren by name in 1841. *Either/Or* got a favourable nod in 1843. In May 1845 it made positive noises about the pseudonymous books, alluding to Kierkegaard as the author. Later that year Hilarius Bookbinder was lauded, and the November 14, 1845, edition immortalised Victor Eremita, claiming that in the annals of literature, his name "will never die." That piece of puffery prompted Søren to draft a response in the guise of Victor, asking the *Corsair* to slay him as it slays everyone else. "To become immortal" through the *Corsair*, Victor claims, "will become the death of me." In the end Søren decided to leave this letter in the drawer. However, he would repeat the same sentiment in public the following year.

From his conversations with Aron and his journals it is evident that there is justice in Søren's claim that his stand against the *Corsair* had been brewing for some time. It was, however, a poison piece from Møller that catalysed the fight. For his part, Møller had been prompted by Kierkegaard's pointed insinuations to Goldschmidt when he distinguished between the author of *A Jew* and the driving force behind the *Corsair*. Møller did not share his friend's fair-minded approach to Søren's foibles, and he seems determined to take the ironist down a peg or two before Søren could do the same to him.

As part of his bid for academic credibility, Møller had started a literary journal of his own called *Gæa*. In the December 22, 1845, edition, Møller published a long review, ostensibly of *Stages on Life's Way*. It was deliberately structured so as to give the impression the piece represented the views of a

Caricature of Søren by Wilhelm Marstrand about 1870. Even after his death in 1855, Søren was dogged by unflattering portraits— with their curved spines and ill-fitting trousers.

number of luminaries from the academy. The review soon expands to take in *Either/Or*, *Fear and Trembling*, *Prefaces*, and other works by Søren, including his letters to newspapers. Significantly, despite alluding to various authors, the only name that prominently appears in the piece is that of "S. Kierkegaard." There are occasional cold words of praise but overall the tone is snide and contemptuous. Møller also steers his review into deeply personal territory, seeing Søren's relations with Regine in the worst possible light:

But to spin another creature into your spider web, dissect it alive or torture the soul out of it drop by drop by means of experimentation—that is not allowed, except with insects, and is there not something horrible and revolting to the healthy human mind even in this idea?

Søren's sexual life (or lack of same) is crudely alluded to more than once: "He satiates himself by writing; instead of reproducing himself with a foetus a year as an ordinary human being he seems to have a fish nature and spawns." Charming.

Cartoon from the Corsair. *Søren stands alone while the universe revolves around him.*

Søren was not one to let personal slights and bad reviews pass unnoticed, but the majority of his responses remained in draft form in his writing desk. This would not be one of those times. Søren's response was swift and decisive. On December 27, 1845, the *Fatherland* contained a rejoinder from Frater Taciturnus. The lengthy article comes out swinging and lands many blows against P. L. Møller. Søren too was adept at wielding rumours, and he paints an unflattering picture of a Møller who is willing to do anything for money and

Cartoon from the Corsair. *A grateful member of the public receives the latest offering from Master Kierkegaard.*

whose *Gæa* article falsely insinuates the author into a company of academics with whom he has no business being associated. Regarding *Gæa*'s interpretation of Søren's authorship, Søren openly questions Møller's basic ability to understand what he is reading: a low blow against a man with pretensions to a professorship in aesthetics. The knockout punch comes at the end of the article. Near the finish of the essay, which until now had been all about Møller and the discussion of *Stages In Life's Way* in *Gæa*, the good Frater Taciturnus concludes:

> Would that I might only get into the *Corsair* soon. . . . My superior Hilarius Bookbinder, has been flattered in the *Corsair*, if I am not mistaken. Victor Emerita has even had to experience the disgrace of being immortalized—in the *Corsair*! And yet, I have already been there, for *ubis spiritus, ibi ecclesia: ubi* P. L. Møller, *ibi* the *Corsair*.

"Where the Spirit is, there is the Church: Where P. L. Møller is, there is the *Corsair*." With these words, Søren launched his attack on the paper and its "loathsome" assaults "on peaceable, respectable men." He did so without drawing Goldschmidt into the fray, and by directly naming and shaming Møller instead. It was a swift jab at the ambitious author's weakest spot, and he meant it to sting.

Møller's involvement with the *Corsair* was an open—yet unspoken—secret. Thus Kierkegaard's phrase was not a revelation so much as it was an intentional trumpet blast where silence usually reigned. Kierkegaard's breach of the etiquette surrounding pseudonymity had its desired effect. The public eye latched on to Møller. Even before the literary spat he was a controversial outsider to the professorship position he most coveted. Møller wrote an insincere conciliatory letter to the *Fatherland* a couple of days later,

Cartoon from the Corsair. *A startled Kierkegaard is confronted on the street by the meek and mild* Corsair, *cap in hand.*

but the damage was done. It is unlikely that he would have got the post in any case, but as the events transpired, Møller perceived that his calling-out in the *Fatherland* was the decisive factor. Aron Goldschmidt agreed, writing years later: "Kierkegaard pounced on him with such vehemence, used such peculiar words, had, or seemed to have, such an effect on the public that the professorship, instead of being brought closer by *Gæa*, was placed at an immeasurable distance."

With nothing left to lose, the *Corsair* struck back. The January 2, 1846, edition contains a satirical conversation between the editor of the *Fatherland* and Frater Taciturnus, who plot the downfall of the *Corsair* and heap praise on "Denmark's greatest mind, the author of Denmark's thickest books." Kierkegaard is named in person in the following issue, where a mocking conversation between Søren and other public figures of Copenhagen soon devolves into a discussion of Søren's tailor, with the joke that Kierkegaard arranges his trouser legs to be uneven "in order to look like a genius." The trouser talk continues, accompanied by pictures from cartoonist Peter Klæstrup. Søren's second and final reply to the *Corsair* appeared in the *Fatherland* on January 10, where Frater Taciturnus names Goldschmidt as an editor and likens the *Corsair* to a streetwalker one must pass by, and as a mercenary paper that attacks people for profit. The allusion brings to mind Møller's infamous dalliances with prostitutes on the one hand, and Aron would later interpret the "mercenary" jab as an allusion to his Jewishness on the other. Whether or not these were indeed Kierkegaard's intentions, in any case his letter ends with a renewed plea, "May I ask to be abused—the personal injury of being immortalised by the *Corsair* is just too much."

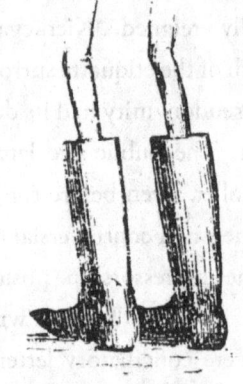

Cartoon from the Corsair. *The notorious legs get another outing.*

Søren stayed silent (at least in public print), but Møller and Goldschmidt continued their onslaught. For the next six months the *Corsair* would keep up the running joke, with most editions containing multiple caricatures and "comic compositions" at Kierkegaard's expense. The pieces share a common quality in that they trade in mocking Søren's awkward physical characteristics and questioning his sanity. Søren is intentionally mistaken for a local eccentric known as "Crazy Nathanson," and the idea that his clothing (especially the trousers) are ill-fitting is driven home in drawing after drawing. It is the cartoons, and not the prose, that stand out the most from the whole affair. The attempts at humorous writing rarely hit their marks, but Klæstrup's caricatures are brutal in their ability to take something true about their target and use it against him. One shows Søren's ungainly attempts to ride a horse, another portrays a lumpen

Søren cowering in the doorway of the *Corsair*'s offices. Another has Søren riding about on the back of a young girl. More pictures show Søren on a pedestal, presenting yet another of his books to a bowing and scraping member of the grateful public. One simply shows a humpbacked figure in silhouette, surrounded by the flotsam and jetsam of Copenhagen life, placing Søren, alone, in his own private universe.

The crude satire eked along until the July 17, 1846, edition, but by then it was clear the *Corsair*'s crew had run out of cannonballs. Goldschmidt and Møller had a falling out over the production of the paper. Møller was excluded from the *Corsair*, and Goldschmidt was growing weary of the whole affair. A few months previous, Aron had chanced upon Søren on the street. They did not speak. There was nothing more that could be said. Kierkegaard, Aron remembers, "walked past me with an intense and extremely embittered look." Aron felt "accused and oppressed: the *Corsair* had triumphed in the battle, yet I myself had acquired a false sense of being number one." Before he got home, Aron made up his mind to give up the *Corsair* for good. Goldschmidt was eventually able to sell off the paper. He went to live abroad in Germany and Italy before returning to Copenhagen as the (publicly named) founder of the respectable political journal *North and South*.

Cartoon from the Corsair. *The picture evokes the image of a real event in Søren's life when he once attempted to ride a horse.*

For his part, Møller continued to write sarcastic reviews of Kierkegaard's works, as well as minor works of poetry of his own. He never received the recognition he thought was owed to him. However dubious and unrealistic Møller's aspirations actually were to academic respectability, he blamed Kierkegaard for the slight. Møller too left Denmark in 1847. Unlike Aron, he never returned home, dying in obscurity and poverty in 1865.

The effects of the feud and mocking campaign are more easily stated than understood. For the principal players, the affair was life-changing. For those not directly involved, it can seem but a trifle. This is not only true for modern observers. Even some of Søren's contemporaries found it difficult to empathise. It was Hans Brøchner's opinion that Søren exaggerated the effects of the *Corsair*: "He [Søren] could reflect on a trifle until it assumed world-historical significance, as it were." However, in his memoirs written thirty years after the fact, Goldschmidt is keen to remind people of the particular historical sweet spot in which the affair of the *Corsair* occurred. "Accustomed as we are now [1877] to vehement and violent newspaper articles, one will have difficulty in understanding how it could sound in that anxious, quiet time [1846]." Søren's nephew Troels Frederik agrees, "In our time it is hard to imagine the chilling vulnerability that could be the lot of a victim of such attacks in those days." The public and popular worlds of Copenhagen in 1846 were on the cusp of change. The moral right of pseudonymity was still largely respected and acted as a bulwark against personal attacks, which wider society frowned on in any case. Furthermore, the political revolutions sweeping Europe were still two years away, with all the ferocious character assassinations and "take no prisoners" rhetoric that come with all culture wars. In Denmark in the '40s, the convention of naming and shaming in print (a matter of course in the modern age) was still relatively new and shocking.

Cartoon from the Corsair. *A famous author rises to prominence by riding on the back of an innocent young girl.*

The active members of Denmark's literary Golden Age were used to lobbing witty and erudite salvos at each other from behind the comfort of their own pseudonyms. The tone and content of the *Corsair* gave license to a level of mockery Kierkegaard did not expect. His walks down the street would be followed by jeering catcalls of "Søren! Søren!" or "Either Or!" from members of the public. "Every kitchen boy feels justified in almost insulting me in accordance with the *Corsair*'s orders," he vented in his journal, "young students titter and grin and are happy to see a prominent person trampled on. . . . The slightest thing I do, if it is merely to pay a visit . . . if the *Corsair* finds out, it is printed and read by everybody, the man I visit is embarrassed, gets almost angry with me, for which he cannot be blamed." On his city walks, Søren encountered groups of people who either would sheepishly stop talking when he approached or call out names as he passed. Matrons with their charges in the park allowed the children to run up to Søren, one after the other, so that they could ask inane questions and run giggling back to the group. Søren would sit in his pew at church, only to overhear his neighbours talking in a loud voice about his trousers.

Cartoon from the Corsair. *Søren's curved spine is mocked here.*

The trousers. Always the trousers. Søren's physicality became a focal point for attention, and his legs especially a matter for scrutiny. This public obsession with how well his ungainly body was clothed was not a figment of Søren's imagination. "Once," Troels Frederik recalls of his uncle, "I was walking behind him and wanted to run up to him to say hello. But just at that moment I heard some passer-by say something mocking about him and saw a couple of people on the other side of the street stop, turn around to look at him and laugh. His one trouser leg really was shorter than the other . . . he was odd-looking. I instinctively stopped, was embarrassed, and suddenly remembered that I had to go down another street." The philosopher George Brandes recalled how when he was growing up, if he tried to leave the house with his socks showing, his Nanny would admonish him, "Don't be such a Søren Kierkegaard!"

Things got so bad that Kierkegaard's tailor hinted that if Søren were to find another garment maker, it certainly would not hurt business. The taunting, grins, gapes, and social embarrassment made Søren's beloved "people baths" untenable. Formerly he had prided himself on his ability to converse with people of all stations. Now "it is the rabble, the utterly brutish humanity, the rowdies, silly women, schoolchildren, and apprentices" who were abusing him. Against his best intentions, Søren had become "eminent," cut off. He could not walk the streets of Copenhagen as before. Søren accrued further travel expenses taking cabs into the country so he could walk in peace. Alas, even these excursions were of no help, for Kierkegaard's reputation was not restricted to his physical appearance.

Thanks to the *Corsair* "Søren" had become "*Søren*," a by-word for a half-mad, lovelorn, and awkward philosopher.

> And so I am wasted on Denmark: and everybody pretends that it is nothing. . . . My first name is now a nickname every schoolboy knows. The same name is more frequently used by authors; it appears in comedies all the time now and everyone knows it is I.

A number of plays began to use this name when they wanted a shortcut to developing a minor comic character. The most overt, pernicious, and popular of these plays was called *Opposite Neighbours* by Jens Christian Hostrup. The first version had hit the stage in 1844 as a student production with a limited run. Here, a character named "Søren Kirk" spouts convoluted jargon filled with "either/or" propositions before being pulled off his perch by a frustrated mob. The play was originally by and for students and was filled with jokes aimed at university insiders. Søren was displeased at the time, but he was just about able to brush off the insult as an example of sophomore hijinks. After the *Corsair* however, it became impossible to pretend that the piece was the lighthearted parody amongst friends that Hostrup claimed it was. In 1845 and '46 Hostrup's play went on tour around the provinces, its success fuelled in part by the publicity that the name "Søren" was currently receiving from that other comic composition. Despite changing the name on the playbill to "Søren Torp. Theologian," it was obvious to everyone who the character was supposed to be. The national hit soon became international, with Holstrup's play touring Norway in 1847. Norwegian reviewers made free use of the name "Søren Kierkegaard" when discussing the character and his foolish speeches.

Søren had expected the great and the good of Danish society to rally to his defence when he took on the *Corsair*, for they too suffered at the hands of the "rabble-barbarians." But even his friends, including Bishop Mynster and Giøwad, the editor of the *Fatherland*, stayed silent, and Søren was left to face the onslaught alone. Søren had picked his fight by calling out the real people behind the anonymous mockery of the pirate paper. Yet the attempt at personalising the beast had led to the rise of a greater monster. The snapping, cackling crowd was threatening to overwhelm. "What I as a public person am suffering is best described as a slow death, like being trampled to death by geese."

It was not just the attention that got to Søren, it was the *manner* of the attention that was so dispiriting. In Søren's reflections on the matter it is evident that it was the cartoons that pained him far more than the prose. Clearly personal sensitivity was an issue: it is not much of a leap to move from "Søren Sock" of schoolboy days to Søren with the uneven trousers of 1846 after all. Yet it was not simply being bullied yet again that irked Kierkegaard. The affair of the *Corsair* drove home to Søren something about the nature of the Christendom in which he was operating. The cartoons had the very real effect of reducing the carefully cultivated intellectual and spiritual edifice Søren had been building with his authorship to a matter of how odd he looked. The members of "the public" proved themselves unwilling (if not incapable) of treating the authorship on its own terms. They did not bother to trace the movements of the separate ideas or weigh one pseudonymous voice up against another in order to own the conclusions inwardly as individuals. Instead, thanks to the *Corsair* and the response it received from all levels of society, it was not their relation to the truth that counted but Søren's relation to his pants.

> I am positive that my whole life will never be as important as my trousers have come to be. Yes, one might almost think that my trousers have become what the age demanded, and, if so, I sincerely hope that the demand of every age may be as moderate for the person concerned, for, good Lord, it does not demand trousers from me, after all, it merely demands that I wear them, and this demand really does not embarrass me, inasmuch as I have made a practice of wearing trousers since I was four years old . . . for someone ardently trying to hold to a concept of the greatness in or potential to every man there is something sad about having an abundance of observations which seem only to bear witness to irresponsibility, silliness, crudity, and the like.

Søren had intended to conclude his authorship with the appropriately named *Concluding Unscientific Postscript*. There were other texts in various states of completion, but these were never considered to be part of the scheme begun with *Either/Or*. The end of the *Postscript* contains Søren's confession that he is indeed responsible for the pseudonyms and finishes with a "wish and prayer" that readers nevertheless respect the pseudonyms as the authors of their works. The bulk of *Postscript* was completed before Søren took up his pen against the pirates, but the decision to include this final authorial confession and plea overlapped with his unmasking and be-trousering by the *Corsair*. In light of the tabloid's crude pre-emptive strike, Søren prevaricated over whether he should take in or leave out the acknowledgement of his authorship. In the end he convinced himself in his journal to leave it in and let the chips fall where they may. "But, no! I owe it to the truth to pay no attention to all this and to do everything as had been decided, leaving the outcome up to God and accepting everything from his hand as a good and perfect gift, refusing to act shrewdly, trusting that he will give me a steady and wise spirit."

It did not take Søren long to realise that his idea of concluding the authorship and taking up a quiet residency as the pastor in a village church was not going to fly. By January 20, 1847, he could write how "the wish to be a rural pastor has always appealed to me and been at the back of my mind. . . . It seems perfectly clear, however, that the situation here at home is becoming more and more confused." He perceives the times demand an extraordinary figure and dares to think this might be him. "When I gave [Regine] up, I gave up every desire for a cosy, pleasant life," he writes, but "from now on I must take being an author to be the same as being at the mercy of insult and ridicule. But to continue along this road is not something self-inflicted, for it was my calling; my whole habitus was designed for this." In this same entry, Søren finds connections between Mynster's "idolization of the establishment," "bourgeois mentality," the "cowardice and envy" of the cultured elite, and the violence of the "rabble-barbarians." The course Søren was setting was nothing less than a collision with all of Christendom.

> Humanly speaking, from now on I must be said not only to be running aimlessly before me but going headlong toward certain ruin—trusting in God, precisely this is the victory. This is how I understood life when I was ten years old, therefore the prodigious polemic in my soul; this is how I understood it when I was

twenty-five years old; so, too, now when I am thirty-four. This is why Poul Møller called me the most thoroughly polemical of men.

The fight to save Goldschmidt's soul and that of the common man from the *Corsair* was not going be an extra project added on to a concluded writing career. Instead, for Søren, the affair and its fallout marked a new turn in the path Governance had set him on years before. The monstrous public had loomed up, and Søren began to think he was the man appointed to slay it.

But to do that he would need to write more books.

CHAPTER 8

An Armed and Neutral Life

It is 1838. The old father has just passed away. The youngest son takes it upon himself to tell the family pastor the sombre news. The father had always revered Mynster and shaped his family's spiritual formation along lines Mynster set. Now, upon being informed of the old man's death, Mynster is puzzled. *Who* has died? It takes him a moment or two to recall how he knows the name of Michael Pedersen Kierkegaard. The preacher is a busy man with many demands on his time and many parishioners. But the son remembers that the bishop forgot.

"Voluntarily exposing myself to attack by the *Corsair* is no doubt the most intensive thing along the order of genius that I have done," Søren reflected in 1849. "It will have results in all my writing, will be extremely important for my whole task with respect to Christianity and to my elucidation of Christianity." In this he was correct. The effects of the *Corsair*, while apparently trivial to some, were in fact deep and long-lasting for Søren's sense of himself, his authorship, and the audience to whom he was writing. It also led to a renewed fascination with what it means to stand apart as a witness to the crowd. "It is frequently said that if Christ came to the world now he would once again be crucified. This is not entirely true. The world has changed; it is now immersed in 'understanding.' Therefore Christ would be ridiculed, treated as a mad man, but a mad man at whom one laughs."

Søren had always known he was singular. Now he was beginning to see himself as a type of potential martyr or witness to the truth. "What Christendom needs at every moment is someone who expresses Christianity uncalculatingly or with absolute recklessness," runs an 1848 entry. "He is then to be regarded as a measuring instrument—that is, how he is judged in Christendom will be a test of how much true Christianity there is in Christendom at a given time." Søren continues, "If his fate is to be mocked and ridiculed, to be regarded as mad, while a whole contemporary generation of clergy (who, note well, do not dare to speak uncalculatingly or recklessly) is honoured and they are also regarded as true Christians—then Christendom is an illusion." Søren is clear in his reflections that his martyrdom—if martyrdom it be—is not for *Christianity* as much as it is for "the truth." The one who presents the truth of the situation as completely and faithfully as he can has made no judgements about his own or anyone else's Christianity, but he has provided the opportunity for a clear choice to be made. "The judgment is not what he says but what is said of him."

The intensified direction of Søren's vocation follows his tentative "conclusion" to the authorship and coincidental "unmasking" in the *Corsair*. Søren was self-conscious about how the loss of his trial at the court of popular opinion marked a new chapter in his life. Literally. On March 9, 1846, he began a new journal with a new system of notation. Each volume was labelled "NB" (from the Latin *nota bene* meaning 'note well') and successively numbered, eventually running to thirty-six books in all. Unlike the pre-*Corsair* journals, which tend to be a jumble of haphazard thoughts and rough drafts, the NB volumes are clearly written with an eye to future readership and often aspire towards a coherence unseen in the earlier journals. A common theme is Søren's reflection on his own mission, as an author and as a witness. Another theme is that of the nature of the Single Individual, Christ, and authentic Christianity. Another is the many "collisions" the trajectory of his life against Christendom was putting in his way. The long, opening entry of the first volume titled "Report" sets the tone. "*The Concluding Postscript* is out; the pseudonymity has been acknowledged . . . Everything is in order; all I have to do now is to keep calm, be silent, depending on the *Corsair* to support the whole enterprise negatively, just as I wish." The Report describes the events from Søren's point of view, straining to put the mockery in as best a light as possible, but he admits "this existence is exhausting; I am convinced that not a single person understands me." Søren is frustrated by the fact that people might think it was because of the *Corsair* that he had ended his authorship, and he is chagrined that luminaries like Bishop Mynster might think he adapted his books for the express purpose of engaging with the low tabloid. Instead, Søren insists the opposite is true. It only looks like he has inserted *Corsair*-specific passages into the *Concluding Unscientific Postscript* because his analysis of the state of things was so astute. The *Corsair* has merely brought to light what was always present in the culture. Søren ends the entry with a reiteration of his conviction that his authorship is concluded, and he expresses the wish once again that he might retire to a quieter life. "If I only could make myself become a pastor. Out there in quiet activity, permitting myself a little productivity in my free time, I shall breathe easier, however much my present life has gratified me." Søren's hesitancy is evident even in the passages where he claims this is what he wants. Despite his occasional assertions that a country parish is the life for him, Søren is too aware of himself and too concerned with truth to push the matter very far.

A visit to Bishop Mynster in the autumn of 1846 confirmed to Søren he was bound for something other than church life. Ironically, it was Mynster's approval of Søren's plan for a pastorate that set the wheels turning. Mynster encouraged Søren to seek a living somewhere in the country. The response immediately put Søren on guard. He sensed Mynster agreed in some way with the treatment Søren was currently receiving at the hands of the *Corsair* rabble, thinking it would do him some good. A spell in a rural parish would take Søren down another peg or two and set him on a more respectable career in the church. These were decidedly not Søren's feelings towards either the *Corsair* or churchmanship. "When

Bishop Mynster advises me to become a rural pastor, he obviously does not understand me." Despite the slight to his father's memory years before, Søren retained the habitual Kierkegaard family reverence for Mynster. Yet at the same time he suspected the bishop had less than pure motives for encouraging Søren to leave Copenhagen. Søren was trouble and Mynster knew it. It would not hurt the old bishop to get the annoying author out of the way. Søren would continue to occasionally meet with Mynster over the coming years, but more often than not the truncated visits would prove dissatisfying. Mynster was clearly not keen to maintain a relationship with his former parishioner's quarrelsome son and he kept Søren at arm's length.

Jakob Peter Mynster, bishop, pastor to the Kierkegaard family and erstwhile mentor to Søren. "You have no idea what sort of poisonous plant Mynster was. . . . He was a colossus. Great strength was required to topple him, and the person who did it also had to pay for it."

The reason is not hard to fathom. Søren's books during this time were filled with hidden and not so hidden critical allusions to Mynster, the church, and the Christian culture over which he presided as primate. And there were a lot of books. Both Søren's plan to take up a pastorate and his idea that his authorship was concluded came to nothing in the years following the *Corsair*. Between 1846 and 1854, under his own name, Søren brought out *Two Ages, Upbuilding Discourses in Various Spirits, Works of Love, Christian Discourses, The Lily of the Field and the Bird of the Air, Three Discourses at the Communion on Fridays, On My Work as an Author*, and *For Self-Examination*. Neither did the practice of pseudonymity cease. Newly invented characters were assigned to *The Sickness Unto Death, Two Ethical-Religious Essays, The Crisis and A Crisis in the Life of an Actress*, and *Practice in Christianity*. Other substantial books did not see the light of day in Søren's lifetime: *The Point of View for My Life as an Author, The Book on Adler, Armed Neutrality*, and *Judge for Yourself!* were written but not published in this period. Newspapers received open letters, old journals were edited, the thirty-six volumes of the NB journals continued apace, and Søren prepared *Either/Or, Works of Love*, and some other texts for their second printing. Far from representing the nadir of his creative life, the years following the conclusion of the first authorship saw an explosion of productivity.

Søren's connection to the voluminous output was now common knowledge—not only for the likes of Heiberg and Mynster but also for all the butcher boys and fishwives in town. In the past, Søren had been able to walk and talk on the streets as a way of keeping a necessary distance between himself and the serious ideas emanating from Victor, Hilarius, Johannes, and the rest. Now, thanks to the *Corsair*, Søren's public personae was no longer separate from his authorship. For the chattering classes obsessed with trousers, his physical presence effectively *was* the authorship. As a result, Søren embarked on a self-conscious effort to reconstruct his image. He took his walks in the empty countryside and, when in the crowded city, tended to stay at home. Søren avoided visitors even more than before. "And now that I have remodelled my external life, am more withdrawn, keep to myself more, have a more momentous look about me, then in certain quarters it will be said that I have changed for the better."

The self-examination that flowed from reflection on the *Corsair* and his dawning realisation that the authorship was not concluded after all saw Søren become more interested in the ways and means of communication and his role as a communicator. Already, before the *Concluding Unscientific Postscript*, Søren had intended to publish a book-length review of a novel by Heiberg's talented mother, Thomasine Gyllembourg. Søren told himself that writing a book review of Madame Gyllembourg's *Two Ages* did not count as being an author, as he was dealing mainly with another person's thoughts. The resulting book, whose full title was *Two Ages: The Age of Revolution and the Present Age, A Literary Review* was half an appreciation of the novel, and half a platform for Søren's own musings on, amongst other things, the present age and its tendency to prefer chatter to meaningful communication and action. The public's predilection to "level" anyone who stands apart from the crowd is also subject to the full force of Søren's considerable critical faculties. What began life as a book review ended as a full length rejoinder to the spirit of the *Corsair* at work in the world.

The "book review" loophole also led to another of Søren's enduring pet projects. In the end, *The Book on Adler* would never be published in his lifetime, but this was not before the manuscript underwent more revisions and rewrites than anything else in the Kierkegaardian canon. Søren received Adolph Peter Adler's latest works in 1846 and began reflecting on them immediately. By the next year he had amassed over 200 pages considering the case of the errant pastor. Adler was a friendly acquaintance of Søren's, a university contemporary who had also studied theology, and had made his mark as a pro-Hegelian. However, in 1840, Adler had a religious experience after which he claimed that God wanted him to promote a new doctrine in opposition to the Hegelian influence at work in Danish Christianity. Adler was widely chastised for his mystical enthusiasm and was forced to retire his parish. In the face of mockery and rejection, Adler then attempted to adapt his new revelation back along Hegelian lines.

It was this last capitulation, more than the claim of divine revelation in the first place, that particularly drew Søren's criticism. He had met with Adler on a few occasions and found him an intelligent but ridiculous figure. On one memorable meeting, Adler sat Søren down and revealed to him that he, Adler, considered Søren to be a John the Baptist figure preparing the way for his new revelation. Adler then proceeded to read out some of the passages that Jesus Christ had supposedly dictated to him. Søren recalled how Adler curiously modulated his voice, alternating between normal speaking and a dramatic stage whisper. When Søren confessed he did not notice anything particularly revelatory in the passages, Adler offered to come back later that evening and read it all again in the special voice. Søren refrained from laughing at the time, but he did later confess to his friend Brøchner that he was quite happy, thank you very much, being John the Baptist as he had no ambitions at all to be a Messiah.

Adler was easy to mock, but Søren was more interested in the serious issues that Adler's case brought up. The bulk of *Adler* considers the "difference between a genius and an apostle" and is in fact an extended reflection on what it means to have and speak with authority. True apostles speak from divine revelation, and thus the quality of their communication is irrelevant. Genius communicators, on the other hand, have to pay attention to form if anything good is to come from their writing. In the end, the main difference between an apostle and a genius is that the genius does not speak with authority but has to rely on skill. The issue was important to Søren's sense of himself and his vocation. The subtitle "without authority" occurs often in the books, becoming a catch-phrase for his entire authorship.

The book on Adler was clearly important to Søren, but there were a few sensitivities to deal with before it could be published. Søren too was a writer with sense of a divine calling and an axe to grind with Hegel and the Hegelians. He too was dogged by accusations of being mentally unbalanced. Thus Søren was understandably ginger about how to deal with Adler, if at all. In the end he decided not to publish, out of deference to his own case but also with due regard for Adler himself. Søren had no desire to commit character assassination for the sake of a rubber-necking public. As he well knew, "it is cruel to slay a person that way." The 200 pages or so stayed in the desk, but an excerpt, "*The Difference Between a Genius and an Apostle*," was published, which took out all mention of Adler by name. The essay appeared as one of the *Two Ethical-Religious Essays*, attributed to the pseudonym H. H. in 1849.

The curious case of Pastor Adler was not the only thing occupying Søren's attention during this time. Besides *Two Ages* and various *Discourses* published in 1847, a major book was underway, laying to rest once and for all Søren's idea of retiring from authorship.

Works of Love came out of an extended reflection on the biblical call to "love one's neighbour" and Søren's renewed appreciation for the "Single Individual." The category began life as a communication to Regine, but he had come to see it was applicable to any and all of his potential readers. Far from being an isolating philosophy, Søren thought the only way to truly love anyone was *as* and *for* individuals apart from any group or crowd to which they might belong. As a result, *Works of Love* is a deeply subversive book dressed up as an apparently innocuous call for everyone to get along. In Søren's hands, the "love of neighbour" is shown to be a radical position in the world, cutting against prior claims of self, family, and nation. The move to inwardness is also a call to action. *Works of Love* is called a "Christian deliberation," a subtitle that Søren intended to differentiate from his other "discourses." The deliberation, he thought, was intended to bring the reader to a point of active decision about controversial ideas rather than reassuring people of established truths.

An upbuilding discourse about love presupposes that people know essentially what love is and seeks to win them to it, to move them. But this is certainly not the case. Therefore a "deliberation" must first fetch them up out of the cellar, call to them, turn their comfortable way of thinking topsy-turvy.

Works of Love was published in September 1847. It sold relatively well and was one of the few books reprinted in Søren's lifetime. The book was barely reviewed, but Søren did not mind as he was writing for Single Individuals, not reviewers filling newspaper space with their chatter. He considered the book itself to be his "work" of love. One section was written for his crippled cousin Hans Peter. Another was written in memory of his dead parents. Brother Peter's ailing wife, Jette, was sent a copy to rally her spirits, accompanied by a sensitive and encouraging letter.

Two high-profile fans were King Christian VIII and his second wife, Queen Caroline Amalie. Søren delivered a copy of *Works of Love* to them in person after its publication. The king had asked Søren to visit him on a few occasions during the writing of the book. He was clearly struck by this author who, much like a king, was also an eccentric figure unable to walk unnoticed amongst the people. Søren had, of course, dutifully obliged, but from lengthy journal entries reflecting on the visits we know he found the audiences largely tiresome. "I firmly decided to visit him as infrequently as possible." The king enjoyed talking about ideas, especially politics, but it was apparent he did not fully understand Kierkegaard's writing. The queen professed to have read some of his works but in conversation persistently referred to "Either *and* Or"; a telling mistake that did not escape Søren's attention. *Works of Love* was delivered in an attempt to improve the situation, but Søren reflected the king seemed content to glance at the table of contents and to be sentimentally moved by a passage Søren read out loud.

A more perceptive reader was also one of Søren's primary intended audience members. Søren was particularly keen to elicit Bishop Mynster's opinion (". . . it would have made me indescribably happy to have him agree with me . . ."), and he went to see him on November 4, 1847. It was to be another dissatisfying meeting. "Today I looked in on Bishop Mynster. He said he was very busy—so I left at once. But he was also very cold toward me. Very likely he is offended by the latest book." Very likely. Mynster was no fool and would have perceived this was yet another thinly disguised critique presuming to tell him and his church what Christianity really was.

There was another intended reader to whom Søren did not dare pay a visit. On the day before Søren's short audience with Mynster, Regine Olsen married Johan Frederik Schlegel at the Church of Our Saviour in Copenhagen.

Regine Schlegel, neé Olsen.
Photograph of Regine from 1855.

The next month, Peter and Søren finally sold the Nytorv family home, splitting the proceeds. The event, coupled with the breach with Mynster and the marriage of the new Mrs. Schlegel symbolically tied up many of the threads of Søren's old life. The following year would prove to be a watershed for the direction the renewed Søren was taking. "Then came the year 1848—for me, beyond all comparison the richest and most fruitful year I have experienced as an author." During this one year Søren began or completed *Christian Discourses*, *The Sickness unto Death*, *Practice in Christianity*, *The Point of View for My Work as an Author*, *Armed Neutrality*, *Two Ethical-Religious Essays*, *The Lily in the Field and the Bird of the Air*, and other occasional pieces.

Søren's fecundity was spurred in large part by the monumental events sweeping Europe. In 1848, the "Springtime of the People" was afoot. Italy, Germany, Austria, and especially France saw waves of violent republican protest against the ruling monarchs. Other European nations saw similar unrest.

Not one to be left out, Denmark too enjoyed its own (bloodless) revolution. By the evening of January 20, 1848, King Christian VIII was dead. Sensing an opportunity for change, a group of Copenhagen's leading republicans (a liberal cause), headed by H. N. Clausen, gathered to draft a scheme for a free constitution. The petition was ignored by Christian's newly enthroned successor, Frederick VII. By February, news of the Revolution sweeping Italy and Paris had reached Denmark. In March a more vigorous group of liberal reformers held a series of mass meetings, this time led by Orla Lehmann. Together, members of the cultured elite, artisans, and peasants thrashed out a National Liberal platform that included as a central plank universal (male) suffrage. On March 20, Lehmann and the reformers met at the offices of the *Fatherland* and drew up another petition. The next day, a crowd of over 15,000 people accompanied Lehmann through the streets to the royal palaces. They demanded a constitution, incorporation of all Slesvig territories into Danish hands, and law from and of "the People." Significantly, this appeal to the common man was accompanied by a thinly veiled threat of the force that the common man could wield if he were not accommodated: Lehmann included in his petition the stark choice between popular revolt or royal assent, imploring the king to save Denmark and "not to force the nation to the self-help of desperation." Lehmann was received, the reforms were accepted, and, with a triumphant roar, the crowd dispersed. By the following year, Denmark had become a constitutional, democratic monarchy.

From the point of view of someone intent on speaking to "the present age," for Kierkegaard two significant developments stemmed from these events. The first was the explosion of the Slesvig-Holstein conflict into open war. In 1848 German nationalists had appealed to the king to recognize the unity of the Slesvig-Holstein region in southern Jutland. They were opposed by Danish republican-liberal-nationalists, led by Lehmann, who supported the so-called "Ultra Danish" party, of which Grundtvig too was a key member. The king was swayed by the Ultra-Danes: an undivided Slesvig would remain constitutionally bound to Denmark. When they heard the news, the German party proclaimed a rival militant Slesvig-Holstein government. The violence would last until 1851, leaving the country in a state of perpetual nationalistic unease. At home it would also deprive Søren of Anders Westergaard, his servant and friend (whom Kierkegaard liked to call "my body") who was drafted into the war.

The second, related, development affected the established Lutheran Church. No longer the state church, it was now to be known as the Danish People's Church. The transition from "State" to "People" marked a shift in emphasis from a constitutional, clerical organization initially favoured by Mynster and Martensen, to one more free-ranging and populist, much to the delight of the Grundtvigians. A lot of the technical detail regarding ecclesiastical constitutions and nomenclature was obscure and largely irrelevant to day-to-day church life. However, Søren was well aware the changes of 1848 marked a significant shift in the cultural imagination. An undefined sense of popular right was pervading politics and religion, where all must bow to a new mass entity called "the People."

Popularity is a dangerous game. It was popular consensus, after all, that kept the *Corsair* in business no less than it kept Danes secure in the assumption that as civilised people naturally they were Christian. The course Søren was plotting diverged both from conservative and liberal assumptions. While Christendom's citizens were getting swept up for or against mass movements in the name of "the People," they were forgetting the real persons, neighbours, and single individuals right in front of their noses. For Kierkegaard this had disastrous consequences: "They are blind to what the year 1848 has made sufficiently clear—that the crowd, the mass, are evil. They still live in the obsolete notion that one battles against the established order with the help of the people." Instead, as Søren wrote in his journal a year before, "'The single individual' is the category through which, in a religious sense, the age, history, the generation must go." His task was becoming clear: to winkle single individuals out from their crowds so they could relate to each other and to God as persons and not as groups. The "established order" certainly needed to be opposed, but it wasn't going to be through yet another faceless movement or mob action. The social and political events of contemporary Denmark furnished Søren with a favourite phrase to describe his strategy. "Armed neutrality" describes a military stance without partisan engagement. Søren wrote a short book by this name (unpublished in his lifetime) articulating his peculiar position:

> *Armed Neutrality.* If my relation were to pagans, I could not be neutral; then in opposition to them I would have to say that I am a Christian. But I am living in Christendom, among Christians, or among people who all say they are Christians. . . . This is why I keep neutral with regard to my being a Christian. . . . The task, then, is to present the ideal of a Christian, and here I intend to do battle.

Two foundational books in Søren's neutrally offensive arsenal are *Sickness unto Death* and *Practice in Christianity*, both substantially written in 1848 but published separately in the ensuing years. Before it was printed, Søren referred to *Sickness unto Death* as an "attack upon Christendom" and Christendom an "altogether un-Christian concept." Early plans for the book included publishing it together with another essay titled "An Attempt to Introduce Christianity into Christendom." The book deals primarily with different forms of despair, original sin, and becoming an authentic self. It was published in the summer of 1849, but not before Søren indulged in yet another extended round of to-ing and fro-ing over what name it should be ascribed to.

Søren's journals and his posthumously published *Point of View* relate the awkward relationship to the pseudonyms the *Corsair* and the collision with Christendom had put him in. Before, Søren had been able to stand above his characters, writing books the content of which he personally may or may not have agreed with. In any case, the point was for readers to weigh and decide for themselves, not look directly to the author for guidance. The signed religious works and the constant presence on the streets was a way of distancing himself from these books. Now, all eyes were on Søren, and the distance between his person and his writing collapsed. What is more, his writing scheme had come up to the point where the highest Christian categories needed to be elucidated, a stage higher than Søren himself felt he occupied. It must not look like he himself was the Christian he was describing in his new books.

Thus a new character, Anti-Climacus, was born with a position and relationship to Søren hitherto unseen in the literature. Although there is a clear connection to Johannes Climacus, *Anti* does not simply mean "against." Instead, the *anti* (as in "anticipate") connotes something greater or prior. Much as a great house will have an anteroom from which all the other doors and corridors lead, so too Anti-Climacus is invested with thoughts and positions higher and more central than that of the other pseudonyms. Anti-Climacus is not intended to hide Søren's involvement (he lists his name as the editor) but it does provide the necessary distance Søren felt he needed between the work and himself. If the readers of Christendom felt weighed and found wanting by this ideal Christian, then so too did Søren. "I would place myself higher than Johannes Climacus, lower than Anti-Climacus."

Days before Anti-Climacus was due to hit the stage with the publication of *Sickness unto Death*, Regine's father, Counsellor Terkild Olsen, passed away. Søren had enjoyed a good rapport with Olsen and the year before had rashly attempted a reunion with him and the family as a first step to seeking an understanding with Regine. Søren had spontaneously taken himself to where he knew the Olsens holidayed. "I was so happy and almost sure of meeting the family there—and that an attempt must be made." Lo and behold, who should pass by but Counsellor Olsen. "The only one," Søren wrote, who "I safely dare become reconciled with, for here there is no danger as with the girl." Søren affected a cheery greeting and offer of friendship, but it was too much for the father, who, with tears in his eyes, said, "I do not wish to speak with you!" and ran away faster than Søren could follow. Søren shouted after him that the responsibility for healing the rift was now on Olsen's shoulders, but it was to no avail. Søren mused later on the event: "We all weep when the pastor preaches about being reconciled with our enemies. Actually to seek reconciliation is regarded as effrontery. Thus Councillor Olsen . . . was furiously incensed over it."

Now he was dead. Rightly or wrongly, Søren had suspected that Olsen was the main barrier to any future friendship with his daughter. With this obstacle out of the way, Søren wondered whether now would be a good opportunity to test the possibility of rapprochement with Regine. They saw each other often on the streets or in church but had not exchanged a word. After many, many drafts and false starts, Søren eventually found the words for his letter, dated November 19, 1849. The draft read in part:

. . . Marry I could not. Even if you were still free, I could not. However, you have loved me, as I have you. I owe you much—and now you are married. All right, I offer you for the second time what I can and dare and ought to offer you: reconciliation. I do this in writing in order not to surprise or overwhelm you. Perhaps my personality did once have too strong an effect; that must not happen again. But for the sake of God in Heaven, please give serious consideration to whether you dare become involved in this, and if so, whether you prefer to speak with me at once or would rather exchange some letters first. If your answer is "No"—would you then please remember for the sake of a better world that I took this step as well.

In any case, as in the beginning so until now,

S.K.

What Regine would have made of this letter, we will never know. She never saw it. Søren, keenly aware that his unusual approach had more than a whiff of the clandestine about it, had enclosed the note in an envelope attached to a cover letter to Fritz Schlegel.

The enclosed letter is from me (S. Kierkegaard) to—your wife. You yourself must now decide whether or not to give it to her. I cannot, after all, very well defend approaching her . . . If you disagree, may I ask you to return the letter to me unopened . . .

I have the honour to remain, etc.

S.K.

This is exactly what Fritz duly did. Søren recorded in his diary, "I then received a moralizing and indignant epistle from the esteemed gentleman and the letter to her unopened." Elsewhere he commented on the need to avoid even the appearance of impropriety with Regine, and he refused to try to enlist her help in persuading Fritz of the possibility that they might talk again. "Now the matter is finished. One thing is sure—without Schlegel's consent not one word. And he has declared himself as definitively as possible."

The door closed to a real-life friendship, all that remained was for Søren to return to conversing with his imaginary Regine. He continued to allude to her in his books and sent her copies of his *Discourses* as they were published. Unbeknownst to him, Fritz and Regine were well aware of the full extent of the one-sided literary conversation. They had read Søren's works out loud to each other during their engagement and continued to purchase his books throughout their married life, following his career with interest.

Around the same time as receiving Schlegel's note and the unopened letter, Søren sustained another unpleasant blow from a source equally close to home. A month before, Peter had delivered a talk in which he unfavourably compared Søren to none other than Martensen. To add insult to the injury, the lecture was published in the *Danish Church Gazette*, a Grundtvigian paper. Søren fired off a letter of protest, complaining of Peter's misrepresentation of the pseudonyms and pointing out that people will wrongly assume that because he is the older brother, readers will be fooled into thinking Peter has reliable access to Søren's mind, which he most certainly does not. Søren was annoyed intellectually but also personally hurt. "Dear Peter," he wrote, "I have now read your article . . . To be honest, it has affected me painfully in more ways than one." He begs his brother that if he is to be compared to Martensen, then "it does seem to me that the essential difference ought to have been indicated, namely this, that I have sacrificed to an extraordinary extent and that he has profited to an extraordinary extent." Finally, "it seems to me that both for your own sake and for mine you should modify your statements about me." Peter's comments only just about applied to a handful of pseudonyms, not to Søren, and he again reiterates his wish and prayer. "I myself have asked in print that this distinction be observed. It is important to me, and the last thing I would have wished is that you of all people should in any way have joined in lending credence to a carelessness from which I must suffer often enough as it is."

Any comparison with Martensen was always going to rankle, but the timing of this spat was particularly frustrating. Martensen's star was rising fast. He had been appointed a full professor of theology at the university and had recently published his *Christian Dogmatics* to international acclaim. Søren had a copy and his marginal notes are, unsurprisingly, disdainful. "All existence is disintegrating," he scribbles on the book. "While anyone with eyes must see that all this about millions of Christians is a sham. . . . Martensen sits and organizes a dogmatic system. . . . Since everything else is as it should be, the most important matter confronting us now is to determine where the angels are to be placed in the system, and things like that." One observation in particular stands out. "Strangely enough, Mynster is frequently quoted . . . And at one time it was Mynster whom 'the system' was going to overthrow." This growing rapport between Martensen and Mynster did not bode well. Ostensibly, the two were theological opponents. Mynster was as opposed to Martensen's Hegelian systematising as was Søren. Yet of late the two churchmen were aligning themselves on the side of exactly the sort of cultured, established, and numerically populous Christendom Søren was warning against. Martensen might be philosophically obtuse, but he was also sophisticated and urbane. In short, he was Bishop Mynster's kind of man, Hegel or no.

Søren had been trying and failing to become Mynster's man for some time. *Practice in Christianity* was his final application for the post. The bulk of the book was written in 1848, but it was published on September 25, 1850, under the name Anti-Climacus. *Practice* sold well (better than most of his other books) but was largely ignored by reviewers. As with *Works of Love*, Søren did not mind, saying of the book, "Without a doubt it is the most perfect and the truest thing I have written." However, he was quick to add, "It must not be interpreted as if I am supposed to be the one who almost censoriously bursts in upon everybody else—no, I must first be disciplined myself by the same thing; there perhaps is no one who is permitted to humble himself as deeply under it as I . . . for the work is itself a judgment."

In retrospect, Søren and others would come to see the book as the beginning of his overt published attack on Christendom. Yet originally Søren had intended *Practice in Christianity* to be an aid to Mynster and a last-ditch defence for the establishment. The book offers extended reflections on various biblical passages where Jesus bids people directly to follow him without taking offence. The language is mild, exhorting, and Christ-centred. It is not fiery or angry. What it is, however, is a clear presentation of the need for the Single Individual to come out of the crowd and stand before Jesus without recourse to hiding behind the distractions of so-called Christian civilisation, either populist *or* cultured. The book includes a stirring "Moral," offering the pastors and leaders of the church to confess their inability to preserve authentic Christianity and to throw themselves upon the grace of God. The primary person who needed to do the admission was the primate of the Danish Church, Bishop Mynster.

Only if the church confesses its guilt can it continue to be the official representative of Christianity in the land, hence the book is a "defence." However, Søren was under no illusions that the book could easily be read as an "attack." Its call to reintroduce Christianity back into Christendom was clearly a bitter pill to swallow for Christendom's existing army of teachers and preachers. He had private conversations with Mynster about the text and its "Moral." The bishop was clearly unhappy with the Moral and with *Practice*'s repeated use of the word "observations," which was an allusion to his own set of popular devotionals published under that name. However, rather than *either* admitting the book was correct, *or* attacking it as blasphemous, Mynster decided to publicly ignore it altogether. The silence was the last straw for Søren who had expected so much and was fast losing all veneration for his father's pastor. "To me it became clear he was powerless."

Regine was never far from Søren's thoughts even while his complaint with Mynster was ramping up. In May 1851 he had been invited to preach at the Church of Our Lady, where his chosen text was his favourite verse from James 1:17: "Every good and perfect gift is from above, coming down from the Father of the heavenly lights, who does not change like shifting shadows." The verse was important to Regine too and featured in the *Discourses*, which Søren had dedicated to her. Søren confesses in his diary of the day that he had picked the passage with her in mind and had half-hoped she would be in attendance during the sermon. Evidently she was not to be seen that day, but Søren would soon see her very often.

In April, for financial reasons, he moved to a house outside of the city walls. From there Søren would make the half-hour walk into the city every morning, where he would regularly pass Regine on the street. They never exchanged a word during these moments, but in his journals Søren would recount every look and detail. Eventually, the daily meetings became a source of concern to Søren, for fear of impropriety. Was Regine arranging to run into him on purpose? Later in the year Søren resolved to alter his walk. "So I was obliged to make a change. I also believed that it would be best for her, for this constant dailiness is trying, especially if she is thinking of reconciliation with me, for which I of course would have to ask her husband's consent." The change worked for a time, but soon Søren reported seeing her again and was obliged to randomize his route. (The run-ins would more or less continue until Søren moved back into the city in October of 1852, this time in cramped apartments behind the Church of Our Lady.) The fresh memories of Regine are undoubtedly on Søren's mind when he publishes more *Discourses* and an explanation of *My Work as an Author* in August 1851. The final two *Discourses* were timed to appear at the same time as Søren's public discussion of the Christian direction of his project. They bore the significant dedication: "To One Unnamed, Whose Name Will One Day Be Named, is dedicated with this little work, the entire authorship as it was from the beginning."

In the main Søren's writing energy was spent on his journals, which by this time were plainly intended for (eventual) publication after his death. An "Open Letter" to one Dr. Rudelbach published in the *Fatherland* on the last day of the year 1851 represents Søren's only foray into the public cut-and-thrust during this period. It is a telling indication of Søren's position at this time. Andreas Gottlob Rudelbach was a renegade reformer who tried to enlist Søren in his schemes to bring about the political separation of church and state. Rudelbach had thought that as a fellow critic of "habitual Christianity," Søren would be a worthy ally to his cause. In his letter, Søren readily agrees, "I am a hater of 'habitual Christianity.' This is true. I hate habitual Christianity in whatever form it appears." However:

> Habitual Christianity can indeed have many forms . . . if there were no other choice, if the choice were only between the sort of habitual Christianity which is a secular-minded thoughtlessness that nonchalantly goes on living in the illusion of being Christian, perhaps without ever having any impression of Christianity, and the kind of habitual Christianity which is found in the sects, the enthusiasts, the super-orthodox, the schismatics—if worse comes to worst, I would choose the first. The first kind has still taken Christianity in vain only in a thoughtless and negative way. . . . The second kind has taken Christianity in vain perhaps out of spiritual pride. . . . One could almost be tempted to smile at the first kind, because there is hope; the second makes one shudder.

Søren has harsh words for the obsession with political solutions to spiritual problems that he perceives in Rudelbach and other enthusiasts:

> There is nothing about which I have greater misgivings than all that even slightly tastes of this disastrous confusion of politics and Christianity. . . . If this faith in the saving power of politically achieved free institutions belongs to true Christianity, then I am

no Christian, or even worse, I am a regular child of Satan, because, frankly, I am indeed suspicious of these politically achieved free institutions, especially of their saving, renewing power.

He ends his letter with a reiteration of his life's task. "I have worked to make this teaching more and more the truth in 'the single individual.' . . . I have aimed polemically throughout this whole undertaking at 'the crowd,' . . . also at the besetting sin of our time, self-appointed reformation."

Any reform Søren wanted was inward, not external. Another short book, *For Self Examination* drove the point home when it was published on September 10, 1851, under his own name. The so-called "silent years" follow the publication of this book. Over three years in which Søren, astonishingly for him, does not print a thing. *Judge for Yourself!* was written at this time but not published, as Søren judged for himself that the time was not right to so openly pursue its theme (more stringent than in *Practice*) of reintroducing Christianity into Christendom. A myriad of journal entries during the silent years reveal that Søren was honing his material. A long entry entitled "About Her" recounts the frequent street meetings (including a smile from Regine on his birthday: "Ah, how much she has come to mean to me!") and a significant event at a church service where the text was once again James 1:17. Before the preacher began his sermon, Søren (who was sitting behind) records that Regine impulsively turned her head to look at him before sinking down in her seat. Søren saw the sermon and the event as a sort of release for them both.

Besides repeated returns to Regine, the Single Individual, and "his task," multiple other entries consider Mynster and Søren's relationship to him. One long entry from 1852 entitled "The Possible Collision with Mynster" is typical insofar as it sketches ways and means for Søren to take the fight further. "My position is: I represent a more authentic conception of Christianity than does Mynster. . . . A little admission from his side, and everything will be as advantageous as possible for him."

Christus *by Bertel Thorvaldsen. The statue is located at the front of Copenhagen's Church of Our Lady. It bears the inscription from Matthew 11:28: "Come to Me." The statue and its invitation are key elements of Søren's book* Practice in Christianity, *which was meant as a wake-up call to Mynster and the Danish Church.*

The plans were all for naught, and Søren would never see the bishop converted to his cause. Mynster died on January 30, 1854. His memorial service was not light on pomp and circumstance. Denmark's finest were out in force, with priests from across the land arriving early in the day to be a part of the proceedings. Martensen, as the royal court chaplain, presided over all. Due to deft manoeuvring on Martensen's part, the gap between Martensen and Mynster had considerably narrowed over the years. Now it was well known that Martensen, although relatively young, had realistic aspirations to be Mynster's successor. As such, his memorial sermon was not without some regard to his own position. Whatever he said about Mynster as bishop was also—whisper it—what Martensen envisioned for himself. So it was that in the memorial address Martensen held forth:

> So let us now then imitate his faith . . . that his memory amongst us in truth must be for upbuilding! Let us admonish ourselves as we say: Imitate the faith of the true witness, the faith of the authentic witness to the truth! . . . [let his precious memory] guide our thoughts back to the whole line of witnesses to the truth, which is like a holy chain stretching itself through the ages from the day of the Apostles until our own day.

One can only imagine Søren's immediate reaction to hearing this speech using his favourite terms like "upbuilding," "apostle," "authentic," and, especially "truth witness." *Of* Mynster, of all people, *by* Martensen, of all people.

Søren vibrates angrily in his pew. He goes home. He writes a scathing response. He leaves it in his desk. And he bides his time.

CHAPTER 9

A Life Concluded

The visitor is perched on an armchair in the sitting room waiting to be called in to Sunday lunch. Anna is in the corridor outside. "I have so little desire to be at the table today," she whispers to her husband, Henrik. "Do you think I can stay away?"

Henrik sadly shakes his head. Duty demands. They both arrange their smiles and bring their guest to the table. "Søren!" Henrik calls out with desperate bonhomie, "Can I tempt you with a little glass of Madeira today?" Anna flutters about, talking about the weather, her children, the servants. Anything at all.

The attempts at deflection fail utterly. Søren will not be put off his course. Immediately he launches into his favourite topic. What do they think about the old Bishop Mynster, now two months dead? Was he *really* a witness? A witness to *the truth*?

"Oh, Søren, let's not go into that old dispute," says Anna. "We are totally familiar with one another's opinions, and to discuss it further can of course only lead to a quarrel."

She should know. Søren has been a guest at their house now every day for a week. And every day the topic is the same.

Søren begins to gesticulate with his fork. He raises his voice. His comments become more pointed. He considers Anna to be a wise person and he respects her sound judgement. He wants to know, was Jakob Mynster a Christian or a poisonous plant? But there is silence. Anna, finally, has had enough. "You know the man of whom you speak so ill is someone for whom we cherish the greatest respect and to whom we are profoundly grateful. I cannot put up with hearing him scorned unceasingly here." Anna stands up, collecting her skirts. "Since you will not stop it, I can escape from it only by leaving the room."

❖

During the "silent years" from September 10, 1851, until December 18, 1854, Denmark's most prodigious prose poet published nothing. "Silence" however, is relative, for Søren never actually stopped writing or talking.

The story of Henrik and Anna comes from their son, Troels Lund. It was Troels' opinion that Søren was trying out his ideas about Mynster on normal people like Henrik and Anna. It is a credible theory. Søren, no stranger to street experiments and performance art, was yet again testing the limits of his audience. If Søren was wondering how upright citizens would react to an unconscionable attack on the memory of the deceased, then he got a clue from his friends. If the good people of Christendom were anything like the Lunds, they would be utterly confused, annoyed, and offended.

Søren's journals during these years see him working out his relationship to himself, to Regine, to Christendom, and to Mynster. The pages return again and again to these familiar topics, with Søren testing out new ways to understand and describe "his task." He is biding his time and gathering his resources—but for what? Books such as *For Self Examination*, *Sickness unto Death*, and *Practice in Christianity* were barely disguised attacks on the modes of life, thoughts, and beliefs that fell under the banner "Christendom." Yet Søren repeatedly insisted to himself and others that his attack was, in fact, a defence. *Practice* had a "Moral," calling the leaders of the church to admit their failing and fall on God's mercy for obfuscating real Christianity. The Moral was the mitigating factor, as Søren told Mynster directly in conversation. He tried to convince Mynster that his writings were intended to support the bishop and his church the only way that it could be—by starting anew after admitting it had failed. Unsurprisingly, Mynster did not feel the need to submit to the entreaties of the upstart son of a former hosier. Needless to say, his admission of his church's guilt was not forthcoming. Søren's silence was due in large part to Mynster's silence. He was waiting for the bishop to act. The longer this did not happen, the more we see Søren's journals sharpen ideas and develop themes that had been long in gestation.

For one thing, Mynster is found, finally, to be powerless. So it is that by March 1, 1854, two months after Mynster's funeral, Søren is ready to write:

> Now he is dead. If he could have been prevailed upon to conclude his life with the confession to Christianity that what he has represented actually was not Christianity but an appeasement, it would have been exceedingly desirable, for he carried a whole age. That is why the possibility of this confession had to be kept open to the end, yes, to the very end, in case he should make it on his death bed. . . . Something he frequently said in our conversations, although not directed at me, was very significant: It does not depend on who has the most power but on who can stick it out the longest.

For another, Søren's long-held antipathy to Christendom hardens during the silent years, as does his conviction that it is now beyond redemption. Ultimately, it is the *Christendom* over which Mynster and his successors preside that is the issue, more than any one priest. The official relationship of state and church, whereby clergymen were effectively civil servants of the country and agents of civilisation is clearly a problem for Kierkegaard:

> A modern clergyman [is] an active, adroit, quick person who knows how to introduce a little Christianity very mildly, attractively, and in beautiful language, etc.—but as mildly as possible. In the New

Testament Christianity is the deepest wound that can be dealt to a man, designed to collide with everything on the most appalling scale—and now the clergyman is perfectly trained to introduce Christianity in such a way that it means nothing; and when he can do it perfectly, he is a paragon like Mynster. How disgusting!

Yet "Christendom" does not begin and end with the established church. In short, the "established church" might well be Christendom, but not all "Christendoms" are established churches. Christendom is a way of being, thinking, and feeling that has far more to do with the cultural appropriation of Christianity than it does with any specific legal agreement between church and state. Christendom is what happens when people presume they are Christians as a matter of inherited tradition, as a matter of nationality, or because they agree with a number of common-sense propositions and Christianised moral guidelines. Kierkegaard sees Christendom as a process by which groups adopt, absorb, and neuter Christianity into oblivion, all the while assuming they are still Christian. Christendom is adept at shielding itself from its own source, for Christianity's original documents offer a deep challenge precisely to the form of civilised life that Christendom represents.

The matter is quite simple. The New Testament is very easy to understand. But we human beings are really a bunch of scheming swindlers; we pretend to be unable to understand it because we understand very well that the minute we understand we are obliged to act accordingly at once. But in order to make it up to the New Testament a little, lest it become angry with us and find us altogether wrong, we flatter it, tell it that it is so tremendously profound, so wonderfully beautiful, so unfathomably sublime, and all that, somewhat as a little child pretends it cannot understand what has been commanded and then is cunning enough to flatter Papa. Therefore we humans pretend to be unable to understand the N.T.; we do not want to understand it.

Here Christian scholarship has its place. Christian scholarship is the human race's prodigious invention to defend itself against the N.T., to ensure that one can continue to be a Christian without letting the N.T. come too close. . . . I open the N.T. and read: "If you want to be perfect, then sell all your goods and give to the poor and come and follow me." Good God, all the capitalists, the officeholders, and the pensioners, the whole race no less, would be almost beggars: we would be sunk if it were not for . . . scholarship!

During this time, Søren begins to sound out medicinal, frequently gastroenterological, ways of talking about the situation. An 1854 entry reads simply: "Christianity in repose, stagnant Christianity, creates an obstruction, and this formidable obstruction is the sickness of Christendom."

Søren Kierkegaard. Artist and wood engraver Hans Peter Hansen drew this likeness in 1854. Søren was unaware that he was being sketched at the time.

Fatal sickness requires radical cure. So it is that during the silent years, Søren's own self-identity as an author, too, undergoes development. He weighs his own communication style and finds it wanting. Up until 1851, Søren would confidently describe himself along poetic lines. His preface to *Two Discourses at the Communion on Fridays* (August 1851) stipulated clearly that he was *not* a witness to the truth, he was *without authority*, and he was *not* claiming to say anything new that the New Testament has not already made clear. What Søren was, however, was "an unusual kind of poet." Now, during this time of waiting and abiding the poet language begins to fall by the wayside. He had long realised that Christendom, with its emphasis on culture, rhetoric, and respectability had become more "art" than "religion." "All modern Christendom is a shifting of the essentially Christian back into the aesthetic." The last thing it needed was more people waxing lyrical. Søren never fully abandons poet language, but he does begin to question its worth and suggest alternative solutions to the problem of Christendom. Significantly, "corrective" language, present since 1849, comes to the fore. Correctives, by necessity, are sharp, effective, and one-sided. Poets are diffuse, subtle, languorous. Poets have all the time in the world. Correctives have to act—*now!*—if they are to be of any use. "After all, the essentially Christian thing to do is not to write but to exist."

Once again, ironically, Søren's sense of urgent, decisive action appears more in his diary than it does in reality. A new manuscript, *Judge for Yourself!*, was completed. The book pulls no punches, but its author did, and the draft was not sent to the publisher. Instead, Søren continued to practice his attacks on his uncomprehending friends. He sharpened his polemics in the privacy of his journals. He wrote a stinging rejoinder to Martensen's sermon a mere few days after Mynster's funeral but the fateful letter was not sent to the newspapers until almost a full year later.

Apart from Søren's habitual prevarication, which accompanied almost every decisive action of his life, an external reason for the delay was political. Bishop Martensen was formally consecrated as Mynster's successor on

Pentecost Sunday, April 1854. (Søren's journal does not disappoint: "you can be sure that there will be a lot of rhetoric about 'the Spirit'—how nauseating, how revolting, when the true situation is that there is not a single one of us who dares pray for the Holy Spirit in earnest.") The happy occasion was marked by fierce political in-fighting. The deeply conservative Prime Minister Ørsted wanted Martensen as Bishop of all Denmark. The National-Liberal opposition did not. Søren kept his powder dry during this time, as he did not want his attack on Christendom *via* Mynster *via* Martensen to be associated with the party politics of either the left or the right. The partisan fight waged on for months even after Martensen's installation and contributed to the sitting government's instability. When Ørsted was ousted on December 12, the liberals gained power, bringing with them, amongst other things, a more relaxed attitude towards public libel. The time seemed right to make a move.

Bishop Hans Lassen Martensen

Søren's article, entitled "Was Bishop Mynster a 'witness to the truth,'—is this the truth?" burst like a bombshell, dropped by the *Fatherland* on December 18, 1854. It opens with more than an insinuation that Martensen's "memorial" address was not in memory of Mynster but in recollection there was a recent job opening. Martensen the protégé has placed himself in the great chain stretching back to the apostles by claiming that Mynster was a witness to the truth:

> To this I must raise an objection—and now that Bishop Mynster is dead I am able and willing to speak . . . one does not need to be especially sharp to be able to see, when the New Testament is placed alongside Mynster's preaching, that Bishop Mynster's proclamation of Christianity (to take just one thing) tones down, veils, suppresses, omits some of what is most decisively Christian.

The article continues for a few pages, spelling out what a "truth-witness" is ("it unconditionally requires suffering for the doctrine") and accusing Martensen outright of "playing at Christianity" by applying this label to the advantages, refinement, and power that Mynster and all clergy in the land enjoy. Martensen's memorial speech was certainly a worthy monument—"I would prefer to say: a worthy monument to Prof. Martensen himself." For his part, Mynster was worldly, "weak, self-indulgent," a good orator who did not live as he preached. The polemic concludes:

> So the silence can no longer continue; the objection must be raised . . . the objection to representing—from the pulpit, consequently before God—Bishop Mynster as a truth-witness, because it is untrue, but proclaimed in this way it becomes an untruth that cries to heaven.

Søren had done his homework. The double assault on the memory of a beloved dead old man and a prominent living public figure elicited exactly the response he doubtless expected: confusion, annoyance, and offence.

The broadside against Martensen and Mynster brought forth an outcry, but not before the gathered masses expressed a sense of befuddlement. The timing of the attack—a year after the events—was strange, as was the target. For the majority of Copenhagen's reading public, the names of Mynster and Kierkegaard were closely connected. Søren had never spoken so brazenly against the old bishop before. Quite the opposite in fact. Attentive readers who had followed the pseudonymous trail may have been less surprised, but they were few and far between. There were, of course, no readers yet of the private journals, so there was no one who could see that this surprise attack had been long, long in the planning, nor see that the "catastrophe" and apparent madness of the action was part of the plan. Perhaps the longsuffering Lunds were the only ones not taken aback.

Between December 1854 and May 1855 Søren would publish twenty-one articles in the *Fatherland*. The public reaction began slowly but soon picked up steam. Letters of protest against Søren began to appear in the newspapers. Martensen published a rebuttal essay in the *Berling's Times* on December 28. Amongst the many things he said in defence of Mynster and against Kierkegaard, Martensen also managed to smuggle in an allusion to Thersites—the vulgar truth-telling social critic from the *Iliad* whom Homer goes out of his way to describe as bow-legged, hunchbacked, and ugly. This low blow elicited a reprimand from some of Martensen's friends, but in general it was obvious that official public opinion was on the bishop's side. Søren fired off another missive on December 30, and then many more over the course of the next five months. Martensen's failure to answer the charges became a running theme of the *Fatherland* material but it was to no avail. Martensen would not be drawn out again. After his one response, Martensen was content to let lesser clergy and university figures take over. He would not break his silence again until well after Søren's death.

One figure who did jump into the fray was Rasmus Nielsen, the university professor who harboured pretensions to be Søren's disciple, a pretension that Søren himself had at one time entertained until he realised Nielsen's plodding nature. Unperturbed, Nielsen tried to position himself as the mediator between Martensen and Kierkegaard, in the process setting himself against both. To the annoyance of both men he made visits and wrote editorials to that effect, offering at one point, bizarrely, to present a public admission of Christendom's failure on behalf of Martensen. Another figure, Dean Victor Bloch, wrote to the *Fatherland*, calling for Kierkegaard to be barred from attending church. "What Cruel Punishment!" came Søren's rejoinder on April 27. "I, the silly sheep who can neither read nor write, and who therefore, excluded in this way, must spiritually languish, die of hunger by being excluded from what can truly be called nutritious, inasmuch as it feeds the pastor and his family!" What Victor perhaps did not know was that Søren had given up attending church long before, ostentatiously sitting in the reading room of his club on Sunday mornings instead. In any case, the world would soon get Søren's clear justification for ecclesiastical absence. "This must be said: by ceasing to participate (if you usually do participate) in the public divine worship as it now is, you always have one and a great guilt less—you are not participating in making a fool of God." Other people would write to the papers, and in similar fashion, whether they wrote for or against Kierkegaard, they would invariably receive short shrift in a subsequent *Fatherland* article.

With each new salvo Søren ramped up the attack on Christendom, moving quickly from Mynster and Martensen to clergymen in general and other Establishment figures who greased society's wheels: capitalists, civil servants, teachers, and the like. The material that had been stocked up over the past three years was now being put to good use. Between themselves, the great and good of Danish society expressed revulsion, incomprehension, and (very occasionally) sympathy with Kierkegaard's polemics. "Naturally, Kierkegaard's battle against the late bishop also has all of us agitated," wrote Hans Rørdam to his brother (and Søren's friend) Peter. "Kierkegaard drags his corpse through the most disgusting filth. It is villainous." "The little war around here," wrote the poet

Ingemann, "has made me very angry, mostly because of the support that the impudence and shamelessness of this sophistry has found among young people." Won't somebody please think of the children! Søren's old friend and teacher Sibbern found only "arrogance and ingratitude" in the attacks. No friend of Mynster or Martensen, nevertheless Grundtvig too weighed in with a thundering sermon against Søren the "blasphemer." Magdalene Hansen, a prominent Grundtvigian supporter, was less sure than her leader. "It has also been a continuing source of sorrow to me to hear people tear S. K. apart," she wrote to a friend, "as if the question were, What sort of person is S. K.? and not, Am I a Christian?"

Not all the ears that Søren's polemics fell on were deaf or hostile. Ingemann's outburst reveals that he, at any rate, thought the youth were listening. So too were many members of that nebulous group classed as "the common man." During the course of his attack Søren received a trickle of humble, nervous well-wishers knocking at his door. Even though his funds were running low, Søren would nevertheless take occasional cabs into the countryside where he made a special point to talk to cow-herders and stone-breakers. A favourite friend on these trips was another Regine, Miss Regine Reinhard, called Tagine by the guests at the inn she kept. Søren would seek her out for long conversations about religion. The matronly Tagine made sure to keep up with Søren's publications. One day someone saw her sitting and reading one of Søren's articles and mockingly asked her whether she understood what she was looking at. "Do I understand it?" she sniffed. "Yes, you can believe I understand every word." Of course she did. Søren had spent enough time writing for cultured literati and their opinion pieces. It was Tagine's turn now. "You common man! I have not segregated my life from yours, you know that; I have lived on the street, am known by all."

A typical charge that people tried to make stick against Kierkegaard during this time was the accusation of hypocrisy. Many of the letter writers and opinion formers took enormous satisfaction in pointing out that Søren was no ideal Christian or truth witness himself. One example was Aron Goldschmidt, who, back from his self-imposed exile and now the editor of the respectable literary journal *North And South*, opined "this new Reformer—who would like even to be called a Hero of the Faith or a Martyr for the Faith—absolutely cannot work with love and disinterestedness for the improvement of the world."

The problem was, of course, that Søren repeatedly, loudly, and in multiple ways never claimed to be any of these things. "Reformer," "Hero," "Martyr," and especially "Christian" are labels of special significance, all the more so because they have been diluted by Christendom. "What Do I Want?" Søren asked in the *Fatherland* on March 31, 1855. "Very simply—I want honesty." The Christianity of Christendom is not the Christianity of the New Testament.

> For this honesty I am willing to venture. However, I am not saying that it is for Christianity I venture. Suppose, just suppose, that I become quite literally a sacrifice—I would still not become a sacrifice for Christianity but because I wanted honesty. But although I do not dare to say that I venture for Christianity, I remain fully and blissfully convinced that this, my venturing, is pleasing to God, as his approval. Indeed, I know it; it has his approval that in a world of Christians where millions and millions call themselves Christians— that there one person expresses: I dare not call myself a Christian; but I want honesty, and to that end I will venture.

Days before this article came out, Søren met Regine for the last time. Fritz Schlegel had accepted an appointment to become the governor of the Danish West Indies. The day of their departure, March 17, Regine deliberately sought out Søren on the streets. Turning a corner, she found him. Startled, Søren had time only to step back as he raised his hat in greeting. Regine pressed close, saying in a low voice, "God bless you— may all go well with you." Then she was gone. The memory is Regine's. Of their final meeting, Søren records not a word.

This act of closure did not in any event mark an end to Søren's zealous attack upon Christendom. If anything, it spurred him on. The *Fatherland* articles continued for a few months more, the title of the last one on May 26, 1855, saying it all: "That Bishop Martensen's silence is, Christianly, (1) unjustifiable, (2) comical, (3) low-cunning, (4) in more than one respect contemptible." The end of the *Fatherland* articles signalled only the close of phase one of the campaign. Phase two belonged to the *Moment*, Søren's self-published, self-financed journal.

For reasons not too difficult to fathom, Søren was wary of the newspaper culture of his day. Giøwad and the *Fatherland* had been good to him, but who knew what twists of fortune might beset the one who got too close to these organs of popular public opinion? Søren's solution was to issue his own newsletter, initially at his own expense with the hope that subscriptions would subsidise the rest. To cover costs he drew from his remaining savings of the sale of the family home. The endeavour was expensive, but it seemed to pay off. By the second edition of the *Moment*, Søren was able to note with satisfaction that his pamphlet had a circulation comparable to the *Fatherland*.

Sometimes translated into English as the "Instant," the journal's original Danish name is *Øieblikket*. It is an important word for Kierkegaard and occurs at key junctures in his philosophy. A prosaic English translation of *Øieblikket* could be "eye-blink," but the more faithful evocation is to the glance or moment of vision in which everything becomes clear. The *Moment* ran for nine substantial issues, from May to September 1855. A tenth was completed but not published in Søren's lifetime. The *Moment* continues all the themes already familiar to *Fatherland* readers but widens its scope to include more trenchant attacks on Grundtvig and the notion of the People's Church. The hits on Grundtvig spilled over to his followers as collateral damage, including Peter Christian. Peter spoke openly against Søren at a pastors' convention, and Søren wrote a rebuttal, which he chose not to publish. Søren met with his brother in the spring, but the two quarrelled and Peter left in anger. Neither was to know their meeting on June 7 would be the last. The issues of the *Moment* continued.

It is in the *Moment* that Søren publicly repudiates his earlier role of "poet," confessing that as Christendom has already turned Christianity into poetry, the role has become useless. Although Søren uses his own name and speaks forthrightly in these texts, it is hardly a straightforward example of direct communication. "S. Kierkegaard" might have given up poetry, but he never gives up playing some sort of role. In the *Moment* he likens himself to an obedient hunting dog who ignores the taunts of the crowd until set loose by his master, a police detective, a fire marshal ringing an alarm, an apothecary with an emetic, a surgeon with a scalpel, a gadfly with a sting—anything that rouses the slumbering public by causing short term pain for a greater good. The language is righteously indignant, spirited, angry, and populist. It is also funny.

> In the splendid cathedral the Honourable Right Reverend Private Chief Royal Chaplain comes forward, the chosen favourite of the elite world; he comes forward before a chosen circle of the chosen ones and, deeply moved, preaches on the text he has himself chosen, "God has chosen the lowly and the despised in the world"—and there is no one who laughs.
>
> Is this the same teaching, when Christ says to the rich young man: Sell all you have and give to the poor, and when the pastor says: Sell all you have and give it to me?
>
> One cannot live on nothing. One hears this often, especially from pastors. And the pastors are the very ones who perform this feat: Christianity does not exist at all—yet they live on it.

The Master of Irony kept a twinkle in his eye. Søren's friends report that during this time of scathing print satire, in person he was warm, jolly, and personable. Hans Brøchner met Søren on the street. "With the greatest clarity and calmness, he spoke of the situation he had provoked,"

Brøchner recalls. "He was able to retain not only his usual equanimity of mind and cheerfulness but even his sense of humour."

The ninth issue of the *Moment* emerged on September 24, 1855. The next day, on a loose sheet of paper tucked into the journal, Søren scribbled a few reflections on his life and task. The entry concluded:

> ... But what, specifically, does God want? He wants souls able to praise, adore, worship, and thank him—the business of angels. Therefore God is surrounded by angels. The sort of beings found in legions in "Christendom," who for a few dollars are able to shout and trumpet to God's honour and praise, this sort does not please him. No, the angels please him, and what pleases him even more than the praise of angels is a human being who in the last lap of this life, when God seemingly changes into sheer cruelty and with the most cruelly devised cruelty does everything to deprive him of all zest for life, nevertheless continues to believe that God is love, that God does it out of love. Such a human being becomes an angel. ... And every time he hears praise from a person whom he has brought to the extremity of life-weariness, God says to himself: This is it. He says it as if he were making a discovery, but of course he was prepared, for he himself was present with the person and helped him insofar as God can give help for what only freedom can do. Only freedom can do it, but the surprising thing is to be able to express oneself by thanking God for it, as if it were God who did it. And in his joy over being able to do this, he is so happy that he will hear absolutely nothing about his having done it, but he gratefully attributes all to God and prays God that it may stay that way, that it is God who does it, for he has no faith in himself, but he does have faith in God.

It was Søren's last act of writing. Late in the month, at a party at Giøwad's, Søren had another of his fits. He fell off a sofa onto the floor, waving away the alarmed offers of help. "Oh, let me lie here till the girl sweeps up in the morning," he joked, before fainting with exhaustion. A few days later Søren collapsed again, this time in the street. On October 2 he checked himself into the Royal Frederik's Hospital. Whether it was delicious irony or chagrin that Søren felt when he was assigned to the "Mynster wing" we will never know.

The diagnosis remained uncertain, but Søren was treated for paralysis of the lower half of his body. Tuberculosis of the spine marrow was suspected with the hospital notes including a prominent question mark after the word "tuberculosis." He was given various medicines to aid his urination and chronic constipation. His legs were subjected to electrical stimulation, to little effect. "The doctors do not understand my illness," said Søren to the visiting Emil. "It is psychical and now they want to treat it in the usual medical fashion."

Emil asked his friend how it was going.

"Badly. It's death. Pray for me that it comes quickly and easily."

How does Søren stand with Regine?

"It was the right thing that she got Schlegel, that had been the earlier understanding, and then I came in and disturbed things. She suffered a great deal because of me." (Emil records that Søren said this last "lovingly and sadly.")

Emil asks, "Are you angry and bitter?"

"No, but sad, and worried, and extremely indignant with my brother Peter. . . . I wrote a piece against him, very harsh, which is lying in the desk at home."

There are lots of other papers at home, including a complete manuscript of the *Moment* number 10, ready to go to the printers, but Søren does not want to bother with them now. His money and his health lasted just long enough for him to get out all the issues he wanted.

"How strange that so many things in your life have just sufficed!" exclaims Emil.

"Yes," agrees Søren. "And I am very happy about it, and very sad, because I cannot share my joy with anyone."

Formerly Royal Frederik's Hospital. Søren Kierkegaard was admitted here on October 2, 1855.

Apart from Emil, Søren restricted his visitors to family members. Henrik Lund took pains to assure Søren that he would take care of money matters and anything else he needed. To this Søren replied, "I have enough. Enough to cover things admirably. Just like your old friendship, for which I sincerely thank you." His niece Henriette, keen to counteract the impression that her beloved uncle was a crabbed and angry man, makes a point of recalling how upon entering the sickroom, she encountered a glow that practically shone from his face, giving the impression of victory mixed with pain and sadness. Nephew Troels reported that Søren had not lost his sense of humour. One day Søren reluctantly agreed to a visit from the boy Troels and Johan, his brother-in-law. Johan Lund was clearly nervous in the presence of illness, and in his hale and hearty fashion exhorted Søren to change his posture and all would be well. "Just straighten your back and stand up and the sickness will disappear! I can tell you that!" During the embarrassed silence that followed, Troels sneaked a peek at his uncle, who winked back at his co-conspirator with a look of tolerance and a subversive sense of fun. Søren brought his awkward visitor back onto an even keel, and it was time for the party to take their leave. Troels was the last to exit the room. Søren took his hand and looked into his eyes. "Thank you for coming to see me Troels! And now live well!" For the nephew, everything was concentrated in the flood of light that came from the eyes—"profound love, beatifically dissolved sadness, an all-penetrating clarity, and a playful smile."

One family member never made an appearance. There are many letters from assorted uncles and nephews to Peter Kierkegaard, updating him on Søren's decline and urging him to come quickly. Finally, Peter arrived at the hospital on October 19, but in the end he was denied entry.

My brother cannot be stopped by debate, only action, Søren told Emil that day. Apart from their old familial conflicts, one of the current pressing issues was the matter of a final Communion, which Søren clearly feared his clergyman brother would force on him.

"Won't you take Holy Communion?" asked Emil. He too was ordained, after all.

"Yes. But not from a pastor, from a layman."

"That will be quite difficult to arrange."

"Then I will die without it. We cannot debate it. I have made my choice. I have chosen. The pastors are civil servants of the Crown and have nothing to do with Christianity."

Emil was filled with pastoral concern for his friend but clearly also had an eye on making a report to history. A day earlier, he had enquired whether Søren believed in Christ and took refuge in him.

"Yes, of course, what else?" came the bemused reply.

But would you change anything, anything at all of what you said? Would you be less stringent?

"That is how it is supposed to be, otherwise it does no good. I certainly think that when the bomb explodes it has to be like this! Do you think I should tone it down, by speaking first to awaken people, and then to calm them down? Why do you want to bother me with this!"

"You have no idea what sort of poisonous plant Mynster was." Søren continued. "You have no idea of it; it is staggering how it has spread its corruption. He was a colossus. Great strength was required to topple him, and the person who did it also had to pay for it."

On October 27, Søren was lying down, incapable of speaking. Emil had to take his final leave and went back to his congregation, wife, and son.

"Søren Kierkegaard died in this building 11 November 1855."

For the next few days Søren slipped in and out of consciousness. He could not eat or drink and he recognised no one. Finally, he fell into a comatose state. Søren Aabye Kierkegaard died at nine in the evening of Sunday, November 11, 1855. He was forty-two years old.

CHAPTER 10

A Life Continued

The complete story of how Kierkegaard got to the world outside of Copenhagen would take volumes to fill, each longer than the tale of his life. Instead, if we imagine Søren's story told as a movie, then it might end something like this, with a montage of people and places running over the credits.

Our image opens with a shot of a spinning globe. Red lines begin from Denmark and arc to Norway, Sweden, and Germany. From there they jump to France, Italy, Spain, and Great Britain. Longer red lines traverse the ocean to Canada and the United States. But even this image, as intricate as it looks with all its red lines leaping, is too simplistic. There are a few false starts to the globe hopping. The name of Kierkegaard had been read in Scotland before most people saw it in Germany. It was heard in the great plains of middle America before Danish school children started reading Kierkegaard in their textbooks. The litany of languages and cultures is also too narrow. We must imagine smaller red lines springing into and out of places such as Mexico, Brazil, China, Korea, Australia, New Zealand, Russia, Bosnia and Latvia, and beyond. There are Muslim, Arab, and Persian Kierkegaard students and ongoing projects to translate his works into Turkish. Japan has enough Kierkegaard scholars to form rival schools of interpretation. And so it goes.

But our image will have to do.

1852. United Kingdom. One of the earliest international notices about Kierkegaard occurred within his lifetime. The Scottish traveller Andrew

Hamilton had spent a lot of time wandering around Denmark. In his travelogue *Sixteen Months in the Danish Isles* he paints a number of pen portraits of Copenhagen characters:

> There is a man whom it is impossible to omit in any account of Denmark, but whose place it might be more difficult to fix; I mean Søren Kierkegaard. But as his works have, at all events for the most part, a religious tendency, he may find a place among the theologians. He is a philosophical Christian writer, evermore dwelling, one might almost say harping, on the theme of the human heart. There is no Danish writer more earnest than he, yet there is no one in whose way stand more things to prevent his becoming popular. He writes at times with an unearthly beauty, but too often with an exaggerated display of logic that disgusts the public. All very well, if he were not a popular writer, but it is for this he intends himself.

It is Kierkegaard's first mention in English. It does not spark a wave of interest.

1855. Denmark. Henrik Lund's contribution to keeping his uncle's memory alive did not stop with his graveside protest. After Søren's death, the young doctor takes it upon himself to act on behalf of the literary remains, of which there are a lot. What he finds is "a great quantity of paper, mostly manuscripts, located in various places." Henrik makes a desultory stab at arranging some of Søren's papers and letters, but it all proves too much. He begs Søren's best friend, Emil Boesen, for help. Perhaps Emil is busy, perhaps he is tired of acting as Søren's literary spy and lapdog, but in any case, he resists the temptation to bury himself in Kierkegaardiana. Eventually in 1857, the papers make their way to Peter Kierkegaard, who, on Martensen's recommendation, is now the newly installed Bishop of Aalborg.

1856. Denmark. Søren Kierkegaard's library, household goods, and assorted possessions are put up for auction. One lucky taker is Mogens

Abraham Sommer, who snaps up a walking stick. Sommer, a Jewish convert to Christianity with a line in schoolteaching, herbology, and itinerant preaching, considers himself a prophet in the Kierkegaardian vein. He uses the staff in his endless missionary trips around the countryside stirring up congregations against their established clergy. Sommer also attacks Martensen in print and gets into trouble with the law for libel. In 1860 Sommer travels to America, where he helps other Danes migrate to the Midwest and where, presumably, he continues to preach his heady mix of Kierkegaard, homeopathy, and Christian socialism.

1859. Denmark. Peter Kierkegaard publishes Søren's *Point of View*, the work in which, amongst other things, Søren retroactively spells out the Christian purpose of his career guided by Governance, a "report to history" helped by some creative juggling of the publishing record. Six years pass with nothing more forthcoming.

Peter Christian Kierkegaard, Søren's brother and last surviving Kierkegaard. In 1875 he relinquished his position as bishop, citing 1 John 3:15 in his resignation letter. Peter died as a ward of the state in 1888.

The Kierkegaard family grave in Assistens Cemetery, Copenhagen. Søren is surrounded by family members. His inscription, leaning against the headstone, reads: "In a little while / I shall have won, / Then the entire battle / Will disappear at once. / Then I may rest / In halls of roses / And unceasingly, / And unceasingly / Speak with my Jesus."

1865. Denmark. Peter enlists his secretary, the former journalist H. P. Barfod, to sort out the papers. Barfod discovers lots of juicy titbits, including the story of father Michael's hilltop cursing of God and evidence that Søren deliberately destroyed pages of his diary he knew would reveal too much of his secret sadness. Barfod is an assiduous editor who thinks of his work on the journals as laying bare the "colossal and clandestine workshop of the soul." It is also he who had the foresight to collect the valuable memoirs of Søren's school chums and contemporaries. However, Barfod and his assistant Hermann Gottsched are responsible for a lot of irreparable confusion. Søren's older, pre-*Corsair* journals were in various states of disarray and seemed incongruous next to the "NB" volumes. Barfod and Gottsched transcribe and arrange the material according to a scheme of their own devising and then—incredibly—destroy the originals. The first collection of papers and letters are published in 1869. The series will eventually run to eight volumes. The publication of the papers and posthumous material leads to a new wave of interest in Søren Kierkegaard. The books sell well, and Peter as literary executioner donates the money to charity. Peter is dogged by indecision about his priestly vocation, guilt over his actions towards his brother, and envy of Søren's success. His mental health deteriorates. In 1875 Peter resigns his bishopric and later hands over his royal decorations. In a move that recalls his reason forty years ago for not taking Communion, he quotes 1 John 3:15 in his resignation letter: "Anyone who hates a brother or sister is a murderer, and you know that no murderer has eternal life residing in him." Peter dies as a ward of the state in 1888.

1866. Norway. Henrik Ibsen publishes *Brand*, a play about an uncompromising Lutheran pastor with reforming zeal. The next year he brings forth *Peer Gynt*. Ibsen read Kierkegaard and knew his story but was cagey about attributing influence. Regardless of Ibsen's protests, the Kierkegaardian connections are widely assumed. Many readers and writers will later claim that the line of Kierkegaard came to them through Ibsen, including the American translator Howard Hong, the Irish novelist James Joyce, and the Spanish philosophical playwright Miguel de Unamuno, who liked to boast that he taught himself Scandinavian languages to read Ibsen, but found Kierkegaard instead.

1871. Denmark. If one were to ask a nineteenth-century British reader to name a famous Danish philosophical and theological writer, a likely name that would come up might be Hans Lassen Martensen. Bishop Martensen is a (relatively) popular figure abroad. His major works were translated into English in his lifetime, including the *Dogmatics* that had so infuriated Kierkegaard. Apart from one newspaper rejoinder, during Kierkegaard's final feud with the Establishment Martensen had kept schtum, much to Søren's contempt. Now Martensen has broken the silence, devoting twenty or so pages of his recently published *Christian Ethics* to laying out and then refuting Kierkegaard's views of sociality and identity. The book is translated into English in 1873 by the Scottish publisher T&T Clark. So it is that Martensen, by answering Søren at last, brings the first extended discussion of Kierkegaard to the English-speaking world. Still, the wave of interest is not sparked. It will take more than this to get the red lines of Kierkegaard arcing over the map of the world.

1877. Denmark. George Brandes is not a supporter of Kierkegaard, but he is the first person in the world to publish a major treatment of Kierkegaard's life and thought. Brandes's aim is to separate what he thinks is good about Kierkegaard—namely the attack on Christendom—from what he thinks is bad—namely the Christian purposes for which Kierkegaard made his attack. It is largely through Brandes that word of Kierkegaard reaches Austria and Germany. For many years the most extensive German translations are taken from Kierkegaard's post-1850 writings, where they are used as fuel for local anticlerical movements.

Bishop H. L. Martensen's grave, Assistens Cemetery, Copenhagen

1888. Germany. Frederick Nietzsche receives a letter from his friend Brandes, recommending that he take a look at Kierkegaard's writings. Nietzsche is intrigued and pledges to seek them out. Before he can do so, he suffers the mental breakdown that will lead to his death.

1896. Denmark. Fritz Schlegel, former governor in the West Indies and lately returned to Copenhagen, dies. His widow, Regine, begins to grant interviews to scholars, biographers, and members of the public hungry for fresh information about Kierkegaard. The conversations all begin with admiration for Fritz, but end with Søren. It is no easy thing being once engaged to Denmark's greatest polemical poet, and Fritz knew what a singular person he had in Regine. Fritz harboured no petty jealousy but instead did all he could to support his wife through it all. Regine would often exclaim to interviewers, "Oh, that he could ever forgive me for being such a little scoundrel that I became engaged to the other one." Of Søren himself, Regine is unfailing in her defence and rebuffs any attempts at vilification. The only thing Regine is insistent on correcting is Søren's insinuation that she was not religiously serious. Regine dies in 1902, with the full realisation—as Søren had predicted—that she had been taken with him into history.

1913. Germany. Interest in the antichurch Kierkegaard has led to the back-catalogue. Theodor Haecker publishes his first monograph. Haecker will go on to become the major German translator of Kierkegaard. A convert to Catholicism and a committed opponent of the Nazis, Haecker is keenly aware of the relevance of Kierkegaard's message for his present age.

It is largely through Haecker that most German readers and writers meet Kierkegaard.

1913. Germany. Karl Jaspers is working in a psychiatric hospital. He is growing disillusioned with the barbaric treatments being meted out on the patients—straps and extended plunges in hot water are commonly used to cure illnesses of the brain. It is from encounters with Kierkegaard now and into the 1920s that Jaspers finds ways to express his idea that mental illness is an "event" in someone's life and part of the development of the existence of that person. Jaspers will become a highly influential philosopher and psychiatrist who will write about Kierkegaard and Kierkegaardian themes for the rest of his career, changing the shape of the establishment's view of mental illness and health.

1918. Czechoslovakia. Franz Kafka writes in his diary about his encounters with Kierkegaard. He is particularly captured by Kierkegaard's treatment of the story of Abraham and wonders at ways of telling this ancient pre-Hebraic story from a modern Jewish perspective. Kierkegaard will remain a major influence for Kafka's entire writing life.

1919. Switzerland. A young pastor in a working-class village parish begins writing his commentary on the apostle Paul. *The Epistle to the Romans* lands like a bombshell on the theological scene, and Karl Barth is appointed to a professorship in Germany as a result. Its emphasis on the radical difference between the revelation of God and the natural endeavours of mankind challenges prevailing theologies of human progress and offers a new way of thinking in light of the devastating Great War. "If I have a system," he writes in the introduction, "it is limited to a recognition of what Kierkegaard called the 'infinite qualitative distinction' between time and eternity."

1929. Germany. The graduate student Hannah Arendt writes her doctoral thesis on Augustine and neighbourly love. She is supervised by Karl Jaspers. A German Jew forced to flee her native country, Arendt will go on to write insightfully about power, violence, and totalitarianism, coining the phrase "the banality of evil" to describe the way heinous crimes can be committed through mass complacency. In a 1964 TV interview conducted by Günther Gaus she recalls eagerly studying politics and philosophy from a young age. "Then I read Kierkegaard and everything fell into place."

c. 1930. United Kingdom. While living in Cambridge, the Austrian philosopher Ludwig Wittgenstein remarks to a friend, "Kierkegaard was by far the most profound thinker of the last century. Kierkegaard was a saint."

1934. Bornholm. Gregor Malantschuk, a Ukrainian orphan who ended up in Germany following the chaos of the Great War, is forced by the rise of Hitler to migrate yet again, this time fleeing to a Danish island in the Baltic Sea. Here he first hears of Kierkegaard from a farm mechanic repairing a threshing machine. He finds in Kierkegaard's "single individual" an alternative to the dehumanising ideologies of both communism and fascism. Later, Malantschuk forms a Kierkegaard study circle where he mentors many influential teachers and translators, including Julia Watkin, and Howard and Edna Hong. After his death, Malantschuk's considerable library seeds the Kierkegaardian centres at McGill University in Canada and at St. Olaf College in the United States.

1935. United Kingdom. E. L. Allen publishes *Kierkegaard: His Life and Thought*. It is the first monograph in English, but like Brandes, Allen is no fan. His portrait damns Kierkegaard with faint praise, and he thinks Kierkegaard's response to Christendom was too pessimistic. The next Dane Allen wrote about reveals where he wants British sympathies to lie. *Bishop Grundtvig: A Prophet of the North* is a glowing endorsement of Grundtvig's view of national, Christian life.

1937. Germany. The dissident theologian Dietrich Bonhoeffer publishes *Discipleship*, his manual for seminary students preparing to become pastors in Nazi-dominated Germany. The book's striking attempt to articulate how to live as Christians in a Christendom seduced by Hitler is similar in theme and structure to *Practice in Christianity*, the book that Anti-Climacus wrote to unsettle the Christians in *his* Christendom. Bonhoeffer was steeped in Kierkegaard's writings. Major tenets of Bonhoeffer's thought such as "cheap grace" and "religionless Christianity" are shaped by his encounters with the Dane, as is Bonhoeffer's choice to opt for real, concrete life against the seduction of triumphalist idealism. For his part in opposing Hitler, Bonhoeffer was executed in 1945.

1938. United Kingdom and the United States. The Anglo-American world is presented with Alexander Dru's *The Journals of Kierkegaard 1834–1854* and Walter Lowrie's monumental biography *Kierkegaard*. They are not the first Kierkegaardian books published in English, but they are the most widely read. Alexander Dru, friend of Theodor Haecker, wrote to the Oxford University Press in 1935 proposing they publish some translated volumes of the philosopher. Dru, an English Catholic (and brother-in-law to the novelist Evelyn Waugh) also enlisted the help of Walter Lowrie, who was labouring on his own translation project. Lowrie, an American Episcopalian pastor and theologian, had found Kierkegaard *via* Barth. In 1932 (at the age of 64) he taught himself Danish and began his translation work shortly thereafter. Some scattered material had been translated by Lee M. Hollander ten years previous, but unsold copies of the pamphlet were collecting dust in Hollander's office. David Swenson (a Swede living in America) had been eking out Kierkegaard translations and essays since 1916 after discovering a Danish-language copy of the *Postscript* in his local library. Professor Swenson's translation of *Philosophical Fragments* came out in 1936 and he was drafted to assist with the OUP project. Although Lowrie was not the first American translator, he proved himself to be an unrivalled powerhouse of public relations and productivity on behalf of the Dane. What his translations lost in elegance or accuracy he gained in vitality and rapid quantity. It is through Lowrie (some of whose translations remain in print today) that most English readers will come to trace their introduction to Kierkegaard. OUP published Lowrie's editions, starting with *Christian Discourses* and *The Point of View* in 1939. Further *Discourses, Training in Christianity, Judge for Yourself!*, and *For Self Examination* soon followed. Dru and Lowrie collaborated on *The Present Age* in 1940. It was not lost on anyone that the book's theme of the malignant mob was especially relevant in light of the looming World War with regimes particularly adept at manipulating the media and popular sentiment. Kierkegaard's philosophical and pseudonymous works emerged in 1941: *Stages on Life's Way, Repetition, Fear and Trembling*, and *Sickness unto Death*. *Concluding Unscientific Postscript* also came out in 1941, mostly translated by Swenson but completed by Lowrie after Swenson's death the year before. Swenson's *Either/Or, Concept of Dread*, and collected material from the *Fatherland* and the *Moment*, which Lowrie called the *Attack upon Christendom*, all came out in 1944. Apart from this final material, the order of the production did not correspond in any way to the timing or pseudonymous scheme painstakingly worked out by Søren a century before.

1939. United Kingdom. *The New Statesman* publishes T. S. Eliot's rave review of an idiosyncratic new book by a niche writer normally associated with "spiritual thrillers." *The Descent of the Dove* by Charles Williams tells the story of the history of Christianity from the point of view of the movement of Goodness and the Holy Spirit across the earth. The high point of the climactic chapter is devoted to Kierkegaard. "His sayings will be so moderated in our minds," predicts Williams, "that they will soon become not his sayings but ours." Other fans of the book include W. H. Auden, who credits Williams for his conversion to Christianity and who embarked on a lifelong appreciation of Kierkegaard as a result. Williams, friend of C. S. Lewis, J. R. R. Tolkien, Dorothy Sayers, and other fellow "Inklings," is no Kierkegaardian novice—in his day job he is an editor for Oxford University Press. It is Williams who first received Dru's proposal and who was an early champion of the project. It is he who oversees the translation work and who manages Lowrie's considerable energy and expectations. It is also Williams we can thank for convincing Lowrie not to lumber his biography with the doggy sounding subtitle, "*the Great Dane.*" During conditions of wartime austerity, Williams labours long and hard to ensure the Press pays for paper at the same time as keeping the price down for the normal reading public. Much of the printing costs are subsidised by Lowrie himself, and Williams often has to broach the subject of money with the translator. "K. may rebuild civilization, but we shall have to be more economical than ever in building K." In the end the war and the prospect of working with a publisher and market closer to home convinces Lowrie to take his work to Princeton University Press, leaving Oxford as the European agent rather than main publisher. The relationship between Williams and Lowrie remains cordial, with Williams suggesting that while the Americans may have bought more actual books, at least the support of the prestigious University of Oxford was a "more intangible but no less effective" vehicle for the reception of Kierkegaard into English.

1940. United States. Recent Roman Catholic convert Thomas Merton notes in his journal: "A week ago today I bought Kierkegaard's *Fear and Trembling* at the Oxford University Press, and have since talked about it so much I feel as if I had been reading Kierkegaard all my life." Merton will go on to become a monk, spiritual writer, nonviolent civil rights activist, and nuclear nonproliferation peace campaigner with worldwide renown. Kierkegaard will remain a constant presence in Merton's life as a source of strength, guidance, and challenge until his death in 1968.

1942. France. The Algerian Albert Camus publishes his novel *The Stranger* and his philosophical treatise *The Myth of Sisyphus*. The works are considered forerunners of French Existentialism, although Camus rejects the label. Camus is forthcoming in his admiration for Kierkegaard, unlike Jean-Paul Sartre, whose book *Being and Nothingness* comes out in 1943. Because of his antipathy to Kierkegaard's Christianity, Sartre often disavows any connection. Rather, his thoughts on the fundamental importance of free will are built on Martin Heidegger's highly influential *Being and Time* (1927). As it happens, the German philosopher *also* went to great lengths to hide his indebtedness to Kierkegaard. *Being and Time* grudgingly mentions Kierkegaard three times in the notes and yet is replete with Kierkegaardian themes, stripped of their Christian orientation. The association of Kierkegaard with the atheistic existentialisms of Camus, Sartre, Heidegger, and others is a powerful one. It led to an explosion of Kierkegaard's popularity in the 1950s and '60s in France and America while at the same time cast a long shadow over his modern reception as a Christian thinker.

1943. United States. Playwright Henry Miller pens a glowing review of Lowrie's *A Short Life of Kierkegaard* in the *New Republic*. His approach is symptomatic of the era in which it is not academics but literate nonspecialists who tend to take up the Kierkegaardian mantle. A lot of the appeal to writers, poets, public intellectuals, artists, and idiosyncratic historians is Kierkegaard's approach to cultural movements that were defining the "modern age." He is heard to be saying something to the dehumanising nature of mass culture in all its forms, whether it be communism, fascism, or jingoistic patriotism. Furthermore, he provides a way to talk about the loss of faith *and* the finding of faith in the shadow of Christianised systems that were proving untenable. Reviews and essays on Kierkegaard begin to appear in places like *The New York Times*, *The New Yorker*, *Esquire*, and, in England, *The Times Literary Supplement*. The literary influence is and will be felt in such diverse figures as Flannery O'Connor, J. D. Salinger, John Updike, and David Lodge, to name but a few twentieth-century authors.

1944. United States. The author Richard Wright, best known for the novel *Native Son* (1940) and the soon to be issued autobiography *Black Boy* (1945), asks his friend Dorothy Norman to instruct him in existentialism and the works of Kierkegaard and others. Norman invites the exiled German theologian Paul Tillich and Hannah Arendt to her home in New York to form a study group with Wright. Wright becomes an enthusiastic reader of Kierkegaard, finding in him a voice for individuals seeking authenticity in the face of a hostile culture. Wright goes on to pen *The Outsider*, his exploration of the black experience in the US and the first American existentialist novel. The book opens with a quote from *The Concept of Anxiety*, and its main character is a conscious embodiment of Kierkegaardian ideas.

1944. United States. Howard A. Johnson, a former student of Lowrie and now curate of St. John's Church, has been invited to a dinner hosted by President Franklin D. Roosevelt. FDR expresses a love for the mystery stories of Dorothy Sayers. Johnson tentatively suggests that she is even more important as a theological writer. "Many moderns like Dorothy Sayers derive from Kierkegaard." A few days later, Roosevelt's Cabinet colleague Frances Perkins finds the president in a thoughtful mood. "Frances, have you ever read Kierkegaard? . . . Well, you ought to read him," he says enthusiastically. "It will teach you about the Nazis.

Kierkegaard explains the Nazis to me as nothing else ever has. I have never been able to make out why people who are obviously human beings could behave like that. They are human, yet they behave like demons. Kierkegaard gives you an understanding of what it is in man that makes it possible for these Germans to be so evil."

1959. United States. Martin Luther King Jr. is invited to write about the influences that have led to him embracing nonviolence as a way of life. In "Pilgrimage to Nonviolence" he talks about how Kierkegaard and others helped shape his thought by introducing him to existentialism. "Its understanding of the 'finite freedom' of man is one of existentialism's most lasting contributions, and its perception of the anxiety and conflict produced in man's personal and social life as a result of the perilous and ambiguous structure of existence is especially meaningful for our time." Shades of Kierkegaard hover behind King's 1964 Nobel lecture, where he says, "Our problem today is that we have allowed the internal to become lost in the external. We have allowed the means by which we live to outdistance the ends for which we live."

c. 1965. United States. The West family lives in Sacramento, California. As African Americans, they face unfair practices in housing and working conditions and are restricted in their access to services such as public libraries. The injustice is not lost on thirteen-year-old Cornel, who is beginning to wonder what he sees in America says about the human condition. Cornel has to get his books from the rotating stock of the bookmobile and it is there he stumbles across a handful of Lowrie's translations. Cornel's discovery helps him make sense of human nature. "In reading Kierkegaard from the Bookmobile . . . here was someone [who was] seriously wrestling with [this] terror, this suffering and [this] sorrow. It resonated deeply with me." Kierkegaard leads West to study philosophy at Harvard and Princeton. West is an admirer of Martin Luther King Jr. and an ally of Malcolm X but was never a member of the Black Panther Party. As an African American and Christian involved in radical politics, he often finds himself on the outside of many circles.

Kierkegaard helps him navigate these ideas, while always maintaining the need to do one's thinking in "existentially concrete situations." In 1982 Cornel West publishes *Prophesy Deliverance! An Afro-American Revolutionary Christianity* where he identifies *Philosophical Fragments* and *Concluding Unscientific Postscript* as amongst the key books primarily informing his viewpoint. West will go on to become a prominent public intellectual figure, infuriating and inspiring in equal measure. A cultural icon, West lent his political and philosophical aura when he appeared in the *Matrix* films, a set of science-fiction movies themselves brimming with Kierkegaardian ideas.

1967. United States. The first of the multivolume *Søren Kierkegaard's Journals and Papers* is published by Indiana University Press to great acclaim. The translators, Howard and Edna Hong, have devoted their lives to the transmission of Kierkegaard. Before the Second World War, Howard had studied under David Swenson in Minnesota, and together he and his wife, Edna, had lived in Copenhagen as part of Malantschuk's study circle. Back in America, the Hongs minister to displaced persons and prisoners of war while nurturing their Kierkegaardian dreams. It was apparent to them that the Lowrie translations and the haphazard method of the OUP production schedule meant the corpus needed another look. Following the success of the *Journals*, between 1978 and 1998 the Hongs would go on to translate all but four of the twenty-five volume series published by Princeton University Press. The completion of the work prompts praise from the *Times Literary Supplement*: "All honour to the Hongs. *Kierkegaard's Writings* is one of the outstanding achievements in the history of philosophical translation."

1976. United States. The Howard and Edna Hong Kierkegaard Library is formally dedicated at St. Olaf College in Minnesota. It houses a replication of Kierkegaard's library, painstakingly collected by the Hongs and others, as well as copies of everything written by and about Kierkegaard from around the world. A major centre for academics and others, past visitors to the Library include Viktor Frankl, Paul Tillich, and the novelist Walker Percy. The philosopher C. Stephen Evans was the Library curator before handing the reigns to Professor Gordon Marino.

1994. Denmark. The Søren Kierkegaard Research Centre opens in Copenhagen. It is a place for academics and researchers to work, but its primary purpose is the production of the definitive editions of Kierkegaard's entire body of work. Overseen by Niels Jørgen Cappelørn, the *Søren Kierkegaard's Skrifter* ("Søren Kierkegaard's Writings," or SKS) project runs to fifty-five volumes of text and commentary. Under the general editorship of Bruce Kirmmse, the English translation of the SKS journals has been well underway since 2007. *Kierkegaard's Journals and Notebooks* will run to eleven volumes, published by Princeton University Press. Unlike the previous versions of Kierkegaard's journals, which were largely hampered by the ham-fisted treatment traceable back to Barfod and even Henrik Lund, these new editions attempt to reproduce on the page what the originals looked like, putting back the large margins (with their marginalia) that Søren created so he could comment on the main text he had written, sometimes years later.

1995. Japan. Kierkegaard is part of Japanese popular culture. For example, *Neon Genesis Evangelion*, created by Hideaki Anno, is a science-fiction anime television series that uses the adventures of young people piloting giant robots in a post-apocalyptic Tokyo as a pretext to tell complex and serious stories about personal identity and existential meaning. The show contains numerous references to Kierkegaard, with one episode named after *Sickness unto Death*. A manga series, also called *Sickness unto Death*, written by Hikaru Asada and illustrated by Takahiro Seguchi, was released in 2010. It tells the story of a psychologist who falls in love with his patient, a woman who suffers from despair and multiple personalities.

2012. Whereabouts Unknown. An anonymous Twitter user gains worldwide attention by mashing vapid phrases in the style of reality television celebrity Kim Kardashian with the thoughts of Søren Kierkegaard. The account, revelling in the name KimKierkegaardashian, is less about making fun of Kim (or Søren) and more about highlighting what happens when the typical banal chatter of self-publicity meets existential angst. "My soul is a hollowness & everything around me is as empty as eternity. Where do I look for fashion inspiration or fun trends?" runs one entry. "We love selfies! The despairing self, by taking notice of itself, tries to make itself more than it already is," runs another.

2013. United States. When not a professor of philosophy, Gordon Marino is a boxing coach and a sports journalist. So it is that one of his books on Kierkegaard makes its way into the hands of former boxing heavyweight world champion Mike Tyson. Tyson makes international headline news when he talks about Kierkegaard on Twitter and in an interview with the *Wall Street Journal*. "He wanted his epitaph to read: 'In yet a little while / I shall have won; / Then the whole fight / Will all at once be done.' I love reading philosophy," said Tyson. The comments lead to widespread derision from some corners of the popular press, revealing a thinly disguised racism and snobbery, clearly incredulous that an African American athlete with a criminal past could possibly get anything out of the intellectual Dane. Doubtless Søren, who had a thing or two to say about the media and who thought that anyone could be the Single Individual, would have had a different opinion.

2013. Canada. The Montreal-based music group Arcade Fire release their fourth studio-album to rave reviews. "*Reflektor* is populated by characters who actively seek to escape systems of control," writes *Pitchfork*, "but the path to the exit leads through the dance floor." The album is inspired by, and named after, Kierkegaard's discussion of the ages of passion and reflection in *The Present Age*. "It sounds like he's talking about modern times," says front man Win Butler to *Rolling Stone*. "He's talking about the press and alienation, and you kind of read it and you're like, 'Dude, you have no idea how insane it's gonna get.'"

2013. Canada. Actor and rapper Donald Glover is in Toronto on a press tour promoting his new hip-hop album released under his pseudonym Childish Gambino.

VICE magazine: Are you reading books right now?

Glover: Yeah, I'm really into Kierkegaard s**t right now.

VICE: Man, that is not going to make you happy.

Glover: It does make me happy, because it makes me feel less alone.

2015. United Kingdom. Simon Munnery is a stand-up comedian, television performer, and occasional "spokesman" for the graffiti artist Banksy (another *agent provocateur* who uses pseudonyms to get a rise out of his urbane audience). Munnery has long admired Kierkegaard and decides rather impulsively one day to perform passages taken from his writing in a comedy show called *Simon Munnery Sings the Songs of Søren Kierkegaard*. Deploying a voice somewhere in the region of Johnny Rotten combined with Kenneth Williams ("an outsider, slightly camp, and scathing"), Munnery reads and recites from memory extended passages, interspersed with his own humorous observations. The professional comedian is keen to point out that Kierkegaard was a master humour writer. "I like the jokes—the conciseness, the really tight language," says Munnery in conversation. "There are points in the recitations where the audience laughs every time." Kierkegaard, he insists, really knew how to write a joke.

❖

Kierkegaard is hardly a household name, yet his fingerprints are everywhere. For most authors, merely being read in Danish, German, French, Spanish, Italian, Japanese, and English would be enough, yet Kierkegaard also stands as a significant figure in these cultures. Not bad for a man who rarely strayed from outside Copenhagen's city walls. The history of modern life and thought cannot be told without the name of Kierkegaard. His words have shaped high art and low, politicians and revolutionaries, churchmen and atheists, missionaries, teachers, journalists, psychologists, therapists, artists, musicians, poets, novelists, comedians, theologians, philosophers, and yes, even academics. Still, Kierkegaard remains a perennial outsider. There is no church or school of Kierkegaard, no movement in his name. How could there be? His thoughts cannot be easily summarised and handed on whole. They scratch and fight and kick against the system, *any* system—even his own. Kierkegaard's thoughts need to be encountered, one by one, person by person, or they are not encountered at all. His insistence on authentic existence is simply stated. It is the consequences of that existence that run amok. The infinite, eternal God is standing before you now with greasy hair and a bit of fish in his beard, bidding you who are weary to come to him and he will give you rest. To turn away in offence from this person is natural, expected, even reasonable. Yet to turn towards such a one is to turn away from all that has a false claim on your identity and into the one who defines what it is to exist. Family, nation, religion, and ideology are "put in their place." It is easy to discover what gods any given established order worships—simply find out what you are not allowed to "put in their place." As long as people continue to live and move and have their being in habitual ideas of their own creation, Kierkegaard will continue to upbuild and provoke wherever he is encountered by the Single One.

The new bishop stands at the window, looking at the crowd milling in the courtyard below. He cannot see, but at the same time he does not want to be seen. That would never do. It is of paramount importance that the newspapers record that the newly minted Bishop of all Denmark, Hans L. Martensen, shepherd to the nation, was not present at the burial of his former student, now scourge of all Christendom, Søren Kierkegaard.

Martensen frowns and returns to his writing desk, where perhaps he has begun to sketch his memoirs. "We may regard it as felicitous that he died when he did," he writes, "or the whole thing might have ended up by being extremely annoying."

Afterword

Kierkegaardians are well aware there are a handful of fault lines in the schools of interpretation. Some of the key questions include whether his pseudonyms are reliable sources of biographical information; whether Kierkegaard's claim of a Christian direction to his work is credible; and whether he ever fully abandoned "indirect communication," even when writing under his own name. To those questions I answer No, Yes, and No and have written this biography as such. I am well aware of the larger academic discussion around these questions, but this is not the place for such a conversation. For those interested in the arguments I would refer them to my other published books and articles on Kierkegaard. These publications also contain the fullest indication of secondary sources I have drawn from over the years. A quick note on sources: translations of Kierkegaard are an ongoing project. For the sake of standardisation and ease of access, unless otherwise indicated, all primary quotes are from the complete and currently academic standard *Kierkegaard's Writings* published by Princeton University Press with Howard and Edna Hong as series editors and translators. Unless otherwise indicated, all quotations from Kierkegaard's letters and journals are taken from the English translation, *Kierkegaard's Journals and Papers* (eds. Howard V. Hong and Edna H. Hong, seven volumes). Following the Hong's convention, this JP material is cross-referenced against the Danish language *Søren Kierkegaards Papirer* (eds. P. A. Heiberg, V. Kuhr and E. Torsting, N. Thulstrup, thirteen volumes). Regarding the views and comments of Kierkegaard's contemporaries: unless otherwise indicated, this material is largely drawn from *Encounters with Kierkegaard*, translator Bruce Kirmmse's peerless compendium of extant eyewitness letters and memoirs. Apart from quoting Kierkegaard's contemporaries, I have avoided excessive footnoting of secondary authors, all of whom appear in any case in the bibliography.

As well as a student of Kierkegaard, I am a social and political theologian. For this reason I am drawn to those places where Kierkegaard's theology abuts against social and political factors. Fortunately for me, Kierkegaard's oft-stated aim to "reintroduce Christianity into Christendom" provides plenty of those places. "Christendom," after all, is nothing if not a theological, social, and political phenomenon. For those who think there is an easy separation between "politics" and "religion," I can only suggest this says more about their anaemic understanding of both church *and* state than it does about the reality of these phenomena. The earliest Christians at least did not think their new citizenship, kingdom, or Lord was operating in an apolitical vacuum, and neither did Kierkegaard, who once wrote, "The religious is the transfigured rendition of what a politician, provided he actually loves being a human being and loves humankind, has thought in his most blissful moment." To my knowledge, Kierkegaard did not talk about Christianity as an "alternative politics." Yet his strategy of drawing single individuals out of their crowds in order that they might be reformed in Christ's image and in relation to each other suggests he would have appreciated this way of speaking about a movement that has massive implications for nationhood and neighbourhood while at the same time resists easy co-option by the partisan politics of the left or of the right.

> The conflict about Christianity will no longer be doctrinal conflict (this is the conflict between orthodoxy and heterodoxy). The conflict (occasioned also by the social and communistic movements) will be about Christianity as an existence. The problem will become that of loving the "neighbour"; attention will be directed to Christ's

life, and Christianity will also become essentially accentuated in the direction of conformity to his life. The world has gradually consumed those masses of illusions and insulating walls with which we have protected ourselves so that the question remained simply one of Christianity as doctrine. The rebellion in the world shouts: We want to see action!

Overviews of the Works of Søren Kierkegaard

From the Papers of One Still Living
September 7, 1838
Søren Kierkegaard

This, Søren's first major published piece, is a critical review not only of Hans Christian Andersen's novel *Only a Fiddler* but of Andersen himself. The work contains a number of themes and ideas that are to become standard for Kierkegaard: an attempt to connect the subject matter with Hegel and with an overarching view of the mood of the historical age; an obsession with art, poetry, and genius; a focus on the individual person as having a value that transcends any group or circumstance to which that person belongs; an emphasis on "authenticity." Following the pattern for much of what will follow in Kierkegaard's authorship, the piece is obscure and complicated. Also, it was not a hit with the public. In his autobiography, Andersen commented that only two people read it straight through—the one who wrote it and the one about whom it was written!

In this short book, Andersen is held up against Kierkegaard's philosophy of art and of the individual and is found wanting. An authentic individual is not simply a passive product of his experiences. His choices, his commitment, and his integrity are essential to his personhood. Andersen's novel tells us its hero is a genius who has been reduced to wretchedness as a result of his circumstances. Nonsense, snorts Kierkegaard, "Genius is not a rush candle that goes out in a puff of air" (88). Andersen's hero (and thus Andersen himself) is charged with being a coward, succumbing to self-pity and weakness all in the name of art and poetry. For Kierkegaard, Andersen is an incomplete person who has produced an unfinished work of art.

Unsurprisingly, the review rankled. Andersen, though young, was already a celebrated author at the time and expected more reverence from an upstart nobody like Søren. The two men moved in similar social and literary circles, and Kierkegaard had broken etiquette with his contentious and highly personal critique. Reared in a family that revelled in the cut-and-thrust of argument for argument's sake, "the Fork" had struck again. By way of revenge, Andersen caricatured Søren as a repetitive, nonsensical parrot in *The Shoes of Fortune*, and wrote a play that quoted extensive passages from Søren's review to comic effect. This was the first time Søren's barbed wit brought literary revenge upon his head. It would not be the last.

Concept of Irony with Constant Reference to Socrates
September 16, 1841
Søren Kierkegaard

The Concept of Irony is the published version of Søren's master's dissertation, which is equivalent to today's doctorate. Apart from its content, the dissertation itself was notable for the fact that Søren sought permission to write in Danish, rather than Latin as was usually required. Søren claimed that as his study included a discussion of European "Romanticism," to write in a language that knew nothing of this cultural movement would be "as unreasonable as asking someone to use squares to describe a circle" (JP 2308).

In the book, Søren enlists Socrates in his critique of the Romantic literature and mind-set that had gripped the imagination of the people of his day. Romanticism is the name given to the cluster of seventeenth- and eighteenth-century artists, writers, thinkers, and politicians who, in a reaction against the soulless rationalism of the Enlightenment, emphasised natural emotion, intuition, and subjectivity. To be ironic is to pretend ignorance, or to adopt a stance opposite from what you know to be the truth for the sake of that truth.

The book is set in two, unequal, parts. The long first part deals with Socrates and argues his life and thought is primarily understood through the lens of irony. This argument is traced through the key Socratic dialogues and is also shown to be the key to explaining Socrates' actions in his own decadent Greek culture. In the face of the Sophists who treated "truth" as a matter of rhetoric and mutual agreement, Socrates pretended to be foolish in order to show the "wise" they had no wisdom at all. In *Irony*, Socrates represents a position of "infinite negativity": always demolishing but not able to build. In his longing for a universal Truth, Socrates rejected all the temporary "truths" of his society. This might be "negative," but at least it does not topple one lesser god only to put another one up in its place.

The second part of *Irony* is much shorter. Here, the concept of "irony" is seen to have taken root in a corrupt form in the literature and mind-set of Romanticism. Søren likes the Romantic displeasure at smug bourgeois life, custom-bound and habitual. The Romantics, he says, breathe fresh air into this spiritless, monotonous existence. Yet the Romantics are portrayed as using their irony for petty, adolescent mockery. They have no conception of Socrates' infinite, absolute negativity, which undermines all assumptions about human ability to produce something True. The Romantics rightly accuse modernity of trapping people in a slavery of social customs, materialism, and shallow religiosity. Yet the Romantics also condemn people to a slavish devotion to their own subjective passions and immature whims. Irony, argues Kierkegaard, is a necessary moment on the way to exposing a lie. But it fails when it becomes the new lie under which people live.

Intellectually, the book suggests a significant future development in Kierkegaard's thought. *Irony* criticises Socrates for not having a vision of the role of the state—he sees only individuals and not commonality. Here, the young Kierkegaard sides with Hegel: a position he would later forthrightly reject: "What a Hegelian fool I was!" (JP 4281). Ironically (!) the focus on the individual, and the Socratic method for drawing individuals from their common crowds, would become the hallmark of Kierkegaard's mature life and work. Personally, Kierkegaard had a vested interest in irony. The book was written during the period leading up to Søren's break up with Regine, with all the elaborate schemes distancing Søren's public actions from his real feelings that accompanied that period. The pseudonymous nature of most of Kierkegaard's authorship is also deeply ironic, as are many of the stances Kierkegaard took under his own name. Significantly, at the end of his life Søren would employ Socratic irony by claiming not to be a Christian, thus exposing the Christianity of Christendom as no Christianity at all.

Either/Or: A Fragment of Life
February 20, 1843
Multiple pseudonymous authors compiled and edited by Victor Eremita

> "It may at times have occurred to you, dear reader, to doubt somewhat the accuracy of that familiar philosophical thesis that the outer is the inner and the inner is the outer" (3).

Kierkegaard considered his authorship proper to have begun with *Either/Or*. It is the first work in a series of pseudonymous and non-pseudonymous books intended to introduce the reader to the various stages of life as expressed by different characters in Christendom.

The book opens with a shaggy-dog tale of how the editor, Victor Eremita (which means "triumphant hermit"), acquired an old writing desk only to find a series of loose papers stuffed into a secret compartment. *Either/Or* purports to be Victor's publication of those papers. Most of the material is attributed to two further pseudonyms. "A," a young man living a hedonistic life of pleasure, and "B," an old man who turns out to be a judge called William. The Judge extols the ethical life to "A," especially as it is found in marriage. The book is peppered with other essays and pieces, most notably the shocking "Seducer's Diary," which details the seduction and then abandonment of a young woman, and a concluding sermon reminding all the characters in the book "in relation to God we are always in the wrong" (350).

Like all of Kierkegaard's books, this one is concerned with the state of our existence and with how to become an authentic person. He identifies three stages of existence—the aesthetic, the ethical, and the religious. *Either/Or* is mostly concerned with the first two, with hints of the religious breaking through. The aesthete lives for experience and lives by appearance. His life finds its highest meaning in drama, music, and sensuous love. *Either/Or* contains the stories of "A," the Seducer, and various operatic figures such as Don Juan. Here, the aesthetic life comes across as appealing and articulate, but also one filled with boredom, selfishness, and callous treatment of others. The second half of the book is given over to the Judge, whose longwinded prose is intentionally supposed to remind the reader of a dull lecture, albeit one that contains much wisdom. The Judge is an "ethical" man, which means he has chosen a life of responsibility for others. The Judge is happier than "A" because his choices are more meaningful and thus more important to him. The ethical person is involved with other people, while the aesthete is confined mostly to his own imagination. Furthermore, the aesthete flits from one temporary experience to the next while the ethical man lives according to eternal principles. In this way, becoming an authentic person is seen to happen only when the individual chooses to live according to a duty external to himself rather than according to some whim of self-satisfaction or human invention.

Except Judge William too is still less than a person. The *Either/Or* of the title is not the choice of *either* aesthetic existence *or* ethical existence. It is a choice between the aesthetic and the ethical on one side, and the religious on the other. "Before God we are always in the wrong" is a reminder that all stages of life rely on adherence to the systems and inventions of man. The ethical Judge might be using the language of "eternity," but in reality he is conforming to the relative moral habits of his culture no less than the aesthete who lives only for sensation. The two stages are necessary for an authentic life, but they need to be brought under a third. *Either/Or* is also a comment on Hegel, who famously proposed that all opposition and contradiction is an illusion. For Hegel, one thesis creates its antithesis, which together in turn becomes a synthesis. That synthesis itself produces an antithesis, and so on and so on. The history of the world is the history of the Big Idea (God) unfolding in this way. Significantly, it is in mankind's highest developed culture that Hegel thinks the Mind of God is best expressed. Instead of seeing either God or man, Hegel sees both/and. It is the idea that human nations and civilisations can generate eternal Truth that Kierkegaard begins to undermine in *Either/Or*.

Eighteen Upbuilding Discourses:

Two Upbuilding Discourses
May 16, 1843

Three Upbuilding Discourses
October 16, 1843

Four Upbuilding Discourses
December 6, 1843

Two Upbuilding Discourses
March 5, 1844

Three Upbuilding Discourses
June 8, 1844

Four Upbuilding Discourses
August 31, 1844
Søren Kierkegaard

When it comes to faith, what is needed is "a different kind of talk" (9).

Søren published these short, theological pieces under his own name. Eventually, he would reissue the eighteen disparate discourses under one title. However, the original publications were designed more or less to accompany the pseudonymous output, with some discourses arriving the same day as other texts. The sequence began four months after the publication of *Either/Or*. Compared to the rapturous reception of Victor Eremita and friends, the religious reflections were not a publishing success. "With my left hand I passed *Either/Or* out into the world, with my right hand *Two Upbuilding Discourses*; but they all or almost all took the left hand with their right" (POV 36).

While it is significant Søren used his own name for these texts, as a "different kind of talk" they are not conventionally straightforward Christian devotional texts. As with everything Kierkegaard wrote, he had "the Single Individual" in mind, intending the reader to follow the thought experiments and exercises as part of their spiritual formation into authentic Christianity and true personhood. "Upbuilding" refers to the building up of the self and is sometimes translated as "edifying." "Discourses" alerts readers to the idea that these pieces are less (or perhaps more) than sermons. The *Discourses* are overtly Christian in a way the pseudonymous texts are not, though they studiously avoid claiming the authority of an apostle or the role of a clergyman ordained by God to preach his Word.

The themes vary widely, but most of the discourses adopt a scriptural verse or biblical character upon which to reflect. A sample of section headings serve as an indication of the whole: "Love Will Hide a Multitude of Sins" (1843); "The Lord Gave, and the Lord Took Away; Blessed Be the Name of the Lord" (1843); "Every Good Gift and Every Perfect Gift Is From Above" (1843); "Think about Your Creator in the Days of Your Youth" (1844); "He Must Increase; I Must Decrease" (1844); "The Thorn in the Flesh" (1844).

Many of the essays contain a similar inscription: "To the late Michael Pedersen Kierkegaard, formerly a clothing merchant here in the city, my father, these discourses are dedicated." Other personal elements are present in these writings. Regine's presence can often be detected, for example in the Second Discourse, entitled "Every Good and Perfect Gift Is from Above." Søren suggests the person who attempts to find their ultimate meaning in a universe that runs along the strict principles of Reward and Punishment will be doomed to frustration. All of God's gifts are perfect, even (perhaps especially) the ones that appear to thwart our desires. Even tragedy needs to be received with thanksgiving for the reason that God can use evil for good. Kierkegaard's description of personal tragedy being redeemed by God is especially poignant in light of the fact that at this time he too was living in the pain of broken love. The *Discourses* are an attempt to articulate how it is a truly religious person can bless the name of the Lord when he gives *and* when he takes away.

Repetition: An Essay in Experimental Psychology
October 16, 1843
Constantine Constantius

> "Hope is a lovely maiden who slips away between one's fingers; recollection is a beautiful old woman with whom one is never satisfied at the moment; repetition is a beloved wife of whom one never wearies" (132).

If God exists, then God is the source of all existence. What is more, if God exists then God is Eternal, not temporary. Thus, if human selves are to realise their authentic existence, they must relate rightly to God, which is to say, to the Eternal. It is the self's identity becoming authentic through a right relationship to Eternity that occupies this book. The idea of "repetition" is crucial for personhood. Without repeated events, there can be no persistent reality, no continuity of a self. Without repetition, life would be one fleeting and unconnected experience after another. Repetition happens when a self commits, and recommits, its new self with the ideals and choices of the past self. By repeatedly choosing oneself, a person unites their past and future selves in the present. Without repetition there can be no meaning—"all life dissolves into an empty, meaningless noise" (149). The continuity of existence through time is what makes "repetition" more a matter of eternity than of temporality. Like the Eternal, repetition is ever-present and ever-future. The self that chooses itself again in the moment is an ever-renewing self: every choice that entails the choices of the past also opens up new avenues in the future. Like Eternity, repetition is pregnant with possibility. However, without a right relationship to the Eternal, repetition becomes bare endurance, much like the pointless task of Sisyphus doomed to roll the same rock up the same hill. Only choices made "before God" give repetition its value and meaning.

Working with the theme that repetition is necessary for meaningful identity, *Repetition* contrasts different ways people attempt to seek this out. Pagans such as Socrates and pre-Christians like the writer of Ecclesiastes adopt the attitude "what is new becomes old." The meaning of existence has to be found by looking (or remembering) the past, for "there is nothing new under the sun" (Ecclesiastes 1:9). The aesthete of Christendom is such a person. The first half of *Repetition* tells the whimsical tale of a young man who, realising he enjoys his memories of his beloved more than he enjoys her, takes a return trip to Berlin to relive his most formative experiences and to rediscover himself. The experiment is a disaster and the young man learns that by attempting to relive the past he has robbed his experiences of the novelty and meaning they held for him. If there is to be true repetition, it cannot be had by replicating external experiences. This leads to the shorter, second section of the book, which explores the ethical approach to repetition. The ethicist realises that meaningful repetition has to do with responsible self-choice. Yet this too is doomed to disaster for the simple reason that no amount of discipline and constancy of character can restore a broken, sinful self to wholeness. Here, the religious possibility of repetition arises. For the one who says, "I am making everything new" (Revelation 21:5), what is old becomes new. The repetition of Eternity does not just repeat a life. It redeems it.

Readers should be forgiven if they read strong autobiographical connections into this book. The subject of a young man aesthetically, ethically, and religiously rethinking his purpose in life after a failed romance hits rather close to (Søren's) home. A few months previous to its publication, Søren had also fled to Berlin when he realised Regine did not hate him. The book is full of allusions to the possibility of restoration of lost love. Yet before the book was sent to the printers, Søren learned the news that Regine had become engaged to Fritz Schlegel. The manuscript editions show evidence of revision and addition in light of this news, expanding the "religious" aspect of spiritual restoration in the face of despair and adding a number of ambiguous comments about the constancy of womanly love. Yet readers would be mistaken to read *Repetition* as straightforward autobiography. As Søren liked to constantly remind his readers, he was a poet who takes the stuff of life (including his own) and spins it into new things. Constantine Constantius is not writing nonfiction, he is writing an experimental essay on what it is to be a self and how one goes about becoming one.

Fear and Trembling
October 16, 1843
Johannes de Silentio

> "The ethical expression for what Abraham did is that he meant to murder Isaac; the religious expression is that he meant to sacrifice Isaac—but precisely in this contradiction is the anxiety that can make a person sleepless, and yet without this anxiety Abraham is not who he is" (30).

Kierkegaard arranged to have this book published on the same day as *Repetition*. It is attributed to the pseudonym Johannes de Silentio, who repeatedly tells his readers he is not a man who has faith. Nonetheless, Johannes de Silentio sets out to explore what he thinks faith might be. He does this primarily through a series of extended reflections on the person of Abraham and the attempted sacrifice of Isaac. *Fear and Trembling* treats the Genesis story seriously, but this is not a work of biblical exposition. Instead, Johannes attempts to get inside the head of this "father of faith," retelling the story from multiple perspectives and comparing Abraham's predicament to other tragic stories drawn from classical myth. It is significant Johannes often admits defeat, thus living up to his name John "the Silent One." "Every time [he considered the story] he sank down wearily, folded his hands and said, 'No one was as great as Abraham. Who is able to understand him?'"(14).

In service of understanding the faith of Abraham, the book introduces some key ideas. One is the idea that "the ethical" can be a temptation away from "the religious." Abraham's religious stance results in his willingness to commit an offence against that which is universally considered to be ethical. It is always true that fathers should not kill their sons. Yet Abraham's right position towards God entails willingness to do just this; hence, faith is something higher than ethics. Here de Silentio introduces the idea of the "teleological suspension of the ethical."

Teleological means "purposeful," and *suspension* implies a temporary pause. Thus faith entails an openness to the possibility that the demands of common morality may be temporally suspended for a higher purpose. De Silentio is quick to point out that faith does not always imply killing—it occurs whenever someone resigns that which is right and good while at the same time believing this will be restored to them. Abraham was willing to sacrifice Isaac while at the very same time believing that God's promise to bless Abraham through Isaac would still be fulfilled. De Silentio likens this double posture of "resigning" and "receiving" to a dancer's leap. (Although the phrase never appears in the original Danish, this is the source of the English idiom "Leap of Faith.") De Silentio calls people who move through life resigning "the ethical" while retaining hope it will be restored "Knights of Faith." The Knights do not call attention to themselves. Indeed, like Abraham, they must remain silent. To justify "faith" by making reference to what is common-sensically and universally considered "ethical" is to succumb to a temptation.

The book contains some of the most striking ideas of Kierkegaard's authorship; however, it is significant how few of them appear in any of his later works. The Knight of Faith and his silent, anonymous faith does not show up again, and de Silentio's vision is subject to criticism by Kierkegaard's later pseudonyms. Although he talks about "faith," it is not actually Christianity with which de Silentio is concerned—he resolutely focuses on characters from pagan antiquity and pre-Hebrew history, and the figure of Jesus Christ is mentioned only once in passing and never named. At the same time, the theme of resigning and receiving is clearly related to the events of Kierkegaard's own life and his tortured relationship with Regine—a connection that did not go unnoticed by her or anyone who knew of their situation.

The thinly veiled personal nature of the book and the lyrical genius Kierkegaard employs to develop his ideas has made *Fear and Trembling* one of the most compelling and influential books, not only of Kierkegaard's career, but in the history of Western thought. Kierkegaard himself was aware of this book's potential to overshadow the rest ("O, once I am dead, *Fear and Trembling* alone will be enough for an imperishable name as an author. Then it will be read, translated into foreign languages as well. The reader will almost shrink from the frightful pathos in the book" (JP 6491), yet the reasons above, and the pseudonymous nature of the piece, should make readers pause before treating Johannes de Silentio's vision of faith as Søren Kierkegaard's last and best word on the subject.

Philosophical Fragments, or a Fragment of Philosophy
June 13, 1844
Johannes Climacus

"... can an eternal happiness be built on historical knowledge?"
(title page).

Philosophical Fragments is attributed to Johannes Climacus, one of Kierkegaard's favourite pseudonyms, and one to whom is entrusted some of the ideas nearest and dearest to Kierkegaard's heart. Søren's journals reveal his prevarication over whether to use a pseudonym at all for this book, and it was only at the last minute he scratched his name from the manuscript and submitted the text to the publishers as "Johannes Climacus" instead. Climacus had been used as a stand-in for Søren in an earlier book with a high autobiographical content (also called *Johannes Climacus*), which Søren had left unfinished. The name will appear a few years later as the author of the magnum opus *Concluding Unscientific Postscript*, which at the time Søren thought would conclude his authorship. *Philosophical Fragments* is a short book, written from the point of view of someone who claims to have faith but who is still uneasy calling himself a Christian. The subject matter revolves around the limits of human reason, methods of learning truth, and the *relationship* between faith, historical events, and paradox. The title is a satirical dig at Hegel and his followers who approached matters of faith, reason, and historical truth from a distinctly systematic angle, offering grand, holistic schemes that allowed for no loose fragments of thought.

One of the major Kierkegaardian themes *Fragments* develops is the difference between "pagan" and "Christian" categories of conveying truth. Socrates, the greatest pagan of all time, embodies the "mauetic," or "midwife," method. His goal was to bring the truth out from within his learners, getting them to effectively recall what was already lodged within. Socrates was not the object of the learning—indeed, he must become less so that the learner can attain self-knowledge. *Fragments* contrasts this with an approach to truth in which the Teacher *is* the message. Here, no amount of midwifery will bring forth truth from within the learner, for the learner exists in a state of sin. Truth must be revealed, not recalled: the condition for receiving Truth is not to gain more knowledge, but to repent and be saved. With the introduction of a Teacher who is himself the Truth, and not merely a vehicle for relaying useful self-knowledge, *Fragments* is led to examine another grand Kierkegaardian theme: offence at—or belief in—the paradox of the incarnation. It is worth noting here that *Fragments* is not an explicitly "Christian" book. As a way of preventing the Christianised reader from making too easy assumptions, the book studiously avoids talking about "God" and instead refers throughout to "the god." The name of Jesus Christ is not mentioned, and the incarnation is discussed wholly in terms of a paradox of mutually conflicting concepts, rather than a specific person with a narrative life. "I shall merely trace [the idea] in a few lines without reference to whether it was historical or not" (45). The Paradox is the presence of the Finite with the Infinite, of the Eternal with the Temporal. It is a thought that reason cannot think, and it is with this paradox that Climacus thinks the learner must reside without being offended if he is to be said to have faith. The time and place of the incarnation is less important to Climacus than is the claim that the incarnation had a time and a place at all. How can faith in any one point in history be the source of salvation? *Fragments* considers whether the first witnesses of the incarnation (the "first-hand disciples") had any advantages over any second-hand disciples who came later. It suggests being a second-hand disciple is impossible only if faith is a matter of accumulating knowledge. Yet faith is not a matter of knowledge. It is a matter of not being offended when confronted with the Paradox. The Paradox of the Infinite residing with the Finite is not a problem that can be solved with more information; thus, the first-hand disciples faced the same challenge as did the second-hand disciples. The incarnation was as offensive to reason one second after it happened as it is thousands of years later.

Concept of Anxiety
June 17, 1844
Vigilius Haufniensis

Søren arranged to have this book published five days after *Fragments* and on the same day as *Prefaces*. Unlike these books, and true to its name, *Anxiety* is a serious, convoluted read. Søren's own anxious inner life clearly informs the work; however, this is no simple autobiography. The book itself is laid out like a sort of textbook, prompting some interpreters to speculate it was intended to be a satire on the Hegelian method that had so gripped Kierkegaard's contemporaries who treated personal subjects with a detached, objective air. The book takes as its subject matter such related topics as freedom, original sin, inherited guilt, and the overriding sense of angst, which Haufniensis thinks affects all humans everywhere.

As an idea, angst can be as difficult to understand as it has been significant in the history of Western thought. Kierkegaard's earliest English translators used the word "dread," while later scholars opted for "anxiety."

Secular existentialist philosophers have made much of Kierkegaardian angst as the fear of death and unavoidable annihilation that looms over all human decisions. Yet angst for Haufniensis was not solely negative. Nor was it fear of an inevitable reality. Instead, angst is about free possibility and is deeply ennobling. Only human beings can experience anxiety about the possibilities of the future because only human beings have the ability to freely choose their lives. "If a human being were a beast or an angel, he could not be in anxiety . . . the more profoundly he is in anxiety, the greater is the man" (155). Angst is not fear of what is real. It is the ambiguous sense of unease people feel when considering the undefined possibilities of life. Specifically for Haufniensis, it is the unease humans face when prompted by the Eternal God to become an Authentic Person. This possibility is attractive and repulsive at the same time. *Attractive*, because it represents the true home for every new self. *Repulsive*, because such a relation to God also requires a death to the old self. Sin is what happens when the person, in fear, turns away from the possibility of relation to the Eternal. Some points that follow from this are worth noting. First, fear comes from angst, but it is not synonymous with it. Secondly, "sin" is seen as the propensity for fearful turning from God (and consequent self-betrayal), which all humans share. Original Sin is the act of the will that occurred first with Adam and occurs every time a self fearfully clutches to itself rather than turns to God. Thirdly, sin follows angst, but the presence of angst does not cause sin. Instead, angst indicates the presence of spiritual freedom. With his prayer "Not my will but yours be done," Jesus Christ faced the possibilities of his future responsibly and authentically. The great angst of Gethsemane revealed a spiritually great Person.

Prefaces: Light Reading for People in Various Estates According to Time and Opportunity
June 17, 1844
Nicholas Notabene

"Writing a preface is like being aware that one is beginning to fall in love ... every event an intimation of the transfiguration" (6).

Spare a thought for poor old Nicholas Notabene. All the chap wants to do is write, but his wife has forbidden it. For her, living with a writer is like being married to man who is never home. "To be an author when one is a husband ... is open infidelity"!

Not wishing to face the wrath of this good woman, Nicholas alights on an ingenious solution. Rather than publish one book of his own, he will write the prefaces to a number of books that have not yet been written. In this way, Nicholas can communicate all he wants to say without succumbing to the temptation to be an author.

Prefaces appeared on the same day as the *Concept of Anxiety*, and a week after *Philosophical Fragments* and *Three Upbuilding Discourses*. As the title and pseudonym imply, it is a lighter work than the others, filled with humorous observations and satirical swipes. While the format of *Prefaces* appears less rigorous than a philosophical or religious text, the content retains themes familiar to any reader of Kierkegaard. Much of the satire is aimed at key literary figures such as J. L. Heiberg and H. L. Martensen. Kierkegaard also has wider targets in mind: Notabene prefaces books that reflect a general cultural intoxication with Hegel's philosophy, as well as Kierkegaard's own reading public, who care more about the appearance of sophistication owning a difficult book provides, than they do about actually reading the book itself.

A literary public intellectual, Heiberg had written reviews of two of Kierkegaard's previous books, *Either/Or* and *Repetition*. The reviews were not good, but more so, Kierkegaard felt that in his misunderstanding of the books, Heiberg had misrepresented them too. *Prefaces* makes fun of Heiberg's pretentious attempts to "go beyond" Hegel, and his pompous predilection to treat his writing as gifts to the reading public. Martensen—never far from Kierkegaard's sights—is satirised for his presentation of the high point of Christian history as producing the sophisticated, cultured chattering class of Golden Age Denmark. Martensen, a Hegelian theologian, was also well-known in Denmark for adopting the phrase "doubt everything" (lifted from the seventeenth-century French philosopher René Descartes). Notabene's fawning *Prefaces* in fact satirise this approach, ironically showing up systematic philosophies that supposedly start with nothing but end up claiming to describe Absolute Truth. Notabene confesses he cannot doubt everything, but at least he can doubt whether the philosophers understand their own thought. The Hegelian philosophy that had so entranced Danish culture was one that proposed an endless development of thought based on opposites: from thesis to antithesis to synthesis.

"I am so obtuse that philosophy cannot become understandable to me. The opposite of this is that philosophy is so sagacious that it cannot comprehend my obtuseness. These opposites are mediated into a high unity, that is, a common obtuseness" (58).

Three Discourses on Imagined Occasions
April 29, 1845
Søren Kierkegaard

These three non-pseudonymous discourses on the occasions of confession, marriage, and a funeral were written at the same time as the pseudonymous *Stages on Life's Way* and came out a day before. Unsurprisingly the occasions correspond in interesting ways with the stages of life in the companion title. True to form, the pseudonymous stuff was more popular than the material in Kierkegaard's own name, a fact not lost on the author.

The first occasion of confession leads Kierkegaard to explore what it means to seek God. It is a reflection on the feelings that arise when one has a truly aesthetic appreciation for nature and the wonder that occurs as a result. The discourse surmises that when a self is alone with itself away from the distractions of human civilisation, it will be more amenable to a godly encounter. Like confession in a church, the appreciation for nature will bring one into contact with God. "When the forest frowns at eventide, then the night's moon gets lost in the trees . . . then the pagan suddenly sees the marvel of a luminous effect that grips him, then he sees the unknown, and worship is the expression of wonder" (19). *Discourses* does not think nature worship is the same as Christianity; instead, Christianity is the completion and attainment of what the honest pagan dimly apprehends and desires. Nature sparks wonder, but it is not itself a fit object of worship. Man is not one with nature. Man in nature is lonely until he finds God. Yet for this he must own up to his guilt and in solitary confession admit his self is not yet a fit home for the Divine.

The occasion of a wedding recalls the earnest ethical discourses of Judge William in *Either/Or*. Like the Judge, Kierkegaard has short shrift for romantic notions and flowery rhetoric. Love does not "conquer all" when it is infatuated happiness, but only when it is a duty of daily commitment. In keeping the marriage vows, a person enters into a relationship that must be renewed again and again in the moment. When men and women live ever-presently, they open themselves up to the Eternal. "So, then, a true conception of life and of oneself is required for the resolution of marriage; but this already implies the second great requirement, which is just like the first: a true conception of God . . . thus a language is required in which they talk to each other. This language is the resolution, the only language in which God will involve himself with a human being" (63).

If Kierkegaard departed from clichéd sentimentality when discoursing on the responsibilities of marriage, the occasion at the graveside finds him departing from the usual sombre tone of a funeral. In the discourse, the reality of death is a route to authentic living. Death is the occasion that brings everyone, equally, before God. Likewise, the certain knowledge of our death is the occasion for hopeful, fruitful living now in the present. This is a form of living every single person can choose, regardless of their station in life, crowd, or culture. Kierkegaard refers to this awakened, aware life as "earnestness." "Death is the schoolmaster of earnestness . . . precisely by its leaving to the single individual the task of searching himself . . . Death says, 'I exist; if anyone wants to learn from me, then let him come to me'" (74–76). The certainty of death is a wake-up call for persons to live in the moment as Single Individuals. "If death is night then life is day . . . the terse but impelling cry of earnestness, like death's terse cry, is: This very day!" (82–83).

Stages on Life's Way
April 30, 1845
Multiple pseudonymous authors compiled and edited by Hilarius Bookbinder

It is evening in the forest. The sun has set, leaving only a cool darkness. Five young, worldly aesthetes gather for a banquet in a fairy-tale hall under the trees. Here we meet a "young man" ambivalent about the possibility of fatherhood, a cynical Ladies' Tailor, Constantine from *Repetition*, and Victor Eremita and Johannes the Seducer from *Either/Or*. The five meet to talk about love, philosophy, and women. Their monologues grow increasingly disdainful of marriage and the female sex. Women are, at best, an inspiration for poems and song. At worst they are mad degenerates. The best thing to do to avoid the trap women represent is to avoid commitment and to treat love of them as an act of momentary enjoyment. By way of sealing their pact, the men throw their wine goblets out into the dark: a libation to the gods of the world.

On their way home, they encounter Judge William and his wife.

William has written a manuscript about marriage, which Victor steals away. The Judge's missive becomes the second stage of *Stages*. In stark contrast to the misogyny of the aesthetes, the moral man urges a view of marriage as the highest of human endeavours. The young men want "love" but they will never have it because they lack resolution. Only a self, choosing daily to dedicate itself to another, will know love. Marriage is a sacred duty.

But there are exceptions. A thing may be good, but still not right for some individuals. Here, *Stages* makes overtures into the other realm of life. The truly religious person does not abide only by what is ethical merely because it is ethical. Existing before God, the Single Individual is set apart from habitually following that which is universal to all, even when the universal is good. "Guilty?/Not Guilty?" is the diary of a young man named Quidam, found and published by Frater Taciturnus (Brother Silence) who fished the manuscript from a lake. Quidam tells of his conflict. He is in love, but he cannot marry. Christian marriage requires openness and honesty, yet if Quidam shares his life with his wife, he will draw his fiancée into a state of suffering, due to an oppressive family secret. In entries marked "morning" and "midnight" and "a year ago today" the work returns again and again to melancholy self-introspection. It recounts the various schemes Quidam alights upon to release himself from this marriage that will doom the beloved. Finally, Quidam decides to bring public shame upon himself, thus allowing the beloved to reject him without hurt to her reputation. A year later, Quidam now wonders whether he is guilty or not. Taciturnus tells us Quidam stands at the doorway to the religious. In *Stages*, the religious person recognises God is not the solution to suffering. A life chosen for God will be distinctly marked by the suffering that comes from being set apart. Unlike the aesthete or the ethicist, the religious man knows misfortune happens to anyone and everyone and is not a source of grief. Truly religious grief is over guilt, not misfortune.

Stages is baffling, elliptical, and monumental. Kierkegaard recognised it as a difficult work. To readers familiar with his life story, the autobiographical elements leap off the page. Søren was fiercely ambivalent about marriage, he laboured under an impeding sense of family doom, and he was convinced his life would be a sort of curse to Regine. Quidam often repeats phrases drawn verbatim from Søren and Regine's communication, including, infamously, a word-for-word reprinting of the note Søren used to break his engagement. The breach of confidence seems almost unforgivable. Yet these are observations gifted by hindsight. In 1845 only two people (Regine and Søren) knew the private phrases for what they were. The convoluted nature of the book and its multiple narrators only hinted at plain truths. More importantly perhaps, they revealed that when it comes to matters of love, identity, and faith, there are no "plain truths" at all.

Concluding Unscientific Postscript to Philosophical Fragments
February 27, 1846
Johannes Climacus

> *"Although an outsider, I have at least understood this much, that the only unforgivable high treason against Christianity is the single individual's taking his relation to it for granted" (16).*

Søren originally intended for this mammoth work to conclude the "authorship" begun with *Either /Or*. The book brings the reader through the stages of life's way, drawing the earlier deliberations on aesthetics and ethics to a close with an extended reflection on the religious forms of existence. The book contains an explanation (of sorts) to the pseudonymous project, and with this revelation and conclusion Søren expected to end his authorial career and begin a new one, possibly as a country parson. Instead, life took over to the extent that, in hindsight, *Postscript* represents the midpoint to a prolific writing career, rather than any sort of conclusion to one.

Like so many of Kierkegaard's works, the book combines humour and polemics with philosophy and intense spiritual reflection. The word "Unscientific" signals Søren's satirical dig at the pompous public figures of his day (such as the "assistant professor" H. L. Martensen and the nationalist, historian, and preacher N. F. S. Grundtvig) who purported to explain all life's questions through their pseudoscientific, systematic worldviews. The first thing a contemporary reader would have noticed about this book is that it physically resembled these rival tomes, mocking their forest of preliminary notes, technical jargon, and convoluted table of contents. The word "Postscript" indicates the place of this book in Søren's scheme as ending what Climacus started with *Philosophical Fragments*. As the postscript is five times the length of *Fragments*, the title is also part of the joke.

The book is wide-ranging but at its heart is the account of what it means for a religiously serious citizen of Christendom to become, finally, a Christian. The opening sections address various ways Christendom usually attempts to defend its religion. The book questions whether history, the church, or Scriptures are sufficient for "proving" Christianity, and, more importantly, it traces the ways these attempts end up betraying and distorting the very thing they are trying to protect. This is because Christianity is not, at its heart, a system, a science, or a cultural worldview. Any attempts to portray Christianity as common sense, patriotic, or objective will fail for the simple fact that God is not an object, and the incarnation is not common sense or culturally acceptable. God, as revealed in the incarnation, is a person—in other words, a Subject.

This is what *Postscript* means by the famous Kierkegaardian idea "Truth is Subjectivity" (discussed at length in Part Two, Section II, Chapter II). It is not a hymn of praise to subjectivism (where truth is generated from within yourself), but instead is an account of the essentially Person-centred nature of authentic Christianity and human existence, where it is recognised that if anyone is to know the truth of the incarnate God, they will have to do so as Subjects. This relation is not only highly personal, it is also highly challenging to the forms of religion and identity usually found in Christendom. "The immorality of our age is perhaps not lust and pleasure and sensuality, but rather a pantheistic, debauched contempt for individual human beings. . . . Just as in the desert individuals must travel in large caravans out of fear of robbers and wild animals, so individuals today have a horror of existence because it is godforsaken; they dare to live only in great herds and cling together *en masse* in order to be at least something" (355–56).

Postscript calls the common-sense religion of cultures and groups "Religiousness A," and differentiates this with "Religiousness B," which recognises the inner and personally reflective nature of Christianity that cannot be had simply by being part of a Christianised culture. The clash between most forms of Christianity and authentic Christianity will become explicit in the latter stages of Kierkegaard's life, yet it is implicit here too. "Now, if someone thinks that this is not quite right, that he is not a Christian, he is considered an eccentric. His wife says to him: 'How can you not be a Christian? You are Danish aren't you? Doesn't the geography book say that the predominant religion in Denmark is Lutheran-Christian? . . . Don't you tend to your work in the office as a good civil servant; aren't you a good subject in a Christian nation, in a Lutheran Christian state? So of course you are a Christian'" (50–51).

Two Ages: The Age of Revolution and the Present Age, A Literary Review
March 30, 1846
Søren Kierkegaard

> "*The public is all and nothing, the most dangerous of all powers and the most meaningless*" *(93).*

A month after concluding his authorship, Søren published *Two Ages*. However, much like the wily author of *Prefaces*, Søren had a loophole. *Two Ages* is not a book. It is a review of one. Thomasine Gyllembourg was a celebrated author, and Søren was an admirer of her novels, which he thought brilliantly captured the tensions of contemporary life. His *Two Ages* is an extended review of her novel of the same name. The first two sections pertain to the novel, while the final section consists of an essay on the theme of the spirits of the age. This last section sometimes appears separately under the title *The Present Age*.

Søren identifies two competing spirits that put their stamp on any given era, an ethos of revolution and decision, and an ethos of reflection, deliberation, and talk. Both spirits have their place, but the contemporary age has gone too far in one direction. "In contrast to the age of revolution, which took action, the present age is an age of publicity, the age of miscellaneous announcements: nothing happens but still there is endless publicity" (70).

In an age overtaken by reflection, talking about doing something important replaces actually doing it. The crowd likes the appearance of decisiveness more than it tolerates the reality of it. Indeed, the crowd works to halt the individual who ventures out on his own. "Entrapped air always becomes noxious, and the entrapment of reflection with no ventilating action or event develops censorious envy" (82). Kierkegaard's name for the way societies work to pull down any member who acts in a way that challenges its common sense is "levelling." Levelling is the process of abstraction, whereby decisive choices are stripped of their power by being morphed into "ideas" or "worldviews," and persons are subsumed into groups. Levelling happens wherever tribes, generations, churches, or countries lay claim to individual allegiance, but Søren has a catch-all term: "For levelling to take place, a phantom must first be raised . . . a monstrous abstraction, an all-encompassing something that is nothing, a mirage—and this phantom is the public" (90). One of the public's most potent weapons in the war to defend itself against individuals taking their existence seriously is an endless stream of celebrity gossip, manufactured ideological conflict, and opinion presented as facts no one owns but everyone has. Søren takes aim especially at the popular press as an agent for levelling. Using the press, the public is preserved through chatter. "What is it to chatter? It is the annulment of the passionate disjunction between being silent and speaking. Only the person who can remain essentially silent can speak essentially, can act essentially. Silence is inwardness. [. . .] But chattering dreads the moment of silence, which would reveal the emptiness" (97–98). It's not all bad however. Although the envious public inevitably opposes anyone who challenges its power, the result is the individual will be, finally, exactly where they need to be if they are to meet God. Stripped of any illusion that "the public" holds any truth, love, or authenticity, the person who has been levelled might find himself catapulted "into the embrace of the Eternal" (89). If any of this seems an unlikely scenario, it is worth noting that in the months leading up to the publication of *Two Ages* Søren himself had been subject to ceaseless mockery by the popular press and had himself experienced a profound realisation of where he stood in relation to the public, his vocation, and his God.

Upbuilding Discourses in Various Spirits
March 13, 1847
Søren Kierkegaard

Søren did not stop writing in 1846, but this was all in his private journals, and it was almost a full year after *Postscript* and *Two Ages* that the public was presented with another publication. *Various Spirits* dispenses with much of the satire and ambiguity of the previous authorship and is more seriously Christian than even the *Eighteen Upbuilding Discourses* of a few years previous. The whole is divided into three distinct parts: purity of heart, the lilies of the field, and the gospel of suffering. The discourses have since developed a reputation as spiritual classics of discipleship and devotion; however, judging by the lack of reviews, they did not make much of an impact on Kierkegaard's first intended audience.

Purity concerns integrity and wholeness of purpose. Part one's constant theme is "purity of heart is to will one thing." The reader is continually reminded they are responsible for the condition of their own souls. It is well-known men are judged at the eleventh hour, but in the eyes of Eternity, "it is always at the eleventh hour" (14). The essay spends less time on "purity" than many people might expect who are used to calls to repentance in the face of judgement. Instead the piece focuses on what it might mean to will one thing. Only one thing is Good, and that is the will of God. There are many barriers to willing the will of God, all of which Søren dubs double-mindedness. The double-minded one might will to be good for men's approval or for godly rewards or out of fear of punishment. No matter what the good intention might be, the self is conflicted because it is not desiring the Good in itself. The self is in rebellion against itself and against God. It needs reconciliation, an act of grace that comes every time an individual repents. What is more, repentance is not a one-off event. The multifarious nature of life means the individual needs to always be on guard: true repentance is accompanied by constant anxiety (in the Kierkegaardian sense), whereby God continually renews the self in wholeness.

Lilies celebrate what it is to be a flourishing, human life. A controlling theme is of contentment and of the solid self in the face of the anxiety of the crowd. Consider the lilies. Once upon a time there was a lily who stood alone in a dell, with only some small flowers and nettles for company. He was happy until one day a malicious bird flitted by, filling the lily's head with tales of more beautiful lilies, growing in masses beyond the dell. The lily grew troubled. Why was it secluded, all alone, with only weeds for company? The lily wished to be magnificent too, so he asked the bird to carry him to the yonder hill. The bird plucked the lily by its roots and duly deposited him amongst the masses of similar flowers. Alas, the lily could not take root. He withered and died.

Suffering is an extended meditation on what it means to follow Christ. Did Jesus suffer so that his disciples might live a life of comfort? Or could it be that, like Job, a life of suffering and a life of righteousness might not be mutually exclusive? It would not be accurate to think this discourse was a celebration of suffering, however. The good news of the gospel is not hardship, but that with Christ, the burden becomes light. There is joy in suffering because God does not cause it, the world does when it feels its authority threatened. The apostles' suffering was a sign of the rightness of their cause. Suffering teaches patient endurance, and, most importantly, it provides the opportunity for that most ancient of Christian prayers "not my will but yours be done" (Luke 22:42).

Works of Love
September 29, 1847
Søren Kierkegaard

With his constant focus on the highly personal aspect of authentic identity and faith, a reoccurring criticism of Kierkegaard is that his thought is irredeemably individualistic. Similar criticisms dogged Søren in his own day. *Works of Love* was written partly in response to contemporaries who accused him of having no feeling for the social life of others. *Works* is a substantial tome. Its subject is Jesus' double love command. Key themes include a comment on the Lutheran culture surrounding "works" and "grace," a searching examination of "love," and an exploration of the prime human target of Christian love—namely "the neighbour."

Søren's favourite book of the Bible was James. The epistle's insistence that "faith without works is dead" informs Søren's observations in *Works* of a Christianised culture that now takes faith for granted. Martin

Luther's great Reformation was based on the idea that salvation is by God's grace and not by anything humans might do to earn it. However, it was Søren's opinion that Danish Lutheranism took such grace cheaply, assuming "faith" was a matter of course. The transforming nature of grace on a life dedicated to Jesus Christ was lost on a culture that assumed becoming a Christian was as easy as being born. *Works* is part of Søren's attempt to rejuvenate a crucial aspect of Christian life that had fallen by the wayside thanks to Christendom. The works in *Works* are not social activism, alms, or indulgences. They are the qualities of love as drawn from the New Testament. For example, love "builds up," it "believes all things," it "hopes," it "abides," and it "covers a multitude of sins."

Besides a healthy sense of the outworking of faith, Christendom has also forgotten what Christian love is. Love's various forms fall roughly into two categories: *eros* (passionate preference) and *agape* (disinterested love). Erotic love does not here mean only sex. Passionate preference is a love of "like for like." It is the love of the patriot, the tribesman, the infatuated couple, the best friend, or the family unit. Such love has its uses; however, it needs to be noted it also tends towards monstrous selfishness. Passionate preference is, by necessity, exclusive. Such love is strongest when it is directed to one, and only one, object, be it a lover, a family, or a country. Yet if my love is primarily directed at those who sound as much like me and look as much like me as possible, then the ultimate horizon of such a love is . . . me. "Erotic love and friendship are the very peak of self-esteem, the I intoxicated in the other I" (56).

Søren identifies this sort of love as "pagan." By contrast, truly other-regarding love that is not based on self-interest is a Christian invention. Agape is the love of God who does not need anything from humans. It is also the love we can have for others regardless of what they can do for us or what sort of relationship they have to us. Indeed, only agape can truly be called "love" because only agape cares about other persons for themselves. Jesus' story of the Good Samaritan furnishes Søren with his term for what to call these "other persons for themselves": neighbours.

"No one in paganism loved the neighbour; no one suspected that he existed. Therefore what paganism called love . . . was preference" (53). *Works* contrasts the so-called love of preference, which is trumped up by poets and politicians, with the apparently mundane love commanded by Jesus. This love might not inspire any pop-stars, but it will result in real persons having their real needs met. "Love for neighbour does not want to be sung about—it wants to be accomplished" (46). Unlike the erotic obsession with identifying who is most deserving of love, Kierkegaard remarks that when one is searching for one's neighbour, all one needs to do is open the door and go out. "The very first person you meet is the neighbour, whom you shall love . . . There is not a single person in the whole world who is as surely and as easily recognised as the neighbour" (51–52).

Christian Discourses
April 26, 1848
Søren Kierkegaard

> *"The sacrifice he offered he did not offer for people in general, nor did he want to save people in general—and it cannot be done in that way either. No, he sacrificed himself in order to save each one individually"* (272).

The year 1848 was an important year for Europe and Denmark politically and Kierkegaard personally. The year saw the rapid success of people's revolutions sweep away old regimes, all of which Kierkegaard observed with an eye to the long view and the implications of popular sentiment and democracy for truth and individual existence. He notes this year was extraordinarily fruitful for him from a writing and thinking point of view; however, only two works were actually published. The first of these, *Christian Discourses*, took its title because, in Kierkegaard's view, "discourses" denotes open-ended discussion whereas a "sermon" suggests the speaker is speaking "with authority." The book's four parts were written at different times over 1847 and 1848, and reflect Søren's deepening mistrust of Christendom's self-satisfaction, which avoided individual responsibility at the expense of abstract historical triumphalism. Section one is titled "The Cares of the Pagans." It focuses on the pre-Christian world and its anxious mind-set. The second section, "States of Mind in the Strife of Suffering," offers a discussion of the joy the Christian life offers in the face of various hardships. The third section, "Thoughts That Wound from Behind," is a polemical attack pointing out the "paganism" that actually informs Christendom. The fourth section, which Kierkegaard intended as a restoring call to worship after the temple-cleansing of the third, is entitled "Discourses at the Communion on Fridays." It contains a number of reflections on seven biblical passages, two of which Søren actually delivered in the Church of Our Lady. The discourse on Matthew 11:28 in particular is noteworthy because the famous Torwaldsen statue of Christ, which bears this verse, stands next to the pulpit from which Søren preached. The passage, in which Jesus bids all who are weary to come and receive rest, will come to play a crucial part in *Practice in Christianity* and Søren's ensuing assault on the distorted religion of Bishop Mynster. Kierkegaard had intended to dedicate part of *Christian Discourses* to Mynster but removed the dedication so as to preserve the possibility that the bishop might respond with an admission of guilt in light of the polemics of part three. The admission was not forthcoming.

The Crisis and A Crisis in the Life of an Actress
Published in the Fatherland over four parts, July 24–27, 1848.
Inter et inter

This was the second of only two pieces Kierkegaard published in 1848. It was deliberately released roughly in conjunction with *Christian*

Discourses as a sort of bookend to the pattern begun with *Either/Or* and the *Upbuilding Discourses* in 1843, where signed works of religious seriousness accompanied pseudonymous philosophic and aesthetic experiments. "I would like to create a little literary mystification," Søren says in his journal of *Crisis* (JP 6060). The pseudonym he chose to run alongside the signed *Discourses* was *Inter et inter* (Latin for "between and between"), which seems to refer to the fact that this little piece stands between the first phase of the authorship leading up to Johannes Climacus and the second phase ushered in by the soon-to-be-inaugurated pseudonym Anti-Climacus. The piece is also important to Kierkegaard for he wanted to signal to readers that although he was indeed a religiously serious author, he had not for that reason left appreciation for poetry, drama, and aesthetics behind.

The actress of the title is Joanna Luise Heiberg, wife of the literary doyen J. L. Heiberg. *The crisis* of the title is one any artist faces: Will they succumb to anxiety or succeed under pressure? *A crisis* is the one specifically for Mrs. Heiberg, who was facing the challenge of taking on the Shakespearean character of Juliet, almost twenty years after she first played the role. The piece interprets and appreciates her work, especially her ability to preserve self-possession in the face of the watching crowd. She does not crumble in the presence of anxiety. The piece moves on to take on art criticism and public appreciation in general, especially when they devolve into obsession over the private lives of artists, their age, or physical characteristics. Instead, *Crisis* puts forward a theory of the timeless quality of the essential ideas the actress conveys, regardless of her age or stage in life. The Heibergs appreciated the piece, and Joanna was especially full of praise for the way Søren, a non-actor, could put into words what she had many times felt but did not express.

The Lily in the Field and the Bird of the Air: Three Devotional Discourses
May 14, 1849
Søren Kierkegaard

To maintain the tradition of printing with the "left hand and with the right," Kierkegaard arranged for these discourses to be published under his own name on the same day the second edition of *Either/Or* hit the shelves.

Kierkegaard loved nature and often reflected on the lessons one can learn from it. He often writes on the biblical treatments of nature and returns to the theme here with his discourses on a number of Jesus' sayings taken from the Gospel of Matthew concerning the lily of the field, the impossibility of serving two masters, the birds of the air, and the grass of the field. There are three discourses. The first is about "silence" as a form of essential communication. Birds and flowers cannot speak, yet their silence is a teacher. The piece is an example of Kierkegaard's mounting frustration with "the poetic" as the best way to communicate, and he pits the romantic notion of truth through poetry against the communication of the lilies endorsed by Jesus. "Because the human being is able to speak, the ability to be silent is an art" (10).

The second discourse concerns "obedience." "Pay attention, then, to nature around you. In nature everything is obedience, unconditional obedience" (25). Birds and flowers are good examples of the peace that comes from only serving one master. But there is one crucial difference between nature and humans. Birds are naturally "obedient" because they do not have a will. People have to choose to obey God, a choice they usually do not make. In this, humans discover an aspect of God the birds and lilies will never know—that he is patient. God commands obedience ("thou shalt") but also patiently takes humans by the hand and shows them the flowers of the field in order for us to learn what it is to live at peace with one, and only one, master.

The third discourse takes on "joy." Birds trill ceaselessly and flowers ever bloom. Nature is filled with joy. This is not because nature is absent of pain and suffering. Kierkegaard is not sentimental enough to think the life of birds and beasts is anything but brutish and short ("The whole creation has been groaning," Romans 8:22). Yet nonetheless, nature is joyful because it does what it is essentially supposed to do. Birds do this without willing it. Humans have to choose to be what they essentially are. "What is it to be joyful? It is truly to be present to oneself; but truly to be present to oneself is this *today*" (39). The joy of existence is the joy of being oneself, which is ultimately to be with and in God, for God is eternally "present to himself in being today" (39). This is the ever-present God of whom it is said, "Today, if you hear his voice, do not harden your hearts" (Hebrews 3:15). "Oh what unconditional joy: his is the kingdom and the power and the glory—forever" (44).

Two Ethical-Religious Essays
May 19, 1849
H. H.

This manuscript was sent to the printers on May 5, 1849, Kierkegaard's thirty-sixth birthday. It comprises two parts: "Does a Human Being Have the Right to Let Himself Be Put to Death for the Truth?" and "The Difference between a Genius and an Apostle." Both essays were originally written in 1847. In his journals, Kierkegaard remarks this book does not belong to his "authorship" proper as it is instead a comment and point of view on the authorship as a whole. He struggled with himself whether the work should be published under his own name or even anonymously. In the end he attributed the work to H. H., who along with Anti-Climacus stands over and above Kierkegaard himself. The second essay is an excerpt of material later published posthumously in *The Book on Adler* and is discussed below. The first essay is drawn from a lot of ideas

Søren had previously worked over in his journals. He tells us the draft of the manuscript was completed in eight hours. The essay is concerned with that most important of all Kierkegaardian categories: the martyr who is a true witness to the truth. Suppose a preacher were to eloquently expound on the glories of the history of martyrdom, and then suppose a naïve man in the pew comes forward and says he is ready to sign up? The preacher will be surprised. Become a martyr? Where in heaven did he get *that* idea? "Travel, find some diversion, take a laxative" (67). Confusion over the matter abounds in Christendom for preachers and audience alike. Kierkegaard tries to shed light on the situation by comparing the heroic death of Socrates with the crucifixion of Jesus. Unlike that merely human philosopher, Christ's death was not martyrdom to an idea but atonement and redemption. Kierkegaard points out Jesus did not die *for* truth. He himself *is* the truth. Socrates died for his limited conception of the truth. Christ died for his enemies; his resurrection was the sign that love and truth (in other words: judgement) were united at that moment. The categorical difference between Jesus' death and the death of anyone else at the hands of the crowd is that only Jesus' death removed the crowd's guilt. The man who willingly embraces martyrdom is bringing the crowd into guilt. Only God can remove guilt, and thus only God has the right to let himself die for the truth. Men, instead, should "lovingly to be concerned for the others, for those who, if one is to be put to death, must become guilty of putting one to death" (69).

Sickness unto Death: A Christian Psychological Exposition for Upbuilding and Awakening
July 30, 1849
Anti-Climacus

The sickness that is unto death is *despair*. Despair is to be differentiated from depression. Depression is sadness, melancholy, or, as modern science now tells us, unbalanced chemicals in the brain. One can be depressed without being in despair, and alternatively, one can live in full comfort but be despairing. Despair has to do with living a life without finding one's true meaning, or, in Kierkegaardian language, without finding one's authentic self. "But what is the self?" asks *Sickness unto Death* in a celebrated opening section. "The self is a relation that relates itself to itself or is the relation's relating itself to itself in the relation; the self is not the relation but is the relation's relating itself to itself" (13). The convoluted formulation is, probably, partly a joke on similar sounding Hegelian terminology. But in the hands of Kierkegaard—or rather *Anti-Climacus*—the formulation also acts as a launch pad for a searching examination of human identity and why it sometimes, often, goes wrong. The self, it should be noted from the formulation, is more of a *verb* than a *noun*. It is an action. Despair is a phenomenon particularly related to the action of the self relating to itself, but in such a way that it is a mis-relation, hence a "sickness." Despair (much like anxiety from the earlier book *Concept of Anxiety* to which this is a companion) presumes and requires a self, thus it represents a certain humanising and superiority of existence. Beasts do not despair because beasts are not capable of personhood. To despair is human, but it is not necessary for humanity. It is a mark of something potentially glorious gone wrong. "The possibility of this sickness is man's superiority over the animal; to be aware of this sickness is the Christian's superiority over the natural man; to be cured of this sickness is the Christian's blessedness" (15). Despair is the action of not willing to be one's authentic self. Enter God. God is the creator of all things and the ground of all existence. If one wants to find one's authentic existence, then one has to be rightly oriented to God. The action of becoming a self happens always before God. Refusal to become a self also happens before God.

Hence, Anti-Climacus begins part two of his book with the heading "Despair Is Sin." Some humans actively rebel against God or are offended at his revelation. They are not in a right relation with existence and thus will never become authentic. They are in despair. Other humans are fearful of the burden of being an individual. They hide in their mass herds and distractions. As a result they do not find authentic existence and are cut off from a right relation to the God who grounds all existence. They too live in despair before God, which is sin.

Sickness unto Death develops a category that will go on to become of great importance to Kierkegaard, namely the "possibility of offence." "There is so much talk about being offended by Christianity because it is so dark and gloomy, offended because it is so rigorous, etc., but it would be best of all to explain for once that the real reason that men are offended by Christianity is that it is too high, because its goal is not man's goal, because it wants to make man into something so extraordinary that he cannot grasp the thought" (83). Anti-Climacus goes to great lengths to counter the common idea (which he calls Socratic and pagan) that sin is ignorance. Christianly, sin is a matter of the will. "Therefore, interpreted Christianly, sin has its roots in willing, not in knowing, and this corruption of willing affects the individual's consciousness" (95).

This is the first book by the pseudonym Anti-Climacus, a character devised by Kierkegaard to stand for an expression of Christianity Søren himself aspired to. He placed himself below Anti-Climacus but above Johannes Climacus. This book sets up major themes such as the becoming of a self as a religious act, the possibility of offence at Jesus, and a veiled "attack upon Christendom": all will be put to great effect in Anti-Climacus's next book, *Practice in Christianity*.

Three Discourses at the Communion on Fridays
November 13, 1849
Søren Kierkegaard

Altogether, Kierkegaard wrote thirteen "Friday Communion" discourses, three of which he delivered in person at the Church of Our

Lady in Copenhagen. Seven Communion discourses were published as part of the *Christian Discourses* in 1848. One was included in *Practice in Christianity* in 1850. Three were issued as *Three Discourses* in 1849 and *Two Discourses* in 1851. A fourteenth piece on the woman who was a sinner in Luke 7 was originally intended as a Communion discourse but was instead published separately as an *Upbuilding Discourse* in 1850. Although the Communion discourses receive relatively little attention in comparison with his other works, Kierkegaard mentions in his journals how he likes to think the rest of his authorship was drawn together here, finding its rest at the altar of contemplation and communal worship.

The three 1849 discourses are "The High Priest" (Hebrews 4:15), "The Tax Collector" (Luke 18:13), and "The Woman Who Was a Sinner" (Luke 7:47). Here, Søren develops the theme that Christ as High Priest is the greatest sufferer who can understand one's affliction more than any friend. In turn, Christ's sacrificial love demands from the follower a new pattern of holiness. The Tax Collector is examined for his humility. Christendom has managed to turn acts of humility into a source of pride: one takes the lowest place with head up and eyes open, waiting to be ushered to the best seat. Instead, the man from Luke 18 stands afar from the crowd. With downcast eyes he waits, and it is thus he meets God. The woman who is a sinner is a favourite of Kierkegaard's themes, and he returns to her often in his discourses. He highlights all the contrasts the story throws up: banquets as a place of confession, the Pharisee's house as a place of grace, and the woman finding salvation by forgetting herself. In her love for Jesus she did not regard herself, and herein precisely lies the salvation of herself. "This woman was a sinner—yet she became and is a prototype. Blessed is the one who resembles her in loving much!" (142–43).

Practice in Christianity
September 27, 1850
Anti-Climacus (with S. Kierkegaard named as editor)

"*If you cannot bear contemporaneity . . . then you are not* essentially Christian" (65).

It is well known Jesus issued a lot of "hard sayings": Turn the other cheek; Sell all you have and give to the poor; If anyone comes to me and does not hate father and mother, wife and children, brothers and sisters, yes, even their own life, such a person cannot be my disciple; and so on. Anti-Climacus in *Practice in Christianity* alights on another saying, not often considered as a difficult command: "Come to me, all you who are weary and burdened, and I will give you rest" (Matthew 11:28).

Christendom has forgotten this is a hard saying, because the citizens of Christendom have forgotten to live in the present with Jesus ever before them. The potential offensiveness of "come unto me" is nullified if we imagine the one speaking is obviously able to give desired rest to suffering souls; if the one speaking is obviously God. Christendom looks to the great number of years that have passed, people who call themselves Christian, or nations that are founded on Christian morality and concludes Jesus was God as a matter of common sense. The only reason someone does not believe in Jesus is because they do not know enough information about him and the history of the culture of his followers. Yet, Anti-Climacus is keen to remind us, this is not the person who the first disciples met. The "obviousness" of Jesus' divinity is not apparent if one is standing directly before him. Thus, to have the faith of the disciples Jesus demanded cannot be to assent to the historical and intellectual data that comprises the Christian religion. Even the miracles recorded in the New Testament are not presented as proof of Jesus' status. They are instead crisis points at which the people around him are brought up short before someone who looks and sounds and smells like a finite person and yet who talks and acts like an infinite one. "It is in the situation of contemporaneity with an individual human being, a human being like others—and he speaks about himself in such a manner! . . . he directly makes himself totally different from what it is to be a human being, makes himself the divine—he, an individual human being" (100).

The rest Jesus offers is authentic rest, which cannot be had apart from faith. *Practice in Christianity* suggests the opposite of faith is not doubt. It is offence. Only if an individual is presented with the potential offensiveness of Jesus the Christ, and wills not to turn away in disgust, can that person be said to have a right relation to the incarnation. This potential for offence can only be encountered in contemporaneity with Christ, by being aware of his call in the moment. The potential offensiveness comes in many forms, and Anti-Climacus charts them all. The first form of offence is the challenge Jesus poses to the institutions and morals of his day and ours. Anti-Climacus does not think this is a minor aspect of Jesus' life by any means, but it is not *the essentially* offensive thing about him as this form of offence is open to anyone who imitates Christ. The essential offence occurs in a "lofty" and a "lowly" form. The lofty offence is that this man before you *is God*. The lowly is that God *is this man*. In all cases, Jesus stands as a figure who represents the impossibility of direct communication. Even when he says direct statements to his divinity ("I and the father are one" [John 10:30]), or acts in divine ways (raising Lazarus from the dead), it is still *this man* who is doing and saying it, and thus the communication is rendered indirect. There is nothing Jesus does that automatically results in faith. The listener must choose how she or he will respond every time. The final section of *Practice* is a long reflection on John 12:32: "And I, when I am lifted up from the earth, will draw all people to myself." Its theme is crucifixion, suffering, and imitation. The cross is a sign of offence. It is also that to which Jesus calls his disciples. The ones who are not offended by the God-Man will obey and imitate him by denying themselves and taking up their own crosses. By doing so, Jesus' disciples will be putting themselves in positions where they too will stand as signs of offence, acting as catalysts for others to be ushered into contemporaneity with Christ. "One becomes a Christian only in the situation of contemporaneity with Christ, and in the situation of contemporaneity everyone will also become aware" (102).

Historically *Practice in Christianity* has not been Kierkegaard's most widely read or reviewed book; however, he considered it "without a doubt [the] most perfect and truest thing I have written" (JP 6501). It is arguably his most important text. The pseudonym Anti-Climacus was invented to represent the highest expression of Christianity—a position to which Søren aspired. The book contains a "Moral" that offers a defence of the established church by calling on the preachers and teachers of Christendom to confess that the Christianity they promote is not the Christianity of the New Testament and potentially offensive contemporaneity. The "Moral" was primarily aimed at Bishop Mynster, who read the book and privately told Søren of his displeasure but who did not address the charges in print or from the pulpit. Mynster's public silence about *Practice* paved the way for Søren's silence. He would soon give up publishing for three years while waiting for Mynster to admit his church's part in the illusion of Christendom. The confession never came and the attack upon Christendom ensued. When the book was re-printed in 1855, Søren claimed if he was to write it again he would leave everything the same, but take away the pseudonym and retract the "Moral."

An Upbuilding Discourse: The Woman Who Was a Sinner
December 20, 1850
Søren Kierkegaard

The short essay was originally part of the longer series of Friday Communion discourses before Kierkegaard decided it worked better as a separate "upbuilding" work. (See the above entry for *Three Discourses at the Communion on Fridays*.) With this 1850 *Discourse* Kierkegaard returns to the woman caught in adultery. Kierkegaard's writings contain many harsh sounding words about women springing from his views on marriage as an example of Christendom's dissipation. However, this *Discourse* is not one of those times. It finds the women of the New Testament, especially the woman caught in adultery, as teachers of authentic Christianity and existential existence. She did not plead or argue with Jesus. She did not do anything to earn forgiveness. She waited with sorrow for her sins. "You can similarly learn from a woman how to sorrow rightly over sin, from the sinful woman whose sins have long, long since ceased to be and have been forgotten but who is herself eternally unforgettable" (149–50).

Two Discourses at the Communion on Fridays
August 7, 1851
Søren Kierkegaard

The *Two Discourses* of 1851 consider how it is that in Luke 7 "The One Who Is Forgiven Little Loves Little" and how in 1 Peter 4:8 "Love Will Hide a Multitude of Sins." The first discourse returns to the sinful woman but this time is intentionally unsettling, aiming for disquiet rather than comfort for the person approaching the Lord's Table. Whereas Jesus' call for people to come to him is a word of rest for people outside the church, his warning here in Luke 7 is for Christianised people who may take their forgiveness for granted. Do you feel little forgiveness? Then perhaps you have little love. The second discourse is addressed to the one who in truth has recognised and confessed their sins. Individual conscience might be able to confess, but it is unable to forget sin. Fortunately, God not only forgives, he *forgets* the sin of the penitent. The book ends with Kierkegaard's view of communion as forgiveness and identity formation: "Only by remaining in him, only by living yourself into him are you under cover . . . it is the communion, this communion that you are to strive to preserve in your daily life by more and more living yourself out of yourself and living yourself into him, in his love, which hides a multitude of sins" (188).

A notable and biographically important element of *Two Discourses* is its opening dedication: "To One Unnamed, Whose Name Will One Day Be Named, is dedicated with this little work, the entire authorship as it was from the beginning." It is significant the discourses were published the same day Kierkegaard issued *On My Work as an Author*. The discourses and their indirect dedication to Regine were intended to be read in the light of this companion piece.

On My Work as an Author
August 7, 1851
Søren Kierkegaard

Later readers of Kierkegaard's journals and posthumous books are well aware how much he wrote about himself and his authorial project. However, contemporary readers had only scattered material to go on, such as the comedic "review of recent Danish literature" in *Concluding Unscientific Postscript*. *On My Work as an Author* was the only piece of autobiographical accounting Kierkegaard released in his lifetime. The occasion springs from the reprinting of *Either/Or* in 1849. The reissue of the earliest and most popular book in the "authorship" led to a new round of self-reflection. Kierkegaard felt the need to reiterate the Christian direction of his life's work, so as not to let the project slip back into the mere aestheticism and moralism of the first book. He considered publishing *The Point of View for My Work as an Author* to accompany the rerelease but then held back, deeming this long work would be too open to misunderstanding. Instead, a shorter version, *On My Work as an Author*, was created. (*Point of View* would be published after his death.) The pamphlet is not part of the authorship *per se*. It is "an act" and thus is supposed to be short and sweet. It runs to just under twenty pages.

In this piece Kierkegaard reiterates his intention to stir up "the crowd" so "the Individual" might emerge. His goal is to introduce Christianity back into Christendom, an aim that can only be done with craftiness thanks to the illusion Christendom has perpetuated. In a world in which everyone assumes they are Christian as a matter of course, Kierkegaard saw fit to pepper his authorship with people who not only are *not* Christian, they know it and can say it. Kierkegaard explains the disunity, obfuscation, and even deception in his authorship as a "godly endeavour" working to communicate the authentically religious in the only way it can be communicated—indirectly and dialectically. Kierkegaard describes his authorship as a "working also to work against oneself" (9). Like a farmer with his plough, Kierkegaard crosses and re-crosses the field several times in order to furrow deeply. Kierkegaard concludes the main section of his accounting by insisting he is a writer "without authority." He asks to be considered not only as the author of the works but as their reader too. The challenges and edification are for him as much as for anyone else. "Before God," he states, "I call my whole work as an author my own upbringing and development, but not in the sense as if I were now complete" (12).

For Self-Examination
September 10, 1851
Søren Kierkegaard

> *"And man, this clever fellow, seems to have become sleepless in order to invent ever new instruments to increase noise, to spread noise, and insignificance with the greatest possible haste and on the greatest possible scale. Yes everything is soon turned upside down: communication is indeed soon brought to its lowest point with regard*

to meaning, and simultaneously the means of communication are indeed brought to their highest with regard to speedy and overall circulation; for what is publicized with such hot haste and, on the other hand, what has greater circulation than—rubbish!" (48).

Kierkegaard half-heartedly tried to conclude his authorship four times in his life. The ink was barely dry on *Concluding Unscientific Postscript* in 1846 before he was finding ways to continue writing. Next he thought *Christian Discourses* and *The Crisis and A Crisis in the Life of an Actress* might mark the end in 1848. Less than a year later, this "end" was followed by another conclusion with *On My Work as an Author* and *Two Discourses* with its thinly veiled dedication to Regine. Finally, he issued *For Self-Examination* in 1851, declining to publish its companion piece, *Judge for Yourself!* The ensuing three years of silence suggested this time Kierkegaard had stuck the landing. The silence can be explained because Kierkegaard considered *Judge!* to be too harsh and *Self-Examination* a fitting final coda to the challenge first issued to Bishop Mynster in *Practice in Christianity*. He was waiting for Mynster to respond. It was not until the Bishop's death and subsequent valorisation as a "truth witness" that Søren would come out swinging with his final attack upon Christendom.

For Self-Examination has three parts, modelled after key dates in the liturgical calendar. The first is a deliberation on Scripture and a celebration of the fifth Sunday after Easter. The second is a reflection on Christ as the Way, in light of Ascension Day. The third, a treatise for Pentecost and a discussion of the Holy Spirit. The book sees Kierkegaard addressing Lutheranism and the Protestant Reformation. The reformation betrays itself when it simply allows one form of anaemic cultural Christianity to replace another. Instead, authentic Christianity is ever new, reforming itself with every generation and every individual. The greatest threat to Christendom's complacency are its own holy texts. Christendom has devised many ways to shield itself from the challenge inherent in Scripture. "Much in the way a boy puts a napkin or more under his pants when he is going to get a licking," (35) people put layers of scholarly research and interpretation between them and the Bible. "I shove all this between the Word and myself and then give this interpreting and scholarliness the name of earnestness and zeal for truth" (35). The Scriptures are not intellectually that hard to understand. It is their *implications* that are difficult. Kierkegaard asks his readers not to think of Scriptures as primarily repositories of historical data or beautiful literature but to use them as a mirror for self-examination. Dare to be alone with the Scriptures! If one dares this, one will invariably meet Jesus Christ in its pages. Christ is the Way. Ascension Day poses a temptation to Christendom as it is too easy to think of Christ glorified rather than the Christ incarnate who came first. Kierkegaard spends time on the difference between the "hard," "narrow" way of Christ and the broad, easy way of destruction. Kierkegaard is keen to point out not all hard and narrow ways are Christ's ways. There can be idolatry and self-delusion in a life of martyrdom too. The followers of Christ are not asked to imitate the life of a sufferer but to imitate the life of Jesus, and that is the difference. Kierkegaard finishes the book with a discussion of the work of the Holy Spirit. "It is the Spirit who gives life" (75). Christendom takes the Spirit's life for granted—as if the role of God was to rubber-stamp whatever comfortable life the citizens have marked out for themselves. "No, no! . . . what blasphemy!" (76). It is not the old life the Holy Spirit endorses but a *new life*. New life requires death of the old life. Kierkegaard here tells a parable of a rich owner who bought a team of horses. He drove them for months, and soon they were tired and lifeless. They "acquired all sorts of quirks and bad habits" and "grew thinner day by day." In desperation the owner calls in a royal coachman. The skilled driver had them for a month. "In the whole countryside there was not a team of horses that carried their heads so proudly." How did this happen? The owner "drove the horses according to the horses' understanding of what it is to drive; the royal coachman drove them according to the coachman's understanding of what it is to drive." Kierkegaard concludes,

"So also with us human beings" (85–86). The Spirit, as the author of life, gives life (faith, hope, and love) where man has come to the end of his own resources.

Kierkegaard deliberately sought as wide a readership as possible for *For Self-Examination*, and it is written in a straightforward, winsome style. It is fitting that this, the last book of the official authorship, is also a very good suggestion for a new reader of Kierkegaard wondering what should be their first.

The "Attack upon Christendom" *and* The Moment and Late Writings
December 18, 1854—September 24, 1855;
Moment no. 10 published posthumously 1881.
Søren Kierkegaard

> *"So the silence can no longer continue; the objection must be raised . . . the objection to be representing—from the pulpit, consequently before God—Bishop Mynster as a truth-witness, because it is untrue, but proclaimed in this way it becomes an untruth that cries to heaven" (8).*

The "Attack upon Christendom" is not the title of a single work, but is instead the collective label for a series of polemical articles that originally appeared in the self-published journal *The Moment* and in the *Fatherland* newspaper between 1854 and 1855. The name applies to the swirl of events, editorials, essays, letters to newspapers, and appeals to the public that characterised the final stage of Kierkegaard's writing career. It also marks the final phase of his life, as he died while in the middle of the attack before the tenth issue of *The Moment* could be published. In these articles, Kierkegaard does not resort to pseudonyms but writes under his own name. However, even this "direct communication" remains in a certain sense indirect, for Kierkegaard adopts a role of "corrective" to the established order. He talks about himself as a fire chief ringing a bell, a detective discovering a great crime, a horsefly rousing its victim with a sting, or a doctor causing his patient to vomit in order to purge them of their poison. The cause of all this urgent imagery is *Christendom*, which for Kierkegaard encompasses not only the Lutheran Church of Denmark but also any and all Christianised cultures. "Oh Luther, you had ninety-five theses—terrible! And yet, in a deeper sense, the more theses the less terrible. The matter is far more terrible—there is only one thesis. The Christianity of the New Testament does not exist at all" (39).

The problem with Christendom is that it tempts its citizens to confuse being a member of a civilisation with being authentically religious and has done away with Christianity as a result. In *The Moment* Kierkegaard maintains he is not a Christian, for under Christendom that term has become meaningless. He also emphasises he is not trying to convert anyone to Christianity—merely to get his readers to face honestly what they are and what they are not. "So let there be light on this matter, let it become clear to people what the New Testament understands by being a Christian, so that everyone can choose whether he wants to be a Christian or whether he honestly, plainly, forthrightly does not want to be that" (97).

In these articles, Kierkegaard appeals to the common man, and he names and shames a number of Christendom's public figures, most notably Jakob Mynster, the recently deceased Bishop of Denmark, and his successor, Bishop Hans Martensen.

> A realistic description of the pastor is: a half-worldly, half-ecclesiastical, totally equivocal officeholder, a person of rank with a family, who (in the hope of a promotion . . .) ensures himself a livelihood, also if necessary, with the help of the police . . . lives on Jesus Christ having been crucified, claiming that this profound earnestness (this "imitation of Jesus Christ"?) is the Christianity of the New Testament . . . (31)
>
> . . . it is easy to see that, Christianly, their whole existence is a malpractice . . . The "pastor" has a pecuniary interest in having

people call themselves Christians, since every such person is of course a contributing member and also contributes to giving the whole profession visible power—but nothing is more dangerous for true Christianity, nothing is more against its nature, than getting people light-mindedly to assume the name "Christians" . . . and "the pastor" has a pecuniary interest in having it rest there, so that by assuming the name "Christians" people do not come to know what Christianity in truth is, since otherwise the whole machinery of 1000 royal offices and class power would come to naught—but nothing is more dangerous for true Christianity, nothing is more contrary to its nature, than this abortion causing it to rest there, so that people assume the name "Christians." (95–96)

The pieces caused great offence as well as admiration from all quarters of society.

Posthumous Works

The Book on Adler
Written, 1846–47; revised 1848; published posthumously 1872
Søren Kierkegaard

Kierkegaard worked and reworked the material for this book many times. Eventually in 1849 he published a short excerpt, "The Difference between a Genius and an Apostle" as one of the *Two Ethical-Religious Essays* attributed to the pseudonym "H. H." The complicated process and Søren's reluctance to publish the full work is due to two factors: Kierkegaard's personal concern for Adolph Peter Adler and Kierkegaard's vocational concern for himself. The book is extraordinarily important as a document about Kierkegaard's self-understanding as a poet who writes Christianly but "without authority." Adler was a contemporary of Søren's, a pastor who began his career as a Hegelian theologian before having a religious experience in which he claimed Jesus wanted him to eradicate the Hegelian influence from all his theology. Adler faced widespread derision and was removed from his pastorate in 1844. He continued to write but went back on his previous claim to be communicating from direct revelation, instead formulating his work as a new philosophical development.

The book is essentially an investigation into the concept of divine revelation, the various ways the modern age gets its categories confused in relation to truth and what the difference is between communicating with divine authority (as an "apostle") and communicating with skill (as a "genius"). Kierkegaard does not question the possibility of revelation, but he does question Adler's original claim, based on his subsequent attempt to dress his divine revelation up as sophisticated philosophy. The words of a "genius" can be critiqued, argued, and appreciated. An "apostle" with a revelation can only be received or rejected. "The question is very simple: Will you obey? or will you not obey; will you in faith submit to . . . divine authority or will you take offence?" (34). Beware! Kierkegaard continues, not taking any side is also an offence.

Kierkegaard draws a distinction between the historical event in Christianity (the appearance of the paradox of the god-man) and the history of Christendom (the development of Christian civilisation and the church). The modern confusion arises because Christendom attempts to prove the plausibility of its foundational event by appealing to common sense, literacy, or intellectual sophistication. Yet, says Kierkegaard, the paradox is not to be tested and proved by men. It is men who are proved and tested by the paradox, which must be encountered afresh in contemporaneity.

Adler claimed he was an apostle with a revelation, but he attempted to communicate as a genius with rhetorical skill. The two categories are qualitatively different. That is Adler's confusion, the confusion he shares with his wider culture. The final chapter of the book thus finds Adler to be a "phenomenon" of the present age. The age confuses aesthetics with the religious—for example, much ink is spilled praising the Apostle Paul for his excellent command of Greek. The age is drunk on seeing itself collectively as an advanced movement of history rather than as individuals continually before the paradox. The present age thinks the more people rally together about something the truer it is or becomes, forgetting that divine revelation, if it exists, remains true whether it attracts the agreement of a million, a hundred, one or none of the human race.

Point of View for My Work as an Author and "The Single Individual": Two "Notes" Concerning My Work as an Author
Written, 1848; published posthumously 1859

Armed Neutrality
Written, 1848; published posthumously 1880
Søren Kierkegaard

> "The Point of View for My Work as an Author *must not be published, no, no!* . . . *The book itself is true and in my opinion masterly. But a book like that can only be published after my death*" (JP 6327).

The popular *Either/Or* was due for reprinting in 1849. Although the money that would come from this publishing was welcome, the event was not wholly positive for Kierkegaard. This aesthetic-moral work lay at the beginning of his authorship. By 1849 the works had moved on to much more religiously serious matters, trenchantly pitting a highly Christocentric understanding of Christianity against the cultural assumptions of Christendom. Kierkegaard was concerned about dragging his authorship back into the aesthetic stage. To make matters more complicated, much of the most Christian material from 1848 still lay on Kierkegaard's desk while he wondered in what manner and under which name to print it. The authorship had used non-Christian pseudonyms to piously deceive readers into Christian edification. The current material awaiting publication was Christian at a higher, more ideal level than Kierkegaard had previously expressed. Some sort of report reminding readers of the full gamut of the authorship and an accounting of his method of indirect and direct communication seemed in order.

Kierkegaard struggled mightily with himself over the form this accounting should take. *Point of View* was complete by November 1848, but Søren was worried it said *too* much about his self-understanding and that it was prone to misunderstanding. Eventually, a much shorter version drawn from *Point of View* was published as *On My Work as an Author* in 1851. The full work, along with its accompanying material on "The Single Individual" and *Armed Neutrality* was eventually published by Peter Kierkegaard years after Søren's death.

The book lays out the case that Kierkegaard was a religious author from the beginning. While there was Christian intent, Kierkegaard does not claim his whole project was fully formed from the start—it developed as the works went on. Kierkegaard again reiterates he is a *reader* as much as the author of the works, and he sees them as a means to his own upbuilding guided by divine Governance. The book justifies the "deception" of the pseudonyms and the necessity of indirectly communicating Christianity. It describes Kierkegaard's relation to the "left" and "right" hands of his writing and devotes ample time tracing "Governance's Part in My Authorship" (71).

The short piece entitled *Armed Neutrality* was intended to supplement *Point of View* but was not in fact published till twenty years later. It spells out Kierkegaard's "Position as a Christian Author in Christendom" (129). The title is an allusion to the conservative and radical upheavals of contemporary Denmark and Kierkegaard's conception that "in relation to the manifold confusion of modern times," the authentically Christian position needs to be fiercely protected from partisan co-option. The essay extols the need for every Christianised culture and generation "to uphold the ideal picture of a Christian" (130). Kierkegaard is not that ideal by any means, but his work tries to present the image. "Humble before God, with my knowledge of what it indeed means in truth to be a Christian, and with my knowledge of myself, I by no means dare to maintain that I am a Christian in any remarkable sense" (134). This is in stark contrast to the thousands of Christians who "have known definitely that they were Christians but did not know definitely what it means to be a Christian" (141).

The notes on "The Single Individual" are often overlooked but contain important discussions on Kierkegaard's posture towards politics. "But although 'impractical,' yet the religious is eternity's transfigured rendition of the most beautiful dream of politics" (103). The essay contains some of Kierkegaard's clearest expressions on what it means to be an individual in the face of the crowd. "The crowd is untruth" (108) when it assumes the mantle of authority merely by dint of its size and numerical strength. Yet truth is not a matter of a "gathering of thousands" or of voting (108). Instead, "truth relates itself to the single individual." This is not elitism: "everyone can be the one" (109). Christ preached so as to draw persons out from their crowds, an action the crowd hates. "That is why everyone who in truth wants to serve the truth is *eo ipso* in some ways a martyr" (109).

Judge for Yourself!
Written, 1851–52; published posthumously 1876
Søren Kierkegaard

Judge For Yourself! was originally written as a sequel to *For Self-Examination* and bears the subtitle "For Self-Examination Recommended to the Present Age: Second Series." In the end, Kierkegaard decided to withhold this more trenchant piece until Bishop Mynster responded to Kierkegaard's repeated calls for confession of Christendom's guilt at portraying authentic Christianity. The confession never happened and *Judge!* stayed amongst Kierkegaard's posthumous papers until published by Peter Kierkegaard in 1876.

The book comes in two parts, with themes familiar to any reader who has encountered Kierkegaard's "attack" material and the ideal Christianity of Anti-Climacus. Part one is a plea for "Becoming Sober," an act defined, eventually, as "to come so close to oneself in one's understanding, in one's knowing, that all one's understanding becomes action" (115). The primary drunken haze from which the reader needs to emerge, of course, is the intoxication of level-headed, sensible, worldly wise Christendom. The second section is a return to the favourite theme of "Christ the Prototype" and another reflection on Matthew 6:24: No one can serve two masters. Christianity is not a doctrine. It is not a set of scholarly data calling for assent or doubt or a set of moral principles. These are all *objective* phenomena. Instead, it has to do with "the subjective" (that is, Persons as subjects not objects). Jesus Christ "as the prototype required imitation" and in this way "expels all anxiety from a person's soul" (209).

The book's "moral" is worthy of note. Here, Kierkegaard (correctly) anticipates the common response to regard him as yet another reformer. In no uncertain terms he rejects the label. Kierkegaard's appeal is to the single individual. He is not seeking disciples or starting a new movement. He states he is happy to let the established order exist in all its forms, but with the *caveat* that it confess before God how far behind it is to imitating the prototype. Unless and until this happens, all "reforming" is but more noise in the present age. The mania for reform is like rearranging deck chairs on a sinking ship. It is a sham "without being willing to suffer and make sacrifices . . . This cannot be God's idea but is a foppish human device, which is why, instead of fear and trembling and much spiritual trial, there is: hurrah, bravo, applause, balloting, bumbling, hubbub, noise—and false alarm" (213).

Notes

Preface

13: "His sayings": Charles Williams, *Descent of the Dove* (London: Longman, 1939), 194.

Chapter 1: A Controversial Life

19–20: "On the evening of Sunday": *Berlingske Tidende* (November 16, 1855) in Bruce Kirmmse, ed., *Encounters With Kierkegaard* (Princeton: Princeton University Press, 1996), 145.

20–21: "He was without a doubt": Goldschmidt, *Encounters*, 130.

21: "I do not wonder": Grundtvig in Joakim Garff, *Søren Kierkegaard: A Biography*, trans. Bruce Kirmmse (Princeton: Princeton University Press, 2005), 796.

21: "I thought it decent": Møller, *Encounters*, 132.

21: "He was said to suffer": Paulli, Garff, 793.

23: "living minute by minute": Lund, *Encounters*, 172.

23: "strongly discordant": Troels-Lund, *Encounters*, 190.

23: "Everyone knew": Troels-Lund, *Encounters*, 190–91.

24: "It was probably in this way": Lund, *Encounters*, 172.

25: "Søren Kierkegaard was buried": Andersen, *Encounters*, 136.

25: "the church was full": Soderman, *Encounters*, 132.

25–26: "A man who": Troels-Lund, *Encounters*, 191.

26: "The tightly packed mass": Lund, *Encounters*, 173.

27: "completely different appearance": Lund, *Encounters*, 173.

27: "They conquered the space": Lund, *Encounters*, 173.

27: "while his face": Lund, *Encounters*, 173.

27: "powerfully delivered": Troels-Lund, *Encounters*, 175.

28: "eulogy": P. Kierkegaard, *Encounters*, 146–50.
28: "became still as glass": Lund, *Encounters*, 173.
28: "Everywhere teemed": Troels-Lund, *Encounters*, 191.
29: "In the name of God . . . Let him speak!": Lund, *Fatherland* (November 22, 1855), *Encounters*, 133–35.
30: "Therefore, both on his behalf": Lund, *Fatherland* (November 22, 1855), *Encounters*, 135.
30: "Bravo!": Troels-Lund, *Encounters*, 192.
30: "The speaker was gone": Troels-Lund, *Encounters*, 192.
30: "As if": Soderman, *Encounters*, 133.
31: "Today, after a service": Martensen, *Encounters*, 135.
31: "great quantity of paper": Lund, *Kierkegaard's Journals and Notebooks: Volume I*, eds. Niels Jørgen Cappelørn, et al. (Princeton: Princeton University Press, 2006), vii.
32: "if anyone wants to talk": Lund, *Encounters*, 131.
32: "The unnamed person": S. Kierkegaard, Garff, 801.
32: "What I wish to express": S. Kierkegaard, *Encounters*, 48.
32–33: "In a little while": Jørgen Bukdahl, *Kierkegaard and the Common Man*, trans. Bruce Kirmmse (Cambridge: William B. Eerdmans, 2001), 130.

Chapter 2: School Life

35: "I don't know . . . I myself belonged to this latter group.": Welding, *Encounters*, 6–8.
37: "I have now read Welding's": Anger, *Encounters*, 10.
37: "In his boyhood": Holst, *Encounters*, 13.
37: "we did not have the least suspicion": Lind, *Encounters*, 11.
37–38: "This young man": Nielsen, 'School Testimony' (September 29, 1830), *Encounters*, 18.
38: "When God speaks": Attrup, *Encounters*, 12.
38: "believed [Søren] lacking": Lind, *Encounters*, 11.
38: "Kierkg is really annoying": Anger, *Encounters*, 10.
39: "Storck's fiancée": Welding, *Encounters*, 9.
39: "will you also tell the professor": Welding, *Encounters*, 9.
39: "Either you leave": Lind, *Encounters*, 11.
39: "Søren had a good eye": Welding, *Encounters*, 8.

39: "deliberately made things difficult": Welding, *Encounters*, 8.
40: "when he was entrusted": Nielsen, 'School Testimony' (September 29, 1830), *Encounters*, 18.
40: "Slight, slender, and frail": Søren Kierkegaard, *Journals and Papers*, eds. Howard V. Hong and Edna H. Hong. 7 volumes (Bloomington: Indiana University Press, 1967–78), 6890 (X.1 A 277).
40: "SK was always one of the first": Welding, *Encounters*, 8.
40: "So what?": Brun, *Encounters*, 6.
40–41: "annoying and provocative": Welding, *Encounters*, 7.
41: "even though it often earned him a beating": Welding, *Encounters*, 7.
41: "with rulers": Meidell, *Encounters*, 4.
41: "Never boots": Welding, *Encounters*, 7.
41–42: "From the very beginning": Nielsen, 'School Testimony' (September 29, 1830), *Encounters*, 15–17.

Chapter 3: Family Life

43: "A fork": Troels-Lund, *Encounters*, 3.
46: "I was born in 1813": JP 5725 (V A 3 n.d., 1844).
"Obedience was for him": Lund, in Joakim Garff and Pia Søltoft, *Søren Kierkegaard: Objects of Love, Works of Love* (Copenhagen: Museum of Copenhagen, 2013), 18.
46–47: "was not to be trifled": unnamed servant, Garff and Søltoft, 24.
48: "a very strict man": JC,120.
48: "While they walked up and down": JC,120.
48: "When I can't sleep": Brun, *Encounters*, 6.
49: Michael in an argument: JC, 121–22.
49: "My father": Thorkild Lyby, "Peter Christian Kierkegaard", *Kierkegaard and his Danish Contemporaries: Tome II Theology*, ed. Jon Stewart (Burlington: Ashgate, 2009), 189.
49: Fuss over sons: Lund, *Encounters*, 153.
50: "Anne Kierkegaard, born Lund": Garff, 130.
51: "deeply humbled": SUD, 112. The insight comes from George Pattison.
51: "It is appalling": JP 6274 (IX A 411).
51–52: "Then it was that the great earthquake occurred": JP 5430 (II A 805 n.d., 1838).

52: "How appalling": JP 5874 (VII.1 A 5).
52: "and ours too." Garff, 136; Alistair Hannay, *Kierkegaard: A Biography* (Cambridge: Cambridge University Press, 2001), 456 n.37.
53: "the temperaments cannot be united": Josiah Thompson, *Kierkegaard* (New York: Alfred A Knopf, 1973), 27.
53: "fall from tree": Lund, *Encounters*, 158.
54: "No, my children have not been brought up like that": Hammerich, *Encounters*, 3.
54: "galloping consumption": Hannay, 32–33.
54: "It is really remarkable": JP 277 (I A 325 January 22, 1837).
55: "I acquired an anxiety": JP 6274 (IX A 411 n.d., 1848).
56: The way of the world: PC, 174ff; WA, 55ff.
57: "As a child": PV, 79.

Chapter 4: Public Life/Private Life

60–61: "strange, confused look": Brøchner, *Encounters*, 225.
61: "witty, somewhat sarcastic face": Sibbern, *Encounters*, 216.
61: "intelligent, lively and superior": Goldschmidt, *Encounters*, 65.
61: Walking with Søren: Brøchner, *Encounters*, 239.
61: "As far as little annoyances are concerned": JP 5092 (I A 72 June 1, 1835).
62: "a man dressed in modern clothes": JP 5094 (I A 63 n.d., 1835).
62: 1262 r.d.: Thompson, 47.
62: "In this way my father": S. Kierkegaard, Thompson, 66.
63: "Peter has always regarded himself as better": JP 6176 (IX A 99 n.d., 1848).
63: March 1834: P. Kierkegaard, Hannay, 53.
63: "when he became morbidly religious": JP 6274 (IX A 411 n.d., 1848).
64: "Søren these days": P. Kierkegaard, Hannay, 90.
64: "Since from the coming first of September": S. Kierkegaard, Thompson, 68.
66: "when the fire gleamed": Sibbern Møller, *Encounters*, 19.
68: "fascinated the youth": Søren Kierkegaard, *Papers and Journals: A Selection*, trans. Alastair Hannay (London: Penguin, 2015), 49 (X 2 155).
68: "a crack in his sounding board": Hans Lassen Martensen, *Af mit Levnet* III, in *Kierkegaard Commentary*, trans. T. H. Croxall (London: James Nisbet, 1956), 244–45.

69: "My mother has repeatedly confirmed . . . the upper hand": Martensen, *Encounters*, 196.
69: "I recognized immediately": Martensen, *Encounters*, 196.
70: Polemical: See for example JP 5961 (VII1 A 221 January 20, 1847).
70: "brilliant dialectic and wit": Ostermann, *Encounters*, 20–22.
71–72: "with one face I laugh": JP 5260 (II A 662 n.d., 1837).
72: "People understand me so little": JP 5119 (I A 123 February, 1836).
72: "I have just now come from a gathering": JP 5141 (1A 161 1836).
73: "Blast it all": JP 5142 (I A 162 n.d., 1836).
73: "One who walked": JP 1672 (I A 158 n.d., 1836).
73: "Situation": JP 5249 (II A 634).
73: "I don't feel like doing anything": JP 5251 (II A 637).
74–75: "What I really need": JP 5100 (I A 75 August 1, 1835).
75: "I grew up in orthodoxy": JP 5092 (I A 72 June 1, 1835).
75–76: "Christianity was an impressive figure": JP 418 (I A 97 n.d. 1835).
76: "When I look at a goodly number": JP 417 (I A 96 n.d. 1835).
77: "Oh how unhappy I am": JP 5225 (11 A 597 n.d. 1837).

Chapter 5: Love Life

79: "the devil of my wit": JP 5219 (II A 67 May 8, 1837).
79–80: Captivated: R. Schlegel, *Encounters*, 34.
80: "angel with the flaming sword": JP 5219 (II A 67 May 8, 1837).
80: ". . . good God": JP 5220 (II A 68 n.d., 1837).
82: "compression of the spinal cord": Johan Schioldann and Ib Søgaard, *Søren Kierkegaard (1813–55): A Bicentennial Pathographical Review*. History of Psychiatry 24 (4) 387–398.
82–83: "When at times": JP 5301 (II A 702 February 9, 1838).
84: "It would be interesting": JP 4400 (II A 163 September 20, 1837).
84: "hackneyed proposition": JP 2313 (II A 159 n.d., 1837).
84: "Philosophy": JP 3251 (II A 11 n.d., 1837).
84: "Such a long period": JP 5302 (II A 209 April, 1838).
85: "To the late Professor Poul Martin Møller": CA, 178 (V B 46, 1844).
85–86: "There is an indescribable joy": JP 5324 (II A 10:30 A. M. May 19, 1838).
86: Pastor Kolthoff: Koltoff to Barfod, letter dated April 19, 1868. Quoted

in Niels Jørgen Cappelørn "Søren Kierkegaard at Friday Communion in the Church of Our Lady", *International Kierkegaard Commentary Volume 10: Without Authority*, ed. Robert Perkins (Macon: Mercer University Press, 2006), 263–64.

86: "Father in Heaven": JP 5328 (II A 231 July 9, 1838).
86: "I am going to work": JP 5329 (II A 232 July 9, 1838).
86–87: "My father died on Wednesday": JP 5335 (II A 243 August 11, 1838).
87: "insane": PV, 79.
88: "Now you will never get your theological degree": Sibbern to S. Kierkegaard, JP 5769 (VI A 8 n.d., 1844–45).
88: "If Father had lived": JP 5769 (VI A 8 n.d., 1844–45).
88: "as long as Father was alive": S. Kierkegaard to Brøchner, *Encounters*, 228.
89: "the longest parenthesis": JP 5446 (III A 35 n.d., 1840).
89: "I must bid farewell": JP 5434 (II A 576 December 20, 1839).
89: "Even before my father died": JP 6472 (X5 A 149 n.d., 1849).
89: "During all that time": JP 6472 (X5 A 149 n.d., 1849).
90: "You, sovereign queen of my heart": JP 5368 (II A 347 February 2, 1839).
90: "Here on the heath": JP 2830 (III A 78 n.d., 1840).
90: "I am so listless": JP 5454 (III A 54 n.d., 1840).
91: "determined to resolve the whole thing": JP 6472 (X5 A 149 n.d., 1849).
91: "O, what do I care about music": JP 6472(X5 A 149 n.d., 1849).
92: "struck completely speechless": R. Schlegel, *Encounters*, 35.
93: "I did not say one single word": JP 6472 (X5 A 149 n.d., 1849).
93: "You could have talked about Fritz": S. Kierkegaard to R. Schlegel, *Encounters*, 35.
93: "a profound, powerful soul": Sibbern, *Encounters*, 215.
94: "discord had already arisen": Sibbern, *Encounters*, 213.
95: Sermon assessment: Hannay, 138.
97: "The exposition suffers . . . it would be fruitless to express a wish about this": Madvig, *Encounters*, 30–31.
97: "Despite the fact": Ørsted, *Encounters*, 32.
97: "For a dedication copy": JP 5322 (II A 749 n.d., 1838).
98: "Above all, forget": SLW, 329–330.
99: "feminine despair": JP 6472 (X5 A 149 n.d., 1849).
99: "In the name of Jesus Christ": JP 6482 (X1 A 667 n.d., 1849).

99: "I have to be cruel": JP 6472 (X5 A 149 n.d., 1849).
99: "scoundrel": JP 6472 (X5 A 149 n.d., 1849).
99: Jonas' angry letter: Hannay, 158.
99: "She fought . . . to have to be so cruel and to love as I did": JP 6472 (X5 A 149 n.d., 1849).
100: "The act . . . I beg you not to break with her": JP 6472 (X5 A 149 n.d., 1849).
101: "Will you never marry? . . . Promise to think of me": JP 6472 (X5 A 149 n.d., 1849).
102: "crying in my bed": JP 6472 (X5 A 149 n.d., 1849).
102: "If you do that": JP 6472 (X5 A 149 n.d., 1849).
102: "I was reminded of her": JP 6472 (X5 A 149 n.d., 1849).
102: "The few scattered days": JP 6163 (IX A 67 n.d., 1848).

Chapter 6: Writing Life

103: "after which I decided to pay": S. Kierkegaard, Garff, 208.
104: "a particular nook": S. Kierkegaard, Garff, 207.
104: German waiters: Brøchner, *Encounters*, 230.
104: "Søren Kierkegaard": Smith, *Encounters*, 58.
104: Doctors: See letters to Emil, JP 5548 (Letters, no. 62 January 16, 1842) and JP 5551 (Letters, no. 68 February 6, 1842).
105: "Here, a groan": JP 5548 (Letters, no. 62 January 16, 1842).
106: "bears a striking resemblance": JP 5542 (Letters, no. 54 December 14, 1841).
106: "I am too old": S. Kierkegaard, Hannay, 163.
107: "Anonymity": JP 5551(Letters, no. 68 February 6, 1842).
107: "I am coming to Copenhagen": JP 5552 (Letters, no. 69 February 27, 1842).
107: "To produce was my life": Joakim Garff, "To Produce was my Life: Problems, Perspectives Within the Kierkegaardian Biography" *Kierkegaard Revisited*, trans. Stacey Elizabeth Axe; eds. Niels Jørgen Cappelørn and Jon Stewart (New York: Walter de Gruyter, 1997), 75 (X 1 A 442).
108: "put everything into": S. Kierkegaard, Garff, 314.
108: Stand writing: Schiødte, quoting Anders, *Encounters*, 195.
108: "I regard the whole city": JP 5763 (VI B 225 n.d., 1844–45).

108: "although I can be totally engrossed": JP 5731 (V B 72:22 n.d., 1844).
109: "He preferred": Schiødte, *Encounters*, 194.
109: "strike up conversations": Brøchner, *Encounters*, 229–30.
109: Coffee cups: Levin, *Encounters*, 208.
110: "He comforted": Brøchner, *Encounters*, 242.
110: "He is so unspeakably loving": H. P. Kierkegaard to Meidell, *Encounters*, 140.
112: "strong attacks": Spang, Garff, 460.
112: "impractical and very self-absorbed": H. Plough, recounting his father's memories, *Encounters*, 56.
112: "my little secretary": JP 5688 (IV A 141 n.d., 1843).
112: "I wager": JP 5688 (IV A 141 n.d., 1843).
115: "healthy, happy": JP 5665 (Letters, no. 82 May 25, 1843).
117: "a little hint": JP 6388 (X1 A 266 n.d., 1849).
117: "in order to clear her out": JP 6388 (X1 A 266 n.d., 1849).
118: "At vespers . . . she has faith in me": JP 5653 (IV A 97 n.d., 1843).
118: "Her eyes met mine": JP 6472 (X5 A 149 n.d., 1849).
118: "After her engagement": JP 6472 (X5 A 149 n.d., 1849).
118: "No doubt": JP 6472 (X5 A 149 n.d., 1849).
118–19: "If I had had faith": JP 5664 (IV A 107 May 17, 1843).
119: "But so my girl": JP 5664 (IV A 107 May 17, 1843).
119: "I have loved her . . . me to do it": JP 5664 (IV A 107 May 17, 1843).
120: "But if I were to have explained myself": JP 5664 (IV A 107 May 17, 1843).
120: "It is my own design": JP 6472 (X.5 A 149).
122: "The Grundtvigian nonsense": JP 4121 (VIII1 A 245 n.d., 1847).
123: "in a legal and literary sense . . . not mine": CUP, 529.

Chapter 7: Pirate Life

127: "looming up": Goldschmidt, *Encounters*, 69.
127: "manned by courageous young men": *Corsaren*, no. 1, cols 5–6 in *Kierkegaard's Journals and Notebooks: Volume 4: Journals NB-NB5* (Princeton: Princeton University Press, 2011), note 7, 445.
127: "six times four days": COR, xi.
128: "read to pieces": Andersen, Garff, 379.

128: "With feelings": Møller to Goldschmidt, Garff, 385.
128: "You are not a riding instructor": Goldschmidt, *Encounters*, 68.
128: "comic composition": Goldschmidt, *Encounters*, 67.
129: "Which of your book's characters . . . *The Corsair* is P. L. Møller": Goldschmidt, *Encounters*, 71.
130: "a bright fellow": JP 588 (VII.1 A 99).
130: "It was my desire": JP 588 (VII.1 A 99).
130: "irreparable harm": TA, 74.
130: "disgusting": Heiberg, Garff, 218.
131: "No, thank you": JP 5944 (VII.1 A 158).
131: Newspaper reviews: JP 2143 (VII.1 A 24).
131: "will never die": COR, ix.
131: "To become immortal": COR, xiv (VI B 192).
133: "But to spin": Møller "A Visit in Sorø", COR, 102.
133: "He satiates himself": Møller "A Visit in Sorø", COR, 100.
134: "Would that I": COR, 46.
135: "Where the Spirit is": COR, 46.
135: "Kierkegaard pounced": Goldschmidt, *Encounters*, 73.
135: "Denmark's greatest mind": *The Corsair*, no. 276, January 2, 1846, COR, 110.
136: "in order": *The Corsair*, no. 27, January 9, 1846, COR, 114.
136: "May I ask": COR, 50.
137: "walked past me": Goldschmidt, *Encounters*, 75.
138: "He [Søren] could reflect": Brøchner, *Encounters*, 235.
138: "Accustomed as we are now": Goldschmidt, COR, xxxi.
138: "In our time": Troels-Lund, *Encounters*, 181–82.
139: "Every kitchen boy": JP 5887 (VII.1 A 98).
139–140: "Once": Troels-Lund, *Encounters*, 183–84.
140: "Don't be such a Søren Kierkegaard": Brandes, *Encounters*, 97.
140: "And so I am wasted": COR, 229 (IX A 370).
141: "What I as a public person": JP 6906 (XI.1 A 484).
142: "I am positive": JP 5863 (VII.1 B 69).
143: "But, no": JP 5872 (VII.1 A 3).
143: "When I gave her up": JP 5961 (VII.1 A 221).
143–44: "Humanly speaking": JP 5961 (VII.1 A 221).

Chapter 8: An Armed and Neutral Life

145: Bishop forgot: Hannay, 390; *Papers and Journals*, 642 (XI2 A 219, 29 June 1855).
145: "It is frequently said": JP 6373 (X.1 A 187).
146: "What Christendom needs": JP 2642 (IX A 165 n.d., 1848).
146: "the truth": Hannay, 369 quoting IX A 302.
146: "The judgment": JP 2642 (IX A 165 n.d., 1848).
146–47: "Report": JP 5887 (VII1 A 98 March 9, 1846).
147: "this existence": JP 5887 (VII1 A 98 March 9, 1846).
147: "If I only could": JP 5887 (VII1 A 98 March 9, 1846).
147–48: "When Bishop Mynster": JP 5947 (VII 1 A 169 November 5, 1846).
149: See JP 5937 (VII1 A 147 September 7, 1846).
150: "And now that I": JP 5894 (VII1 A 107 n.d., 1846).
151: John the Baptist: Brøchner, *Encounters*, 234.
152: "it is cruel": JP 6049 (VIII 1 A 264 n.d.,1847).
153: "An upbuilding discourse": JP 640 (VIII1 A 293 n.d., 1847).
153: Reprinted: Historical introduction, WL, xv.
153: "I firmly decided": JP 6310 (X1 A 42 n.d. 1849).
153: King and Queen: JP 6310 (X1 A 42 n.d. 1849).
153: Intended Reader: WL, xvi.
154: ". . . it would have made me": JP 6071 (VIII1 A 390 November 4, 1847).
154: "Today I looked in": JP 6071 (VIII1 A 390 November 4, 1847).
155: "Then came the year 1848": PC, xi quoting X6 B 249.
155: "the People": Bruce Kirmmse, *Kierkegaard in Golden Age Denmark* (Bloomington: Indiana University Press, 1990), 66.
156: "not to force the nation": Roar Skovmand. *De folkelig bevaegelser i Danmark* (Copenhagen: Shultz, 1951), 24; Kirmmse *Golden Age*, 66.
157: "They are blind": JP 2960 (X4 A 93 n.d., 1851).
157: "The single individual": JP 2004 (VIII1 A 482 n.d., 1847).
157: "Armed Neutrality": PV, 138–39.
158: "attack upon Christendom": *Papers and Journals,* 395 (X1 A 533, 1849).
158: "An Attempt": JP 6271 N.B. (IX A 390 n.d., 1848).
159: "I would place myself": JP 6433 (X1 A 517 n.d., 1849).
159: "I was so happy": JP 6247 (IX A 262 n.d., 1848).

159: "I safely dare": JP 6247 (IX A 262 n.d., 1848).
159: "I do not wish": JP 6247 (IX A 262 n.d., 1848).
159: "We all weep": JP 6536 (X2 A 205 n.d., 1849).
160: ". . . Marry I could not": JP 6537 (Letters, no. 239).
160: "The enclosed letter": JP 6537 (Letters, no. 239).
160: "I then received": JP 6537 (Letters, no. 239).
161: "Now the matter": JP 6538 (X.2 A 210).
161: Peter protested: JP 6559 (X6 B 131 n.d., 1849).
161–62: "I myself have": JP 6560 (Letters, no. 240 December, 1849).
162: "All existence is disintegrating": JP 6448 (X1 A 553 n.d., 1849).
162: "Strangely enough": JP 6449 (X1 A 556 n.d., 1849).
162–63: "Without a doubt . . . the work is itself a judgment": JP 6501 (X2 A 66 n.d., 1849).
163: "To me it became clear": M, 70 (*Fatherland* 112, May 16, 1855).
164: "So I was obliged": JP 6800 (X.4 A 540).
165: "habitual Christianity": COR, 52.
165–66: "There is nothing": COR, 54.
166: "I have worked": COR, 56.
166: Regine looks around: JP 6800 (X.4 A 540).
166: "The Possible Collision": JP 6795 (X4 A 511 n.d., 1852).
168: "So let us now": Hans Lassen Martensen, *Leilighedstaler. (Prædiken holdt i Christiansborg Slotskirke, paa 5te Søndag efter Hellig-Tre Konger, Søndagen før Biskop Dr. Mynster's Jordefærd).* [Special Occasion Talks. (Sermon held in Christiansborg palace chapel . . . the Sunday before Bishop Dr. Mynster's funeral)] (Kjøbenhavn, 1884), 20.

Chapter 9: A Life Concluded

169: "I have so little desire . . . leaving the room": Troels-Lund, *Encounters*, 184–86.
171: "Now he is dead": JP 6853 (XI.1 A 1 March 1, 1854).
171–72: "A modern clergyman": JP 6860 (A 69 n.d., 1854).
172–73: "The matter is quite simple": JP 2872 (X3 A 34 n.d., 1850).
173: "Christianity in repose": JP 2731 (XI1 A 345 n.d., 1854).
174: "an unusual kind of poet": See the preface to *Two Discourses at the Communion on Fridays*.

174: "All modern Christendom": JP VI 6466 (X1 A 617).
174: "Corrective": Hannay, 406.
174: "After all": JP 6840 (X5 A 105 March 28, 1853).
175: "you can be sure": JP 6862 (XI1 A 72 n.d., 1854).
176: "To this I must raise an objection . . . an untruth that cries to heaven": M, 3–8.
177: "catastrophe": JP 615 (XI2 A 263 n.d., 1854).
178: "What Cruel Punishment": M, 56.
178: "This must be said": M, 74.
178–79: "Naturally": Rørdam, *Encounters*, 102.
179: "The little war": Ingemann, *Encounters*, 103.
179: "arrogance and ingratitude": Sibbern, *Encounters*, 103.
179: "blasphemer": Grundtvig in Hannay, 408.
179: "It has also been": Hansen, *Encounters*, 106.
179: "Do I understand it": Rosted, *Encounters*, 110.
179: "You common man": M, 346.
180: "this new Reformer": Goldschmidt, *North and South*. Sept. 15, 1855.
180: "What Do I Want": M, 49.
180–81: "God bless you": R. Schlegel to Meyer, *Encounters*, 42.
181: "That Bishop Martensen's silence": M, 79.
181: "circulation": Garff, 753.
182: "In the splendid cathedral . . . Is this the same teaching . . . One cannot live": M, 203–5.
183: "With the greatest clarity": Brøchner, *Encounters*, 248.
183: "But what, specifically": JP 6969 (XI2 A 439 September 25, 1855).
184: "Oh, let me lie": Levin, *Encounters*, 210.
184: "Mynster wing": Garff, 783.
184: "The doctors . . . share my joy with anyone": Boesen, *Encounters*, 121–28.
185: "I have enough": Troels-Lund, *Encounters*, 186.
185–86: Victory: Lund, *Encounters*, 172.
186: "Just straighten . . . a playful smile": Troels-Lund, *Encounters*, 190.
186: "Brother stopped by debate . . . person who did it also had to pay for it": Boesen, *Encounters*, 125–26.

Chapter 10: A Life Continued

190: "There is a man": Andrew Hamilton, *Sixteen Months in the Danish Isles*. London: Bentley, 1852, 269 in George Pattison, "Great Britain: From 'Prophet of the Now' to Postmodern Ironist (and after)", *Kierkegaard's International Reception: Tome 1 Northern and Western Europe*, ed. Jon Stewart (Burlington: Ashgate, 2009), 237.

190: "a great quantity of paper": Lund, in *Kierkegaard's Journals and Notebooks Vol 1*, eds. N. J. Cappelørn, et al. (Princeton: Princeton University Press, 2001), vii.

192: "colossal and clandestine": Barford, *Written Images: Søren Kierkegaard's Journals, Notebooks, Booklets, Sheets, Scraps, and Slips of Paper*, eds. Niels Jørgen Cappelørn, Joakim Garff, and Johnny Kondru (Princeton: Princeton University Press, 2003), 56.

193: "Martensen answering Søren at last": The insight is George Pattison's. "Great Britain: From 'Prophet of the Now' to Postmodern Ironist (and after)", *Kierkegaard's International Reception: Tome 1 Northern and Western Europe*, ed. Jon Stewart (Burlington: Ashgate, 2009), 239; On early reception of Martensen see also Stephen Backhouse "State and Nation, the Theology of H.L. Martensen," *Hans Lassen Martensen: Theologian, Philosopher and Social Critic*, ed. Jon Stewart (Copenhagen: Tusculanum Press: 2012).

195: "Oh, that he could ever forgive me": Regine to Meyer, *Encounters*, 41.

195: "religiously serious": Regine to Neiiendam, *Encounters*, 54.

196: "If I have a system": Karl Barth, *Epistle to the Romans* (Oxford: Oxford University Press, 1968), 10.

196: "Then I read Kierkegaard": Marcio Gimenes de Paula "Hannah Arendt," *Kierkegaard's Influence on Social-Political Thought*, ed. Jon Stewart (Burlington: Ashgate, 2011), 32.

196: "Kierkegaard was by far": Maurice Drury 'Some Notes of Conversations with Wittgenstein', *Recollections of Wittgenstein*. eds. Rhees, Rush (Oxford: Blackwell, 1981), 87.

197: "threshing machine": Jack Schwandt, *The Hong Kierkegaard Library* (Northfield: Friends of the Kierkegaard Library, 2011), 34.

199: "spiritual thrillers": T. S. Eliot "A Lay Theologian" [review of *The Descent of the Dove* by Charles Williams], *The New Statesman* (9 December 1939).

199: "His sayings": Williams, *Descent*, 194.
199: "K. may rebuild": Williams to Lowrie, September 7, 1939, WLP. In Michael J. Paulus Jr. "From a Publisher's Point of View: Charles Williams's Role in Publishing Kierkegaard in English", *Charles Williams and his Contemporaries*, eds. Suzanne Bray and Richard Sturch (Newcastle: Cambridge Scholars Publishing, 2009), 33.
200: "more intangible": Williams to Lowrie, June 3, 1940, WLP. In Michael J. Paulus Jr. "From a Publisher's Point of View: Charles Williams's Role in Publishing Kierkegaard in English", *Charles Williams and his Contemporaries*, eds. Suzanne Bray and Richard Sturch (Newcastle: Cambridge Scholars Publishing, 2009), 35.
200: "A week ago": Thomas Merton, *Run to the Mountain: The Journals of Thomas Merton Volume 1*, (San Francisco: HarperCollins, 1997), 259.
201: "Many moderns . . . to be so evil": Frances Perkins, *The Roosevelt I Knew* (New York: Viking Press, 1946), 147–49.
202: "Pilgrimage to Nonviolence": Nigel Hatton, "Martin Luther King", *Kierkegaard's Influence on Social-Political Thought*, ed. Jon Stewart (Burlington: Ashgate, 2011), 102, quoting *The Papers of Martin Luther King Jr.* vol. 5, 419–24.
202: "Our problem today": Hatton, 104; Martin Luther King Jr. 'The Quest for Peace and Justice' *Nobel Lecture* December 11, 1964.
202: "In reading Kierkegaard": West interview with George Yancy quoted in Marcia C. Robinson "Cornel West", *Kierkegaard's Influence on Social-Political Thought*, ed. Jon Stewart (Burlington: Ashgate, 2011), 236. See note. 27, 237.
203: "existentially concrete": Robinson, 238.
203: "viewpoint": Cornel West, *Prophesy Deliverance! An Afro-American Revolutionary Christianity* (Philadelphia: Westminster, 1982), 167, n2.
203: "All honour to the Hongs": Jonathan Ree, *Times Literary Supplement* (June 26, 1998, no.17).
205: "He wanted his epitaph": "Mike Tyson Explores Kierkegaard" *Wall Street Journal*, December 13, 2013.
205: "Reflektor": Zoe Camp "The 100 Best Albums of the Decade So Far (2010–2014)" *Pitchfork*. August 2014.

205: "It sounds like": Patrick Doyle, "Win Butler Reveals Secret Influences Behind Arcade Fire's 'Reflektor'" *Rolling Stone Magazine*, October 22, 2013.
206: "Donald Glover": http://noisey.vice.com/en_uk/blog/donald-glover-childish-gambino-interview. 31 October 2013.
206: "Simon Munnery": Recorded interview with the author. March 18, 2015.
207: "We may regard it": Hans Lassen Martensen, Af mit Levnet: Meddelelser [From My Life: Communications] 3 volumes, København: Gyldendal, 1882–83.

Afterword

210: "the religious": PV, 103.
211: "The conflict about Christianity": JP 4185 (X3 A 346 n.d., 1850).

Abbreviations

BA	Book on Adler	**M**	The Moment and Late Writings
CA	Concept of Anxiety		
CD	Christian Discourses	**PC**	Practice in Christianity
CI	The Concept of Irony	**PF**	Philosophical Fragments
COR	The Corsair Affair	**PV**	The Point of View
CUP	Concluding Unscientific Postscript	**R**	Repetition
		SLW	Stages on Life's Way
EO	Either/Or	**SUD**	Sickness unto Death
EP	Early Polemical Writings	**TA**	Two Ages
EUD	Eighteen Upbuilding Discourses	**TDIO**	Three Discourses on Imagined Occasions
FSE	For Self-Examination	**UDVS**	Upbuilding Discourses in Various Spirits
FT	Fear and Trembling		
JC	Johannes Climacus	**WA**	Without Authority
JFY	Judge for Yourself!	**WL**	Works of Love
JP	Kierkegaard's Journals and Papers		

Bibliography

Kierkegaard

Søren Kierkegaard: Samelede Værker [Collected works]. Eds. A. B. Drachmann, J. L. Heiberg, et al. 20 vols. København: Gyldendal, 1962–64.

Søren Kierkegaards Skrifter [Writings]. Eds. Niels Cappelørn, Niels Jørgen, Joakim Garff, et al. 55 volumes in process. København: Gads Forlag, 1997 to present.

Søren Kierkegaards Papirer [Papers and journals]. Eds. P. A. Heiberg, V. Kuhr, E. Torsting, and N. Thulstrup, vols. I–XIII. København: Gyldendal, 1909–48; 1968–70; 1975–78.

Kierkegaard Translations

Kierkegaard's Journals and Papers. Eds. Howard V. Hong and Edna H. Hong. 7 volumes. Indiana: Indiana University Press, 1967–78.

Kierkegaard's Journals and Notebooks. Eds. Niels Jørgen Cappelørn, Alastair Hannay, David Kangas, Bruce H. Kirmmse, George Pattison, Vanessa Rumble, and K. Brian Söderquist. 8 volumes. Princeton: Princeton University Press, 2011.

Kierkegaard's Writings. Series eds. Howard V. Hong and Edna H. Hong. 26 volumes. Princeton: Princeton University Press, 1978–98.

> I. *Early Polemical Writings.* Edited and translated by Julia Watkin.
>
> II. *The Concept of Irony, with Continual Reference to Socrates/ Notes of Schelling's Berlin Lectures.* Edited and translated by Howard V. Hong, Edna H. Hong.

III. *Either/Or*. Edited and translated by Howard V. Hong, Edna H. Hong.
IV. *Either/Or* Part Two. Edited and translated by Howard V. Hong, Edna H. Hong.
V. *Eighteen Upbuilding Discourses*. Edited and translated by Howard V. Hong, Edna H. Hong.
VI. *Fear and Trembling/Repetition* (Two books in one volume). Edited and translated by Edna H. Hong, Howard V. Hong.
VII. *Philosophical Fragments, or a Fragment of Philosophy/ Johannes Climacus, or De omnibus dubitandum est* (Two books in one volume). Edited and translated by Edna H. Hong, Howard V. Hong.
VIII. *Concept of Anxiety: A Simple Psychologically Orienting Deliberation on the Dogmatic Issue of Hereditary Sin*. Edited and translated by Reidar Thomte.
IX. *Prefaces: Writing Sampler*. Edited and translated by Todd W. Nichol.
X. *Three Discourses on Imagined Occasions*. Edited and translated by Edna H. Hong, Howard V. Hong.
XI. *Stages on Life's Way*. Edited and translated by Howard V. Hong, Edna H. Hong.
XII. *Concluding Unscientific Postscript to Philosophical Fragments*. Edited and translated by Howard V. Hong, Edna H. Hong.
XIII. *The Corsair Affair and Articles Related to the Writings*. Edited and translated by Edna H. Hong, Howard V. Hong.
XIV. *Two Ages: The Age of Revolution and the Present Age, A Literary Review*. Edited and translated by Howard V. Hong, Edna H. Hong.
XV. *Upbuilding Discourses in Various Spirits*. Edited and translated by Howard V. Hong, Edna H. Hong.
XVI. *Works of Love*. Edited and translated by Howard V. Hong, Edna H. Hong.

XVII. *Christian Discourses: The Crisis and a Crisis in the Life of an Actress*. Edited and translated by Howard V. Hong, Edna H. Hong.

XVIII. *Without Authority* (containing *Lily in the Field and the Bird of the Air*; *Two Ethical-Religious Essays*; *Three Discourses at the Communion on Fridays*; *An Upbuilding Discourse*; *Two Discourses at the Communion on Fridays*). Edited and translated by Howard V. Hong, Edna H. Hong.

XIX. *Sickness unto Death: A Christian Psychological Exposition for Upbuilding and Awakening*. Edited and translated by Edna H. Hong, Howard V. Hong.

XX. *Practice in Christianity*. Edited and translated by Howard V. Hong, Edna H. Hong.

XXI. *For Self-Examination/Judge for Yourself!* (Two books in one volume). Edited and translated by Howard V. Hong, Edna H. Hong.

XXII. *The Point of View*. Edited and translated by Howard V. Hong, Edna H. Hong.

XXIII. *The Moment and Late Writings*. Edited and translated by Howard V. Hong, Edna H. Hong.

XXIV. *The Book on Adler*. Edited and translated by Howard V. Hong, Edna H. Hong.

XXV. *Letters and Documents*. Edited and translated by Henrik Rosenmeier.

XXVI. *Cumulative Index to Kierkegaard's Writings*. Compiled by Nathaniel J. Hong, Kathryn Hong, Regine Prenzel-Guthrie.

Papers and Journals: A Selection. Trans. Alastair Hannay. Penguin: London, 2015.

Other Select Sources

Aiken, David. "Kierkegaard's Three Stages: A Pilgrim's Regress?" *Faith and Philosophy* 13 (1996).

Allen, E. L. "Grundtvig and Kierkegaard." *The Congregational Quarterly* vol. XXIV (1946): 205–12.

———. *Bishop Grundtvig: A Prophet of the North*. London: James Clarke & Co., 1949.

Antonio, Edward P. "Søren Kierkegaard." *Empire and the Christian Tradition: New Readings of Classical Theologians*. Eds. Kwok Pui-lan, Don Compier. Minneapolis: Fortress Press, 2007.

Arbaugh, George E., and George B. Arbaugh. *Kierkegaard's Authorship*. London: Allen and Unwin, 1968.

Auken, Sune. *Sagas Spejl: Mytologi, historie og kristendom hos N. F. S. Grundtvig*. København: Glydendal, 2005.

Backhouse, Stephen. *Kierkegaard's Critique of Christian Nationalism*. Oxford: Oxford University Press, 2011.

———. "Kierkegaard and Politics in Golden Age Denmark." *Blackwell's Companion to Kierkegaard*. Ed. Jon Stewart. Oxford: Blackwell, 2015.

———. "Nationalism and Patriotism." *The Oxford Handbook of Theology and Modern European Thought*. Eds. Nicholas Adams, George Pattison, and Graham Ward. Oxford: Oxford University Press, 2011.

———. "State and Nation in the Theology of H. L. Martensen." *Hans Lassen Martensen: Theologian, Philosopher and Social Critic*. Ed. Jon Stewart. Copenhagen: Tusculanum Press, 2012.

Barth, Karl. *Church Dogmatics* IV/2. Trans. G. W. Bromiley. Edinburgh: T & T Clark, 1958.

———. *Epistle to the Romans*. Trans. Edwyn C. Hoskyns. Oxford: Oxford University Press, 1968.

———. *Fragments Grave and Gay*. Trans. Martin Rumscheidt. London: Collins, 1971.

Bellinger, Charles K. "Toward a Kierkegaardian Understanding of Hitler, Stalin and the Cold War." *Foundations of Kierkegaard's Vision of Community*. Eds. George Connell and C. Stephen Evans. New Jersey: Humanities Press, 1992.

Best, Steven, and Douglas Kellner. "Modernity, Mass Society, and the Media: Reflections on the Corsair Affair." *International Kierkegaard Commentary: The Corsair Affair*. Ed. Robert L. Perkins. Macon: Mercer University Press, 1990.

Bonhoeffer, Dietrich. *The Cost of Discipleship*. London: SCM, 2011.
Brookfield, Christopher. "What Was Kierkegaard's Task? A Frontier to be Explored." *Union Seminary Quarterly Review* vol.18 (1962): 23–35.
Bukdahl, Jørgen. *Søren Kierkegaard and the Common Man*. Trans. Bruce H. Kirmmse. Cambridge: William B. Eerdmans Publishing, 2001.
Camp, Zoe. "The 100 Best Albums of the Decade So Far (2010–2014)." *Pitchfork*. (August 2014).
Cappelørn, Niels Jørgen, Joakim Garff, and Johnny Kondrup, eds. *Written Images: Søren Kierkegaard's Journals, Notebooks, Booklets, Sheets, Scraps, and Slips of Paper*. Princeton: Princeton University Press, 2003.
Christensen, Dan C. 2013. *Hans Christian Ørsted: Reading Nature's Mind*. Oxford: Oxford University Press.
Collins, James. *Mind of Kierkegaard*. London: Secker and Warburg, 1954.
Croxall, T. H. *Kierkegaard Commentary*. London: James Nisbet, 1956.
Daise, Benjamin. *Kierkegaard's Socratic Art*. Macon: Mercer University Press, 1999.
de Paula, Marcio Gimenes. "Hannah Arendt." *Kierkegaard's Influence on Social-Political Thought*. Ed. Jon Stewart. Burlington: Ashgate, 2011.
Dooley, Mark. *The Politics of Exodus: Søren Kierkegaard's Ethics of Responsibility*. New York: Fordham University Press, 2001.
Doyle, Patrick. "Win Butler Reveals Secret Influences Behind Arcade Fire's 'Reflektor.'" *Rolling Stone* (October 22, 2013).
Dru, Alexander, trans. *The Journals of Kierkegaard 1834–1854*. Oxford: Oxford University Press, 1938.
Drury, Maurice. "Some Notes of Conversations with Wittgenstein." *Recollections of Wittgenstein*. Ed. Rush Rhees. Oxford: Blackwell, 1981.
Eliot, T. S. "A Lay Theologian" [review of *The Descent of the Dove* by Charles Williams]. *The New Statesman* (December 9, 1939).
Evans, Stephen C. *Kierkegaard's Ethic of Love*. Oxford: Oxford University Press, 2004.
Fenger, Henning. *Kierkegaard: The Myths and Their Origins*. Trans. George Schoolfield. London: Yale University Press, 1980.
Ferreira, M. Jamie. "Faith and the Kierkegaardian Leap." *The Cambridge Companion to Kierkegaard*. Eds. A. Hannay and G. Marino. Cambridge: Cambridge University Press, 1997.

Garff, Joakim. *Søren Kierkegaard: A Biography*. Trans. Bruce H. Kirmmse. Princeton: Princeton University Press, 2005.

———, and Pia Søltoft. *Søren Kierkegaard: Objects of Love, Works of Love*. Copenhagen: Museum of Copenhagen, 2013.

———. "To Produce Was My Life: Problems, Perspectives within the Kierkegaardian Biography." *Kierkegaard Revisited*. Trans. Stacey Elizabeth Axe; eds. Niels Jørgen Cappelørn and Jon Stewart. New York: Walter de Gruyter, 1997.

———, Niels Jørgen Cappelørn, and Johnny Kondru, eds. *Written Images: Søren Kierkegaard's Journals, Notebooks, Booklets, Sheets, Scraps, and Slips of Paper*. Princeton: Princeton University Press, 2003.

George, Peter. "Something Anti-Social about Works of Love." *Kierkegaard: The Self in Society*. Eds. George Pattison and Steven Shakespeare. London: Macmillan, 1998.

Hamilton, Andrew. *Sixteen Months in the Danish Isles*. London: Bentley, 1852.

Hannay, Alistair. *Kierkegaard: A Biography*. Cambridge: Cambridge University Press, 2001.

Hartshorne, M. Holmes. *Kierkegaard, Godly Deceiver*. New York: Columbia University Press, 1990.

Hatton, Nigel. "Martin Luther King." *Kierkegaard's Influence on Social-Political Thought*. Ed. Jon Stewart. Burlington: Ashgate, 2011.

Holm, Anders. *Historie og Efterklang: En studie i N. F. S. Grundtvigs tidsskrift 'Danne-Virke.'* Odense: Odense Universite-forlag, 2001.

Holm, Søren. *Søren Kierkegaard's Historiefilosofi*. København: Bianco Luno Bogtrykkeri, 1962.

Holmer, Paul. "On Understanding Kierkegaard." *A Kierkegaard Critique*. Ed. Howard Johnson and Niels Thulstrup. New York: Harper, 1962.

Huntington, Patricia J. "Heidegger's Reading of Kierkegaard Revisited." *Kierkegaard in Post/Modernity*. Eds. Martin Matuštík and Merold Westphal. Bloomington: Indiana University Press, 1995.

King, Martin Luther, Jr. "The Quest for Peace and Justice." *Nobel Lecture* (December 11, 1964).

Kirmmse, Bruce. "'But I am Almost Never Understood . . .' Or, Who Killed Søren Kierkegaard?" *Kierkegaard: The Self and Society*. Eds. George Pattison and Steven Shakespeare. London: Macmillan, 1998.

———, ed. and trans. *Encounters With Kierkegaard: A Life as Seen By His Contemporaries*. Princeton: Princeton University Press, 1996.

———. *Kierkegaard in Golden Age Denmark*. Indianapolis: Indiana University Press, 1990.

Koch, Hal. *Grundtvig*. Trans. Llewellyn Jones. Yellow Springs: Antioch Press, 1952.

Lindhardt, P. G. "Martensen, Hans Lassen." *Dansk Biografisk Leksikon*. Tredje Udgave, Bind 9, [Danish Biographical Dictionary third edition, Volume 9] København: Gyldendal, 1981.

Lowrie, Walter. *Kierkegaard*. London: Oxford University Press, 1938.

———. *A Short Life of Kierkegaard*. New York: Anchor Books, 1961.

Lübke, Poul. "Kierkegaard and Indirect Communication." *History of European Ideas* vol. 12, 1990: 30–40.

Lyby, Thorkild. "Peter Christian Kierkegaard." *Kierkegaard and His Danish Contemporaries: Tome II Theology*. Ed. Jon Stewart. Burlington: Ashgate Publishing, 2009.

Mackey, Louis. *Kierkegaard: A Kind of Poet*. Philadelphia: University of Pennsylvania Press, 1971.

———. *Points of View*. Tallahassee: Florida State University Press, 1986.

Malantschuk, Gregor. *Kierkegaard's Thought*. Trans. Howard and Edna Hong. Princeton: Princeton University Press, 1971.

Malik, Habib C. *Receiving Søren Kierkegaard*. Washington: Catholic University of America Press, 1997.

Martensen, H. L. *Af mit Levnet: Meddelelser* [From My Life: Communications] 3 vols. København: Gyldendal, 1882–83.

———. *Christian Dogmatics*. Trans. William Urwick. Edinburgh: T&T Clark, 1866.

———. *Christian Ethics*. Trans. C. Spence. Edinburgh: T&T Clark, 1873.

———. *Christian Ethics: Special Part, First Division; Individual Ethics*. Trans. William Affleck. Edinburgh: T&T Clark, 1881.

———. *Christian Ethics: Special Part. Second Division; Social Ethics*. Trans. Sophia Taylor. Edinburgh: T&T Clark, 1882.

———. *Outline to a System of Moral Philosophy*, printed in *Between Hegel and Kierkegaard: Hans L. Martensen's Philosophy of Religion*. Trans. Curtis L. Thompson and David J. Kangas. Atlanta: Scholars Press, 1997.

Merton, Thomas. *Run to the Mountain: The Journals of Thomas Merton Volume 1*. San Francisco: HarperCollins, 1997.

Michelsen, William. "Grundtvig's Place in Danish Intellectual Thought— With Particular Reference to Søren Kierkegaard." *N. F. S. Grundtvig: Tradition and Renewal*. Copenhagen: The Danish Institute, 1983.

"Mike Tyson Explores Kierkegaard." *Wall Street Journal* (December 13, 2013).

Mooney, Edward. *On Søren Kierkegaard: Dialogue, Polemics, Lost Intimacy and Time*. Aldershot: Ashgate, 2007.

Munro, R. "Bishop Martensen." *Methodist Review* 68 S, 1886: 701–17.

Nordentoft, Kresten. *'Hvad Siger Brand-Majoren?' Kierkegaards Opgør Med Sin Samtid*. København: G.E.C. Gad, 1973.

Pastuk, Slava. "Donald Glover: Fear and Trembling." Posted October 31, 2013. *Vice Magazine*. http://noisey.vice.com/en_uk/blog/donald-glover-childish-gambino-interview.

Pattison, George. "Great Britain: From 'Prophet of the Now' to Postmodern Ironist (and After)." *Kierkegaard's International Reception: Tome 1 Northern and Western Europe*. Ed. Jon Stewart. Burlington: Ashgate, 2009.

———. *Kierkegaard: Religion and the Nineteenth-Century Crisis of Culture*. Cambridge: Cambridge University Press, 2002.

———. *Kierkegaard's Upbuilding Discourses*. London: Routledge, 2002.

Paulus, Michael J., Jr. "From a Publisher's Point of View: Charles Williams' Role in Publishing Kierkegaard in English." *Charles Williams and His Contemporaries*. Eds. Suzanne Bray and Richard Sturch. Newcastle: Cambridge Scholars Publishing, 2009.

Perkins, Frances. *The Roosevelt I Knew*. New York: The Viking Press, 1946.

Perkins, Robert L., ed. *International Kierkegaard Commentary: Eighteen Upbuilding Discourses*. Macon: Mercer, 2003.

———. *International Kierkegaard Commentary: The Concept of Anxiety*. Macon: Mercer, 1985.

———. *International Kierkegaard Commentary: Concluding Unscientific Postscript*. Macon: Mercer, 1997.

———. *International Kierkegaard Commentary: The Corsair Affair*. Macon: Mercer, 1990.

———. *International Kierkegaard Commentary: For Self-examination and Judge for Yourself!* Macon: Mercer, 2002.
———. *International Kierkegaard Commentary: Philosophical Fragments.* Macon: Mercer, 1994.
———. *International Kierkegaard Commentary: Practice in Christianity.* Macon: Mercer, 2004.
———. *International Kierkegaard Commentary: Two Ages.* Macon: Mercer, 1984.
———. *International Kierkegaard Commentary: Upbuilding Discourses in Various Spirits.* Macon: Mercer, 2005.
———. *International Kierkegaard Commentary: Without Authority.* Macon: Mercer University Press, 2006.
———. *International Kierkegaard Commentary: Works of Love.* Macon: Mercer University Press, 1999.
Plekon, Michael. "Kierkegaard, the Church and the Theology of Golden-Age Denmark." *Journal of Ecclesiastical History* vol. 34, 1983: 245–66.
Poole, Roger. *Kierkegaard: The Indirect Communication.* Charlottesville: University Press of Virginia, 1993.
———. "The Unknown Kierkegaard: Twentieth-Century Receptions." *The Cambridge Companion to Kierkegaard.* Eds. A. Hannay and G. Marino. Cambridge: Cambridge University Press, 1997.
Ree, Jonathan. *Times Literary Supplement* no. 17. (June 26, 1998).
Rerup, Lorenz. "Grundtvig's Position in Danish Nationalism." *Heritage and Prophecy.* Ed. A. M. Allchin, et al. Norwich: Canterbury Press, 1994.
Robinson, Marcia C. "Cornel West." *Kierkegaard's Influence on Social-Political Thought.* Ed. Jon Stewart. Burlington: Ashgate, 2011.
Rogan, Jan. "Keeping Silent Through Speaking." *Kierkegaard on Art and Communication.* Ed. George Pattison. London: St Martin's Press, 1992.
Schilling, Peter A. *Søren Kierkegaard and Anglo-American Literary Culture of the Thirties and Forties.* Doctoral Thesis: Columbia University, 1994.
Schioldann, Johan, and Ib Søgaard. *Søren Kierkegaard (1813–55): A Bicentennial Pathographical Review. History of Psychiatry* 24(4) 387–98.
Schjørring, J. H. "Martensen" in *Kierkegaardiana 10, Kierkegaard's Teachers.* Eds. Niels Thulstrup and Marie Mikulová Thulstrup. Copenhagen: C. A. Reitzel, 1982.

Schwandt, Jack. *The Hong Kierkegaard Library.* Northfield: Friends of the Kierkegaard Library, 2011.

Skovmand, Roar. *De folkelig bevaegelser i Danmark.* Copenhagen: Shultz, 1951.

Smith, Ronald Gregor. *The Last Years: Journals 1853–1855.* London: Collins, 1965.

Stewart, Jon. *Kierkegaard's Relations to Hegel Reconsidered.* Cambridge: Cambridge University Press, 2003.

Thanning, Kaj. *N. F. S. Grundtvig.* Trans. David Hohnen. Copenhagen: The Danish Institute, 1972.

Thompson, Curtis L., and David J. Kangas. *Between Hegel and Kierkegaard: Hans L. Martensen's Philosophy of Religion.* Atlanta: Scholars Press, 1997.

Thompson, Josiah. *Kierkegaard.* New York: Alfred A Knopf, 1973.

Thulstrup, Niels. *Kierkegaard's Relation to Hegel.* Trans. G. Stengren. Princeton: Princeton University Press, 1980.

Thyssen, Anders P. "Grundtvig's Ideas on the Church and the People 1848–72." *N. F. S. Grundtvig: Tradition and Renewal.* Copenhagen: The Danish Institute, 1983.

Veninga, Jennifer Elisa. "Richard Wright." *Kierkegaard's Influence on Social-Political Thought.* Ed. Jon Stewart. Burlington: Ashgate, 2011.

West, Cornel. *Prophesy Deliverance! An Afro-American Revolutionary Christianity.* Philadelphia: Westminster Press, 1982.

Westphal, Merold. *Kierkegaard's Critique of Reason and Society.* Pennsylvania: Pennsylvania University Press, 1991.

Williams, Charles. *Descent of the Dove.* London: Longman, 1939.

Index

Adler, Adolph Peter, 150, 151, 152, 263, 264, 265
Allen, E. L., 197
Andersen, Hans Christian, 19, 24, 25, 65, 71, 87, 88, 127, 128, 215, 216
Anger, Edward, 37
Anno, Hideaki, 204
Arendt, Hannah, 196, 201
Asada, Hikaru, 204
Auden, W. H., 199
Bakunin, Mikhail, 106
Banksy, 206
Barfod, Hans Peter, 35, 36, 37, 40, 52, 192, 193, 204
Barth, Karl, 11, 196, 198
Bloch, Victor, 178
Boesen, Emil, 100, 104, 105, 190
Bonaparte, Napoleon, 45
Bonhoeffer, Dietrich, 197
Brandes, George, 140, 194, 197
Brøchner, Hans, 88, 89, 109, 110, 151, 183
Butler, Win, 205
Camus, Albert, 200
Cappelørn, Niels Jørgen, 204
Caroline Amalie (queen), 153
Christensen, P. V., 112
Christian VIII, 153, 155
Clausen, H. N., 155
Congreve, William, 45
de Unamuno, Miguel, 193
Descartes, René, 84, 232
Dru, Alexander, 197, 198
Eliot, T. S., 199
Engels, Friedrich, 106
Evans, C. Stephen, 204
Frankl, Victor, 203
Frederick VI, 45
Frederick VII, 155
Garff, Joakim, 12
Gaus, Günther, 196
Giøwad, J. F., 112, 141, 181
Glover, Donald, 205
Goldschmidt, Meïr Aron ("Aron"), 20, 21, 125, 126, 127, 128, 129, 130, 131, 132, 135, 136, 137, 138, 180
Gottsched, Hermann, 192, 193
Grundtvig, Nicolai Frederik Severin ("N.F.S."), 21, 75, 120, 121, 122, 123, 156, 179, 181, 197, 237
Gyllembourg, Thomasine, 150, 239
Haecker, Theodor, 195, 197
Hamilton, Andrew, 189, 190
Hannay, Alastair, 12
Hansen, Hans Peter, 173
Hansen, Magdalene, 179
Harvey, Lincoln, 11
Hegel, Georg Wilhelm Friedrich, 66, 67, 71, 96, 122, 152, 162, 215, 217, 220, 228, 232
Heiberg, Johan Ludvig ("J.L."), 70, 71, 75, 85, 88, 100, 114, 130, 149, 231, 232, 246
Heiberg, Joanna Luise, 246
Heidegger, Martin, 200
Hollander, Lee, 198
Holst, Hans, 37
Hong, Howard, 193, 197, 203, 209
Hong, Edna, 197, 203, 209
Hostrup, Jens Christian, 140, 141
Ibsen, Henrik, 193
Ingemann, Bernhard Severin, 179
Jaspers, Karl, 195, 196
Jesus Christ, 23, 29, 33, 54, 56, 63, 76, 80, 86, 94, 99, 145, 146, 151, 163, 182,

187, 192, 226, 228, 230, 242, 243, 244, 245, 247, 249, 251, 252, 253, 254, 255, 256, 259, 260, 262, 264, 267, 268
Johnson, Howard, 201
Jørgensen, Jørgen, 64
Joyce, James, 193
Kafka, Franz, 196
Kardashian, Kim, 204, 205
Kierkegaard, Peter Christian (brother), 18, 24, 27, 28, 30, 32, 35, 37, 39, 43, 49, 52, 54, 55, 60, 61, 63, 64, 72, 75, 83, 86, 87, 94, 100, 102, 106, 120, 121, 155, 161, 181, 182, 184, 186, 190, 191, 192, 193, 266, 268
Kierkegaard, Michael Pedersen (father), 19, 41, 43, 44, 45, 46, 47, 48, 49, 50, 51, 52, 53, 54, 55, 56, 57, 60, 62, 63, 64, 73, 83, 86, 87, 88, 90, 93, 117, 145, 192, 222
Kierkegaard, Maren (sister), 43, 52, 53
Kierkegaard, Søren Michael (brother), 43, 53
Kierkegaard, Niels Andreas (brother), 43, 47, 48, 54
Kierkegaard, Søren Aabye, *passim*; works of (**boldface** numbers reference the discussion of that title in the "Overviews of the Works of Søren Kierkegaard," 215–268):
 "A Defence of Woman's Superior Capacity," 70
 "Our Journalistic Literature," 70
 "Public Confession," 112
 "The Single Individual": Two "Notes" Concerning My Work as an Author, **265–267**
 An Upbuilding Discourse: The Woman Who Was a Sinner, **255–256**
 Armed Neutrality, 149, 155, 157, **265–267**
 Book on Adler, 149, 150, 151, 248, **263–265**, 285
 Christian Discourses, 149, 155, 198, **244–246**, 252, 259, 285
 Concept of Anxiety, 85, 107, 114, 115, 116, 201, **229–230**, 231, 250, 285
 Concept of Dread, 198. See *Concept of Anxiety*
 Concept of Irony with Constant Reference to Socrates, 95, 96, 128, **216–218**, 285
 Concluding Unscientific Postscript to Philosophical Fragments, 107, 122, 123, 142, 146, 147, 150, 198, 203, 227, **236–238**, 240, 257, 259, 285
 Discourses, 107, 110, 116, 117, 131, 149, 152, 155, 161, 164, 174, 198, 220, 221, 222, 231, 232, 233, 240, 241, 244, 245, 246, 247, 251, 252, 255, 256, 257, 259, 285. See the specific entries for *An Upbuilding Discourse: The Woman Who Was a Sinner*; *Christian Discourses*; *Eighteen Upbuilding Discourses*; *Four Upbuilding Discourses*; *The Lily in the Field and the Bird of the Air: Three Devotional Discourses*; *Three Discourses at the Communion on Fridays*; *Three Discourses on Imagined Occasions*; *Three Upbuilding Discourses*; *Two Discourses at the Communion on Fridays*; *Upbuilding Discourses in Various Spirits*
 Eighteen Upbuilding Discourses, **220–222**, 241, 285
 Either/Or: A Fragment of Life, 95, 107, 111, 112, 113, 116, 117, 123, 130, 131, 132, 142, 149, 198, **218–220**, 221, 231, 233, 234, 246, 247, 257, 265, 285
 Fear and Trembling, 107, 114, 116, 118, 119, 131, 132, 198, 200, **225–227**, 285
 For Self-Examination, 149, **258–261**, 267, 285
 Four Upbuilding Discourses, **220–222**
 From the Papers of One Still Living, 87, **215–216**
 Johannes Climacus, 48, 227, 285
 Judge for Yourself!, 149, 166, 174, 198, 259, **267–268**, 285
 On My Work as an Author, 149, **257–258**, 259, 266
 Philosophical Fragments, or a Fragment of Philosophy, 107, 114, 116, 122, 131, 198, 203, **227–229**, 231, 236, 237, 285

Practice in Christianity, 149, 155, 158, 162, 163, 166, 167, 170, 197, 245, 251, **252–255**, 259, 285
Prefaces: Light Reading for People in Various Estates According to Time and Opportunity, 107, 114, 116, 132, 229, **231–232**, 239
Present Age, 198, 205, 239. See *Two Ages: The Age of Revolution and the Present Age, A Literary Review*
Repetition: An Essay in Experimental Psychology, 107, 114, 116, 118, 119, 198, **222–224**, 225, 231, 234, 285
Sickness unto Death: A Christian Psychological Exposition for Upbuilding and Awakening, 51, 149, 155, 158, 159, 170, 198, 204, **249–251**, 285
Stages on Life's Way, 98, 107, 114, 116, 123, 132, 134, 198, 232, **234–236**, 285
The "Attack upon Christendom," 198, **261–263**, 285. See also *The Moment and Late Writings*
The Battle Between the Old and New Soap Sellers, 84
The Crisis and the Crisis in the Life of an Actress, 149, **245–246**, 259
The Difference Between a Genius and an Apostle, 152. See *Two Ethical-Religious Essays*
The Lily in the Field and the Bird of the Air: Three Devotional Discourses, 149, 155, **247–248**
The Moment and Late Writings, 181, 182, 183, 184, 198, **261–263**, 285 see also The "Attack Upon Christendom"
The Point of View for My Life as an Author, 110, 149, 155, 158, 191, 198, 257, **265–267**, 285
Three Discourses at the Communion on Fridays, 149, **251–252**, 255
Three Discourses on Imagined Occasions, 116, **232–234**, 285
Three Upbuilding Discourses, **220–222**, 231
Training in Christianity, 198. See *Practice in Christianity*
Two Ages: The Age of Revolution and the Present Age, A Literary Review, 149, 150, 152, **238–240**, 285

Two Discourses at the Communion on Fridays, 174, **256–257**
Two Ethical-Religious Essays, 149, 152, 155, **248–249**, 263
Two Upbuilding Discourses, **220–222**
Upbuilding Discourses in Various Spirits, 110, 149, **240–242**, 285
Works of Love, 149, 152, 153, 162, **242–244**, 285
Kierkegaard, Hans Peter ("Peter," cousin), 110, 153,
Kierkegaard, Paul (nephew), 120
Kierkegaard (née Boiesen), Marie, 63, 64, 83, 120
Kierkegaard (née Glahn), Sophie Henriette ("Jette"), 120, 153
Kierkegaard (née Lund), Anne Sørensdatter (mother), 19, 43, 49, 50, 51, 52, 53, 54, 62, 68, 69
Kierkegaard (née Røyen), Kirstine, 45, 49
King, Martin Luther, Jr., 202
Kirmmse, Bruce, 204
Klæstrup, Peter, 136
Kolthoff, E. V., 86
Lehmann, Orla, 155, 156
Levin, Israel, 109
Lewis, C. S., 199
Lind, Peter, 37
Lodge, David, 201
Lowrie, Walter, 12, 198, 199, 201, 203
Lund, Henriette (niece), 22, 23, 26, 46
Lund, Henrik (nephew), 29, 30, 31, 54, 185, 190, 204
Lund, Charlotte, 39
Lund, Johan Christian, 54, 186
Lund, Michael, 54
Lund, Sophie, 54
Lund, Carl, 54
Lund, Peter Severin, 54
Lund, Henrik Ferdinand, 54
Lund, Vilhelm, 54
Lund, Peter Christian, 54
Lund, Henrik (father of Troels), 169, 170
Lund, Anna, 169, 170
Lund (née Kierkegaard), Nicoline (sister), 47
Lund (née Kierkegaard), Petrea Severine (sister), 43, 54
Luther, Martin, 243, 262
Malantschuk, Gregor, 196, 197

Malcolm X, 202
Marino, Gordon, 204, 205
Martensen, Hans Lassen, ("H.L."), 17, 27, 31, 67, 68, 69, 71, 75, 77, 85, 89, 97, 114, 122, 156, 161, 162, 167, 168, 174, 175, 176, 177, 178, 179, 191, 193, 194, 207, 231, 232, 237, 262,
Merton, Thomas, 200
Miller, Henry, 200
Møller, Poul Martin, 66, 67, 70, 71, 84, 85, 96, 115, 127, 144
Møller, Peter Ludvig, 127, 128, 129, 130, 132, 134, 135, 136, 137, 138
Munnery, Simon, 206
Mynster, Jakob Peter, ("J.P."), 35, 55, 56, 75, 111, 117, 120, 121, 131, 141, 143, 145, 147, 148, 149, 154, 155, 156, 162, 163, 164, 166, 167, 168, 169, 170, 171, 172, 174, 175, 176, 177, 178, 179, 184, 187, 245, 255, 259, 261, 262, 268
Nielsen, Rasmus, 26, 30, 31, 177, 178
Nielsen, Michael, 37, 38, 39, 41, 64
Nietzsche, Frederick, 194
Norman, Dorothy, 201
O'Connor, Flannery, 201
Olsen, Terkild, 93, 94, 101, 159
Olsen, Cornelia, 99
Olsen, Jonas, 99
Ørsted, Hans Christian, ("H.C."), 71, 97
Ørsted, Anders Sandøe, 175
Ostermann, J. A., 70
Pattison, George, 271, 281
Percy, Walker, 204
Perkins, Frances, 201
Plough, Carl, 112
Reinhard, Regine ("Tagine"), 179
Roosevelt, Franklin, 201
Rørdam, Peter, 79, 125, 178
Rørdam, Bolette, 79
Rørdam, Catrine, 125, 128
Rørdam, Hans, 178
Rotten, Johnny, 206
Røyen, Mads, 45

Rudelbach, Andreas Gottlob, 165
Salinger, J.D., 201
Sartre, Jean-Paul, 200
Sayers, Dorothy, 199, 201
Schelling, Friedrich, 106
Schlegel, Johan Frederik, ("Fritz"), 93, 118, 154, 160, 161, 180, 184, 195, 224
Schlegel (née Olsen), Regine, 32, 33, 77, 79, 80, 81, 89, 91, 92, 93, 94, 95, 98, 99, 100, 101, 102, 103, 104, 105, 107, 117, 118, 119, 120, 125, 132, 152, 154, 159, 160, 161, 164, 166, 170, 180, 181, 184, 195, 218, 222, 224, 226, 236, 257, 259
Schleiermacher, Friedrich, 68
Seguchi, Takahiro, 204
Sibbern, Frederick Christian, ("F.C."), 65, 67, 88, 94, 95, 97, 98, 99, 179
Smith, Caspar, 104
Socrates, 216, 217, 223, 228, 249
Sommer, Mogens Abraham, 191
Swenson, David, 198, 203
Thomas à Kempis, 94
Thompson, Josiah, 12
Thorvaldsen, Bertel, 167
Tillich, Paul, 201, 203
Tolkien, J. R. R., 199
Troels-Lund, Troels Frederik ("Troels," nephew), 23, 25, 26, 27, 28, 29, 30, 138, 139, 170, 186
Tryde, Eggert, 25, 27, 28, 29, 31
Tyson, Mike, 205
Updike, John, 201
Watkin, Julia, 197
Waugh, Evelyn, 198
Welding, Frederik, 35, 36, 37
Wesley, John, 56
West, Cornel, 202, 203
Westergaard, Anders, 108, 156
Williams, Charles, 13, 199,
Williams, Kenneth, 206
Wittgenstein, Ludwig, 196
Wright, Richard, 201

Permissions and Credits

The author and publisher would like to acknowledge the following sources for the images used in this book:

Cover photo of Stephen Backhouse: Sophie Francisco.

The Copenhagen City Museum: 44.

The Corsair: 139 (Jan. 9, 1846, issue 277), 136–38 (Jan. 16, 1846, issue 278), 135 (Jan. 23, 1846, issue 279), 133–34 (March 6, 1846, issue 285).

The Danish National Historical Museum, Frederiksborg: 47 (artist; F. C. Camrath), 50 (artist: F. C. Camrath).

The Library of Congress: 20 (LC-DIG-ppmsc-05749), 71 (LC-DIG-ppmsc-05746).

The Royal Library, Copenhagen: 22, 26, 60, 81, 105, 121, 126, 154, 173, 175, 191.

Stephen Backhouse: 167, 185, 187, 192, 194.

Wikimedia Commons: 24 (photograph by Thora Hallager, 1867), 69 (artist: David Monies), 92, 96, 113, 148 (artist: Vilhelm Gertner, 1842), 192.

www.ingramcontent.com/pod-product-compliance
Lightning Source LLC
Chambersburg PA
CBHW011949150426
43194CB00019B/2852